The Republic of Vietnam, 1955–1975

The Republic of Vietnam, 1955–1975

Vietnamese Perspectives on Nation Building

Edited by Tuong Vu and Sean Fear

SOUTHEAST ASIA PROGRAM PUBLICATIONS
an imprint of Cornell University Press
Ithaca and London

Southeast Asia Program Publications Editorial Board
Mahinder Kingra (ex officio)
Thak Chaloemtiarana
Chiara Formichi
Tamara Loos
Kaja McGowan

Copyright © 2019 by Cornell University

All rights reserved. Except for brief quotations in a review, this book, or parts thereof, must not be reproduced in any form without permission in writing from the publisher. For information, address Cornell University Press, Sage House, 512 East State Street, Ithaca, New York 14850.

First published 2019 by Cornell University Press

Library of Congress Cataloging-in-Publication Data
Names: Vu, Tuong, 1965– editor. | Fear, Sean, 1984– editor.
Title: The Republic of Vietnam, 1955–1975 : Vietnamese perspectives on nation building / edited by Tuong Vu and Sean Fear.
Description: Ithaca : Southeast Asia Program Publications, an imprint of Cornell University Press, 2019. | Includes bibliographical references and index.
Identifiers: LCCN 2019012613 (print) | LCCN 2019013608 (ebook) | ISBN 9781501745140 (pdf) | ISBN 9781501745157 (epub/mobi) | ISBN 9781501745126 | ISBN 9781501745126 (cloth) | ISBN 9781501745133 (pbk.)
Subjects: LCSH: Vietnam (Republic)—Politics and government. | Vietnam (Republic)—Civilization.
Classification: LCC DS556.9 (ebook) | LCC DS556.9. R47 2019 (print) | DDC 959.7/7043—dc23
LC record available at https://lccn.loc.gov/2019012613

Contents

Introduction   1
TUONG VU AND SEAN FEAR

Chapter 1

Coping with Changes and War, Building a
Foundation for Growth   13
NGUYỄN ĐỨC CƯỜNG

Chapter 2

The Birth of Central Banking, 1955–1956   25
VŨ QUỐC THÚC

Chapter 3

Reform or Collapse: Economic Challenges
during Vietnamization   35
PHẠM KIM NGỌC

Chapter 4

Land Reform and Agricultural Development,
1968–1975   47
CAO VĂN THÂN

Chapter 5

Striving for a Lasting Peace: The Paris Accords
and Aftermath   57
HOÀNG ĐỨC NHÃ

Chapter 6

Public Security and the National Police   71
TRẦN MINH CÔNG

Chapter 7

Reflections of a Frontline Soldier   81
BÙI QUYỀN

Chapter 8

The Philosophies and Development
of a Free Education 93
NGUYỄN HỮU PHƯỚC

Chapter 9

Personal Reflections on the Educational System 105
VÕ KIM SƠN

Chapter 10

Life and Work of a Journalist 117
PHẠM TRẦN

Chapter 11

The Vietnam War in the Eyes of a
Vietnamese War Correspondent 127
VŨ THANH THỦY

Chapter 12

Sóng Thần's Campaign for Press Freedom 139
TRÙNG DƯƠNG

Chapter 13

Writers of the Republic of Vietnam 155
NHÃ CA (TRANSLATED BY TRÙNG DƯƠNG)

Chapter 14

The Cinema Industry 165
KIỀU CHINH

Chapter 15

The Neglect of the Republic of Vietnam
in the American Historical Memory 173
NU-ANH TRAN

Chapter 16

Political, Military, and Cultural
Memoirs in Vietnamese 179
TUAN HOANG

About the Editors 189

Index 191

The Republic of Vietnam, 1955–1975

INTRODUCTION

Tuong Vu and Sean Fear

From its origins as a guerilla struggle, the Vietnam War rapidly evolved into the definitive conventional military encounter of the Cold War era. The final stages featured tanks, artillery, helicopters, perhaps the world's most sophisticated air defenses, and round-the-clock bombardment on an unprecedented scale. Despite this show of arms on both sides, however, the core underlying conflict was always primarily political in nature. Central to the struggle were the competing visions of "nation building" in the South advanced by rival Vietnamese communist and noncommunist actors, each supported to varying degrees by their respective international allies.

Although scholarship on the role of the United States and the communist side has been substantial, republican Vietnamese contributions and perspectives have only recently attracted in-depth scholarly attention. The vast majority of academic works devoted to the Vietnam War have been centered on American decisions and experiences.[1] A series of recent studies has begun reversing this trend, but they have been limited to certain periods or particular state projects.[2] Few works address how local actors interpreted and shaped events, either in tandem or at cross-purposes with the Americans. And fewer still have explored the role of civil society and the population at large in South Vietnam.

Far from puppets or incidental players in the conflict, however, the Republic of Vietnam (RVN, or South Vietnam) and its constituents were committed to a robust nation-building agenda of their own. This often took the form of top-down state-driven projects, including involuntary population resettlement; experimentation with state- and market-oriented economic reform; agrarian development and land registration; modernization of the national educational system; and, in 1967, a sweeping political restructuring consisting of a new constitution, a bicameral legislature, and national- and village-level elections.

Everyday citizens also had a part to play, as the testimonies in this volume attest. The military, boasting well over one million soldiers at peak strength, was swelled by conscription but also by thousands of dedicated volunteers, who at times fought bravely against often unfavorable odds. Desertion, corruption, and administrative ineptitude posed persistent challenges, but rank-and-file soldiers at times also demonstrated great commitment, their determined resistance against communist offensives in 1968 through 1975 proving critical to prolonging the state's survival.[3]

Meanwhile, despite the government's recurring if generally ineffective harassment and censorship, South Vietnamese artists, writers, musicians, and even film and television stars contributed to a burgeoning cultural scene in Saigon, their works regarded by many as a welcome alternative to the communists' statist agitprop. South

Vietnamese journalists likewise resisted state efforts to stifle an independent press, resulting in a lively print media scene that contested recurring government crackdowns until the very end. Through brave opposition to the government's authoritarian tendencies, South Vietnam's vibrant civil society demonstrated a firm commitment to constitutionalism and republican values. And long before the guns of war fell silent, a distinctly anticommunist national identity had emerged and crystallized in the South.

This volume emerged from a symposium held at the University of California, Berkeley in October 2016, which aimed to promote a deeper understanding of the Republic of Vietnam. This two-day event was not an ordinary academic meeting: in addition to academic presentations, the speakers included fifteen prominent South Vietnamese administrators, politicians, military officers, educators, writers, artists, and journalists.

It was quite a challenge for the organizers of the symposium to assemble these historical figures from around the world, the youngest of whom were in their late sixties and the oldest in their mid-nineties.[4] In fact, two of the confirmed speakers—Mr. Võ Long Triều, the former owner and editor of the Saigon-based newspaper *Đại Dân Tộc* (The great nation) and an opposition legislator in the RVN's National Assembly, and Nguyễn Thanh Liêm, former vice minister of education in the RVN—passed away only a few months before the symposium. Two other speakers, Vũ Quốc Thúc and Cao Văn Thân, were well enough only to greet symposium participants from their hospital beds in Paris and Montreal, respectively. (Their papers were read by others and are included in this volume.) And both Mr. Lâm Lễ Trinh, professor of law and former minister of the interior, and Mr. Huỳnh Văn Lang, former director of the Foreign Exchange Agency and founder of the journal *Bách Khoa* (Polytechnics), presented via Skype from southern California. (Their presentations have not been included in this volume.)[5]

Especially significant is that these RVN figures have had few previous opportunities to express themselves, despite having played such important roles in the history of their country. Even today, the presenters remain largely obscure in the English-language scholarship on the war, reflecting the field's long-standing tendency to dismiss noncommunist South Vietnamese perspectives. Indeed, this symposium represents one of the first events to include such a wide range of former RVN military and civilian officials in a respectful academic environment.[6] The range of authors also reflects the diversity of South Vietnamese society, featuring accounts from men and women, soldiers and civilians, and elites and everyday citizens alike. Readers may agree or disagree with the viewpoints of these historical figures, but it is our hope that this volume will provide insight for researchers and general readers alike, both by illuminating the historical events that the authors shaped and experienced and by recording the memories and reflections of a generation that is rapidly passing away. Accordingly, apart from minor editing for length and clarity, the testimonies presented here have been kept intact.

Nation Building in War

Nation building can be defined either as the deliberate efforts to create a community within a nation-state or the abstract process by which such a community emerges. The basis for the community is a sense of solidarity built on shared beliefs, cultural practices, or political principles.[7] As an abstract process, nation building may take place over centuries in tandem with other processes such as war, state formation, urbanization, and industrialization. As a deliberate process, it can be championed either by local elites or by foreign powers.

These efforts can be observed in Africa and Asia following World War II, as local elites sought to expel colonial rulers and form new nation-states. As the world's superpower, the United States led many nation-building projects abroad to contain communism (for example, South Vietnam) or to accompany regime change (for example, Afghanistan and Iraq).

The importance of the postcolonial context for any discussion of post-1945 nation building cannot be overstated. As newly formed states emerged in Asia and Africa following the end of World War II, most faced extraordinary challenges including widespread illiteracy, deep social divisions, economic dependency, and political instability. Given these obstacles, it is perhaps unsurprising that many struggled to establish cohesive polities, sustained economic prosperity, or social equality.

Postcolonial nation building also proved challenging because rival elites and their constituents often held competing national visions, leading to violent confrontations and civil war. Beyond the threat to political stability, war also deprived postcolonial states of the resources required for development. Especially challenging during wartime is the preservation of democratic norms and institutions. This is not an abstract issue, but a challenge that involves real dilemmas: how to provide sufficient security for elections to take place despite violent threats by the enemy; whether to tolerate civilian protests against the government's conduct of war that can be exploited by the enemy; how to prosecute war crimes without affecting the morale of troops on the front lines; and how to protect civil rights while preventing enemy infiltration. These are taxing dilemmas even for long-established democracies, let alone young governments that lack democratic traditions. The more protracted and intense the war, the likelier it becomes for democratic norms and institutions to be compromised.

Like other young postcolonial states in Asia and Africa, the Republic of Vietnam confronted a largely illiterate population, an underdeveloped agrarian economy dominated by foreign influence and dependent on trade with the metropole, and a diverse society beset by deep ethnic and class cleavages. These were the objective conditions that made radical revolutions attractive and popular in much of the postcolonial world, and Vietnam was no exception. In fact, when the republic was established in 1955, a revolutionary government was already consolidating power in North Vietnam, posing a critical threat to the South Vietnamese state's survival. Nonetheless, there was much more to the Republic of Vietnam than its involvement in a war. Central to its story, we believe, were the collective efforts of many men and women dedicated to nation building. This volume explores their efforts and the many challenges they faced.

Challenges of Nation Building in the Republic of Vietnam

The Republic of Vietnam was founded in October 1955 under the leadership of President Ngô Đình Diệm and with the support of many Vietnamese political groups. The republic emerged from the protracted war (1946–54) between France and the Democratic Republic of Vietnam (DRV), an anticolonial coalition led by Hồ Chí Minh and increasingly controlled by communist partisans. In great part due to concern over communist influence within the DRV, many nationalists rallied instead during the war behind Bảo Đại, the former emperor of Vietnam, demanding a united, independent Vietnamese state free of French and communist domination. Meanwhile, fighting a losing battle against the Chinese-trained and Chinese-equipped DRV, which likewise claimed the mantle of national independence, French colonial authorities established a Vietnamese auxiliary army of some 167,000 soldiers by 1954.[8]

Defeated by Hồ Chí Minh's forces at the Battle of Điện Biên Phủ in 1954, France began withdrawing from Indochina following peace accords signed later that year in Geneva. The Geneva Accords also left Vietnam divided along the seventeenth parallel, with DRV authority established in the North, and Bảo Đại's fledgling State of Vietnam recognized in the South. While communist forces quickly consolidated control over the DRV, or North Vietnam, Ngô Đình Diệm—a Catholic nationalist—emerged victorious in a struggle against Bảo Đại for control over the South. By 1955, Diệm had swept Bảo Đại and his supporters aside, using a needlessly rigged referendum to proclaim his authority and inaugurate the new Republic of Vietnam—widely known as South Vietnam.

The republic that Ngô Đình Diệm founded was not created from scratch; instead, it inherited the remnants of both the colonial bureaucracy and the French-trained Vietnamese military. Its territory extended up to the seventeenth parallel—the effective border with the communist DRV in the North—and contained roughly fourteen million inhabitants, including, at least initially, a small number of committed communist partisans.

The newborn Southern republic initially seemed outmatched. Its most intractable challenge was to secure widespread popular legitimacy. After all, despite Ngô Đình Diệm's impeccable nationalist credentials, the state he inherited had evolved under the shadow of the French military. The armed forces required thorough reorganization, and their loyalty to the government in Saigon had yet to be tested. Association with the United States was also a double-edged sword, undermining the republic's assertions of sovereignty both at home and abroad. Moreover, while many in the South were apprehensive about the Vietnamese communists, they were also divided over long-standing ethnic, ideological, religious, and regional differences. As a result, upon proclaiming his presidency, Ngô Đình Diệm was still far from earning widespread allegiance among the South's diverse non-communist-aligned political communities.

In rural areas, the Diệm government's position was less certain still. Significant pockets of the Southern countryside had embraced communist rule during the war with France, and many noncommunist Southerners nonetheless respected Hồ Chí Minh. Additionally, following Vietnam's 1954 partition, the communists maintained clandestine weapons caches and cadres, in anticipation of future political or military mobilization. Meanwhile, in a further challenge to the new state's internal unity and legitimacy, nearly one million Northern refugees had migrated to the South, requiring urgent assistance and posing the risk of a native Southern backlash.

Despite these daunting odds, the state proved relatively capable during its first five years in power. South Vietnam achieved a degree of political stability and military security, enabling notable economic and cultural development. The economic transition from French control to Vietnamese sovereignty went relatively smoothly, complemented by educational reforms aimed at asserting a postcolonial Vietnamese national identity (see chapters 2 and 8 in this volume).[9] The migration of Northern writers, artists, and intellectuals to the South also stimulated new ideas and movements such as the Sáng Tạo (Creativity) literary group and the magazine *Bách Khoa* (Polytechnics) (see chapter 13).[10]

Yet the Ngô Đình Diệm government's increasing nepotism, corruption, and perceived Catholic favoritism created deep discontentment among the political elites.

Equally significant, communist attacks on government targets and the assassination of local officials escalated sharply in 1958 and 1959, claiming the lives of hundreds of government supporters.[11] Though this communist revolt was increasingly under Hanoi's direction, it was fueled in part by native Southerners' growing dissatisfaction with Diệm, especially after a draconian 1959 crackdown saw former anti-French guerrillas condemned as communists and summarily detained, tortured, or executed by government forces.

By 1960, the legitimacy of the Ngô Đình Diệm government was in crisis, with unrest in some provinces and urban anticommunists publicly decrying Diệm's authoritarianism. Although the government made impressive counterinsurgency gains in 1962, this military success was overshadowed by the mounting political tensions, compounded by renewed communist momentum.[12] Widespread Buddhist protests in the summer of 1963 combined with Diệm's resistance to American demands for reform prompted President John F. Kennedy and several advisers to lend secret support to a South Vietnamese military coup. On November 1, 1963, Ngô Đình Diệm was deposed, and then murdered the following day along with his brother.

The Central Intelligence Agency–backed coup resulted in four years of political chaos, as a procession of rival generals and weak civilian leaders competed to fill the void. Seizing the opportunity, Hanoi escalated its military campaign in the South, with the goal of achieving immediate victory. The White House, alarmed that South Vietnam was on the brink of collapse, prepared a massive expansion of the war to follow the 1964 presidential election. In response, Moscow and especially Beijing rushed to aid Hanoi, helping it to meet the American challenge.

But while U.S. military intervention may have forestalled Saigon's capitulation in 1965, it generated a new set of debilitating long-term obstacles. The war destabilized South Vietnam's countryside, forcing millions to seek refuge in mushrooming urban slums. The influx of American wealth, personnel, and consumer goods prompted deep resentment toward the corrupting effects of foreign culture, and American largesse created deep imbalances in the Southern economy (see chapters 1, 3, and 13).

Faced once again with formidable overlapping challenges, South Vietnam's leaders and civilians managed an unlikely if qualified recovery. Following a second Buddhist uprising in 1966, which saw much of the central coast defying central government authority, the military junta was compelled to make political concessions in order to both regain popular legitimacy and shore up wavering American support. Accordingly, 1967 saw a new constitution, a bicameral assembly, and presidential elections. Though widely seen in the South as a fig leaf to legitimize de facto military rule, the 1967 reforms helped restore political stability, enshrining the state's pledge to uphold administrative transparency, political pluralism, and the rule of law.

Following the elections, South Vietnamese officials made unheralded progress, promoting economic development and introducing social and administrative reform. In the countryside, long-standing land claims by tenant farmers were recognized and legalized, at the South Vietnamese government's initiative (see chapter 4). And despite constant tension and surveillance by an apprehensive military regime, a vibrant civil society also emerged in Saigon during this phase of the war, resulting in a blossoming in arts, science, and the humanities (see chapters 13 and 14). American technology, material goods, and media were avidly consumed, provoking intense cultural and philosophical debates. Though the government still wielded great power over society, opposition voices and parties were afforded relative tolerance between 1967 and 1971, especially in urban centers.

The communist Tết Offensive of 1968 provided a profound test of the South's political institutions, which largely weathered the crisis intact. The Tết attacks generated a wave of passionate if short-lived anticommunist solidarity. Exposed to often indiscriminate American firepower, the communists suffered substantial casualties, affording the Saigon government an opportunity to increase its rural presence. Communist atrocities, particularly the massacre of nearly three thousand civilians in Huế, repulsed previously ambivalent Southerners, particularly among the urban population.[13] From then on, urban Southerners fled en masse wherever communist forces advanced.

In the United States, however, Tết shocked a public subject to years of official deception about the war, leading to renewed doubts over the conflict's merits and prospects, and a clamor for American withdrawal. In response to mounting popular demands, incoming U.S. president Richard Nixon began reducing the American presence, expanding and equipping South Vietnamese forces to bear a greater share of the defense burden (see chapters 3 and 7). This approach appeared to pay off when, in 1972, a number of Army of the Republic of Viet Nam (ARVN) units performed effectively against a massive well-armed communist attack, albeit bolstered by decisive American air and logistical support. Nonetheless, reduced American aid and a spiraling defense budget left the South's economy plagued by simultaneous inflation and recession, though a new team of young Vietnamese technocrats worked to mitigate the damage (see chapters 1, 3, and 4).

But with global public opinion already turning against the war, military infighting and accelerated corruption saw the South's fledgling civil society once again brought into conflict against the state. A turning point came with the 1971 presidential election, a markedly different contest than the 1967 affair. As Bùi Diễm, South Vietnam's ambassador to the United States recalled, it marked the moment when "the search for a vivifying national purpose was finally discarded in favor of the chimerical strength of an autocrat."[14] After President Nguyễn Văn Thiệu's written vote-rigging instructions were inevitably leaked, both opposition candidates withdrew in protest. Ignoring even devout anticommunists' howls of remonstration, Thiệu proceeded apace, insisting that the now unopposed contest represented a referendum on his rule. This one-man show, however, greatly damaged the international and domestic legitimacy of his government.

Predictably reelected but faced with mounting public outrage and a renewed communist offensive, the government imposed harsh new legal decrees, effectively silencing opposition parties and the press (see chapter 12). The measured optimism of 1967 now contended with anxiety and despair. And by the mid-1970s, even fanatically anticommunist Northern refugee parties had taken to the streets demanding President Thiệu's resignation.

All the while, plummeting U.S. public support for South Vietnam pressured Washington and Saigon to reach an agreement with Hanoi. The Paris Peace Accords of 1973—signed by the United States and North Vietnam, with South Vietnam resisting until the last minute—left a large communist military force in the South, replenished with fresh troops from the North and backed by supplies from China and the Soviet Union (see chapter 5). Meanwhile, South Vietnam's chronic dependence on American aid, weapons, and air support proved a fatal liability. Though U.S. economic assistance to Saigon remained substantial until the very end, the changing political climate in Washington saw Congress cut U.S. aid in half and prohibit any form of military support for the republic in 1974—an abrupt about-face that few states in South Vietnam's position could have withstood.

Still, if the republican experiment remained uncertain up until the communists' final victory, the ideals that inspired it were real and are essential to understanding the complexity of the war. Their proponents often mirrored the sacrifice and commitment long misattributed solely to the communist side. Among Southern republicans, imprisonment at the hands of French colonial authorities, the South Vietnamese military, and ascendant communist officials after 1975 was not uncommon.

And it was under the Republic of Vietnam that urban Southerners had, at times, enjoyed a relatively liberal environment. Targeted for infiltration if not assassination by communist agents, and for surveillance and harassment by their own government, student, religious, ethnic, or professional organizations clung to their hard-fought autonomy. Inspired by democratic ideals and the antiwar movement in the West, many war-fatigued Southerners rallied behind calls for peace. Repeatedly frustrated by their government, Southern civil society groups reliably took to the streets to protest, at times managing to effect meaningful political change. If only fitfully attained, these republican visions were nonetheless widespread and powerful, and worthy of more serious consideration than most studies of the war have afforded them thus far.

Featuring testimonies and recollections from across the duration of the Republic of Vietnam, by high-ranking officials and everyday citizens alike, this volume is uniquely equipped to document the challenges, setbacks, and aspirations that informed the republican project. It demonstrates that South Vietnam's fate was far from preordained, its prospects ebbing and flowing over time. And it preserves for posterity the voices of a generation that played a pivotal but long overlooked role in one of the twentieth century's most tragic and dramatic encounters.

Overview of the Book

This volume is divided into five themes: economic development; politics and security; education; journalism and media; and culture and the arts.

Chapters 1–4 cover banking, finance, and economic development. Minister of Trade and Industry Nguyễn Đức Cường offers a sweeping overview of the key challenges faced by RVN leaders over two decades in building a foundation for economic growth. Vũ Quốc Thúc describes the challenges he faced while establishing the banking and financial sector during the First Republic's turbulent transition from French colony to independent state. Phạm Kim Ngọc, minister of the economy during the Second Republic, describes his team's attempts to avert financial disaster following the withdrawal of U.S. aid beginning in 1969. And former minister of agriculture and land reform Cao Văn Thân reveals his contributions to agricultural modernization and to the 1970 Land to the Tiller land-reform campaign.

Politics and security are the themes of chapters 5–7. Present during the critical diplomatic showdowns that helped seal South Vietnam's fate, Hoàng Đức Nhã considers the trials of contending with a superpower central to South Vietnam's foreign relations. Trần Minh Công, meanwhile, recounts the challenges he faced at the helm of the National Police Academy during a period of political unrest and guerilla insurgency. Finally, Bùi Quyền reflects on his experiences as a frontline soldier, his assessment of the South Vietnamese military, and his insights from working with American advisors.

Chapters 8–9 are discussions of education by Nguyễn Hữu Phước and Võ Kim Sơn, two teachers and school administrators in the Second Republic. Nguyễn Hữu Phước discusses the philosophical tenets underlying the educational system. His chapter covers high-profile developments such as the comprehensive high schools, community colleges, teacher-training methods, and the use of objective tests for high school graduates. Võ Kim Sơn focuses on her personal experiences as a teacher in the diverse educational environments of South Vietnam, including the National Wards Schools, the College of Education in Saigon University, and the private Catholic school Thánh Mẫu in Gia Định Province.

In chapters 10–13, journalists Phạm Trần, Vũ Thanh Thủy, and Trùng Dương offer their perspectives on the media scene in the RVN. As a journalist and editor with a career spanning both the First and Second Republics, Phạm Trần provides an overview of major issues relating to press freedom in South Vietnam and also discusses the control of the press in Vietnam today. Vũ Thanh Thủy was a young war correspondent in the 1970s, and her chapter describes her battlefield observations and the role of the media (both South Vietnamese and international) in the war. Trùng Dương, a novelist who was a cofounder of the daily *Sóng Thần* in Saigon in the 1970s, discusses how the paper played an aggressive watchdog role in the late Second Republic and how journalists bravely challenged the government's attempt to muffle the press.

Finally, the last two chapters are testimonies from novelist Nhã Ca and actress Kiều Chinh. Both authors capture the vibrant and rich literature and arts scene in the RVN. Nhã Ca particularly highlights the relative freedom writers enjoyed at the time and the challenges facing them during and after the war. While Kiều Chinh focuses primarily on the remarkable growth of cinema under the Second Republic, her chapter also offers valuable memories of cinematic development during the colonial and early postcolonial years in both North and South Vietnam.

The individuals who offer their testimonies in this volume represent a range of professions and perspectives, and their diverse voices and deep experiences contribute to a nuanced understanding of South Vietnamese society and the Vietnam War. Most of the authors were relatively young at the time of the events they describe, coming of age or beginning their careers during the First Republic. They came from middle-class backgrounds, and many were educated in the West. Some displayed strong adherence to liberal values; others showed a deep commitment to a capitalist economy; and many were optimistic about the future of the RVN until the very end. They faced massive challenges in their work, whether from shifting American strategy, communist threats, or their own government's repressive policies.

More broadly, their testimonies present a continually evolving and at times seemingly viable nation-building project with significant South Vietnamese agency. The various authors emphasize its liberal constitution, certain functioning representative institutions, modern military and police force, technocratic bureaucracy, dynamic educational and economic systems, dedicated journalists, and lively community of artists and writers. Their accounts portray a complex society that strove to overcome regional, religious, and political schisms while struggling to establish republican institutions. Despite their diverse and sometimes opposing political positions, many of these contributors shared a vision of a national community free from war, communist and authoritarian rule, and foreign intervention—whether French, American, Soviet, or Chinese.

Several testimonies offer their authors' personal views of their communist enemies and American allies, as well as their explanations for the ultimate defeat of South Vietnam. These authors see communist North Vietnam as part of the Communist Bloc bent on imposing a communist regime all over Vietnam. They admit the popularity of the North Vietnamese leader Hồ Chí Minh, yet attribute the communist advantage primarily to their skills in psychological warfare and their use of violence and coercion.

Americans appear in mixed light in the testimonies of RVN government officials. American support is noted, but some authors take issues with the imperious attitude of certain American officials and advisors such as Henry Kissinger and John Paul Vann. South Vietnamese journalists and educators admired American values and institutions, but some profoundly question the attitude of the American media toward the republic.

Some authors believe that American reduction of support after 1973 led to the fall of South Vietnam in April 1975 to the communists, who continued to receive full backing from their allies. Five authors did not leave Vietnam after that loss, and three of them were incarcerated for as long as thirteen years. Whether or not they were the targets of communist retributions, several authors feel strongly vindicated in their lost cause, given what happened in postwar Vietnam since 1975.

In providing their testimonies, the contributors were constrained by time, health conditions, and the limitations of their memories. As editors, we asked them to recount events to the best of their knowledge, checked the facts to the extent possible, and helped them to follow academic writing norms. However, we value their testimonies not only for their potential use as primary sources by historians but also for their perspectives and sentiments. The latter may be fair or biased, insightful or misguided, but more importantly, they enable both specialists and general readers to gain a sense of the difficult yet exciting period in which they helped make a difference.

To contextualize and enhance the value of their testimonies, we commissioned two additional chapters written by professional historians who are Vietnamese-Americans. Chapter 15 by Nu-Anh Tran of the University of Connecticut explains the neglect of the Republic of Vietnam in the American historical memory and makes a personal appeal to the diasporic community for help in addressing this problem. Echoing our view about the importance of memories, Tran urges "everyone who lived under the RVN to write memoirs, to grant interviews, and to share their memories." The most important kind of help from the community, Tran believes, is to provide primary sources for historians, which is what this volume aims at. In addition, the community should support Vietnamese studies, value the humanities and the social sciences as possible careers for their children, and support intellectual freedom.

In chapter 16, Tuan Hoang of Pepperdine University discusses how historians view the values and limitations of personal memoirs. Hoang also reviews some of the most important memoirs written in the Vietnamese language by former government and civil society leaders of the RVN; these are not the same figures who contribute to this volume but were no less prominent. These memoirs have been published in the United States for many years, but scholars have hardly used them. Hoang's review helps not only to provide a broader context for the testimonies in this volume but also to draw out the major themes in those memoirs that parallel our discussion above on the challenges facing nation-building efforts in the republic. These themes include communist violence that explains the harsh anticommunist policies in the early years of Ngô Đình Diệm, contested views of the First Republic, and a generally more positive assessment of the Second Republic. The bourgeois values embraced by the RVN, Hoang points out, drew support from many Vietnamese at the time and are a source of nostalgia for many in Vietnam today.

Looking Forward

For too long the Vietnam War has been popularly understood as a conflict primarily between the United States against a unified Vietnamese nation, presumed to have been led by Hồ Chí Minh. The underlying Vietnamese ideological and political clash, in which the United States played a shifting role over a thirty-year period, has often been obscured by scholars who exaggerate American importance on the one hand, and assume overwhelming Vietnamese support for the communists on the other.

But new scholarship since the end of the Cold War reveals that North Vietnam's leaders were often motivated more by communist doctrine than pragmatic nationalism, contrary to what many opponents of the American war effort presumed.[15] Conversely, historians have traced the emergence of republican constitutionalism—championed by many of South Vietnam's diverse political groups—back to the early twentieth-century colonial era.[16] No mere Cold War proxy struggle, the communist/republican schism in Vietnam was irreconcilable long before American intervention began in earnest, and it lingers among Vietnamese across the globe even today. The South Vietnamese state struggled to overcome its dependence on U.S. assistance, and its republican nation-builders drew from long-standing intellectual traditions and vehemently resisted foreign interference, not least of all from Washington. Given the deep historical and ideological roots of the civil war in Vietnam, and the critical role played by South Vietnamese actors in shaping its outcome, it is no longer possible to ignore the impact of Vietnam's republican heritage to the origins and the outcome of the war. We welcome readers to join us in exploring that experience in the rest of the book.

NOTES

1 Examples of U.S.-centric scholarship are Andrew J. Gawthorpe, *To Build as Well as Destroy: American Nation Building in South Vietnam* (Ithaca: Cornell University Press, 2018); Jessica Elkind, *Aid under Fire: Nation Building and the Vietnam War* (Lexington: University Press of Kentucky, 2016); James Carter, *Inventing Vietnam: The United States and State Building, 1954–1968* (Cambridge: Cambridge University Press, 2008); Christopher T. Fisher, "Nation Building and the Vietnam War," *Pacific Historical Review* 74, no. 3 (2005): 441–56; Jefferson P. Marquis, "The Other Warriors: American Social Science and Nation Building in Vietnam," *Diplomatic History* 24, no. 1 (2000): 79–105.

2 For example, Geoffrey Stewart, *Vietnam's Lost Revolution: Ngô Đình Diệm's Failure to Build an Independent Nation, 1955–1963* (Cambridge: Cambridge University Press, 2017); Phi Vân Nguyen, "Fighting the First Indochina War Again? Catholic Refugees in the Republic of Vietnam, 1954–59," *Sojourn* 31, no. 1 (March 2016): 207–46; Van Nguyen-Marshall, "Student Activism in Time of War: Youth in the Republic of Vietnam, 1960s–1970s," *Journal of Vietnamese Studies* 10, no. 2 (Spring 2015): 43–81; Edward Miller, *Misalliance: Ngo Dinh Diem, the United States, and the Fate of South Vietnam* (Cambridge, MA: Harvard University Press, 2013); Jessica Chapman, *Cauldron of Resistance: Ngo Dinh Diem, the United States, and 1950s Southern Vietnam* (Ithaca: Cornell University Press, 2013); and Philip Catton, *Diem's Final Failure: Prelude to America's War in Vietnam* (Lawrence: University Press of Kansas, 2002). Several studies are recently completed dissertations, including Sean Fear, "The Rise and Fall of the Second Republic: Domestic Politics and Civil Society in U.S.–South Vietnamese Relations, 1967–1971" (PhD dissertation, Cornell University, 2016); Nu-Anh Tran, "Contested Identities: Nationalism in the Republic of Vietnam (1954–1963)" (PhD dissertation, University of California–Berkeley, 2013); and Tuan Hoang, "Ideology in Urban South Vietnam, 1950–1975" (PhD dissertation, University of Notre Dame, 2013).

3 For accounts of ARVN performance in these battles, see Andrew Wiest, *Vietnam's Forgotten Army: Heroism and Betrayal in the ARVN* (New York: New York University Press, 2008); Lam Quang Thi, *Hell in An Loc: The 1972 Easter Invasion and the Battle that Saved South Vietnam* (Denton: University of North Texas Press, 2009); George Veith, *Black April: The Fall of South Vietnam, 1973–1975* (New York: Encounter Books, 2012).

4 The main organizers were Tuong Vu, Peter Zinoman, Sarah Maxims, Nguyễn Đức Cường, Hoàng Đức Nhã, and Trần Quang Minh. We are indebted to the advice, collaboration, and support of Phan Công Tâm, Nu-Anh Tran, Trùng Dương, Bùi Văn Phú, and the late Trần Văn

Sơn. The organizers also are greatly indebted to the assistance provided during the symposium by Nguyễn Nguyệt Cầm, Trần Hạnh, Alex-Thai Vo, Trinh Luu, and Kevin Li.
5 Interested readers are strongly encouraged to consult their rich memoirs and (for Mr. Lâm Lễ Trinh) numerous videos of his interviews with key RVN figures available on YouTube. See Lâm Lễ Trinh, *Thức Tỉnh: Quốc Gia và Cộng Sản* [Nationalism and communism] (self-published, 2007); Huỳnh Văn Lang, *Ký Ức Huỳnh Văn Lang* [Huynh Van Lang's memoirs], 2 vols. (self-published, 2012).
6 A similar but smaller symposium, which inspired our own, took place at Cornell University in 2012 resulting in the publication of *Voices from the Second Republic of South Vietnam (1967–1975)*, ed. Keith W. Taylor (Ithaca: Cornell University, Southeast Asia Program, 2014). This event was organized by Keith Taylor, a prominent historian of Vietnam.
7 See also Norbert Kersting, "Nation-Building," in *International Encyclopedia of Political Science*, ed. Bertrand Badie, Dirk Berg-Schlosser, and Leonardo Morlino (New York: Sage Publications, 2011), 5:1645–50; Francis Fukuyama, "Nation-Building and the Failure of Institutional Memory," in *Nation-Building: Beyond Afghanistan and Iraq*, ed. Francis Fukuyama (Baltimore: Johns Hopkins University Press, 2006), 1–16.
8 Christopher Goscha, *Vietnam: A New History* (New York: Basic Books, 2016), 260.
9 For a comparative study of North and South Vietnam's educational systems, see Olga Dror, *Making Two Vietnams: War and Youth Identities, 1965–1975* (Cambridge: Cambridge University Press, 2018).
10 See Võ Phiến, *Văn Học Miền Nam Tổng Quan* [An overview of South Vietnamese literature] (Westminster, CA: Văn Nghệ Publishers, 2000).
11 Miller, *Misalliance*, 200.
12 David Elliott, *The Vietnamese War: Revolution and Social Change in the Mekong Delta, 1930–1975* (New York: M. E. Sharpe, 2003), 1:407–24; Miller, *Misalliance*, 249–51.
13 Olga Dror, "Translator's Introduction," in Nha Ca, *Mourning Headband for Hue: An Account of the Battle for Hue, Vietnam 1968*, trans. Olga Dror (Bloomington: Indiana University Press, 2014), xxxi.
14 Bui Diem with David Chanoff, *In the Jaws of History* (Boston: Houghton Mifflin, 1987), 293.
15 For example, see Tuong Vu, *Vietnam's Communist Revolution: The Power and Limits of Ideology* (New York: Cambridge University Press, 2017).
16 For examples, see Goscha, *Vietnam*, concluding chapter; Peter Zinoman, *Vietnamese Colonial Republican: The Political Vision of Vũ Trọng Phụng* (Berkeley: University of California Press, 2014); Nu-Anh Tran, "Contested Identities"; Tuan Hoang, "Ideology in Urban South Vietnam."

Chapter One

COPING WITH CHANGES AND WAR, BUILDING A FOUNDATION FOR GROWTH

Nguyễn Đức Cường

Nguyễn Đức Cường graduated summa cum laude from the University of New Hampshire with a bachelor of science in electrical engineering in 1963. He went on to graduate studies at the Massachusetts Institute of Technology where he earned a master of science in electrical engineering and completed the PhD course requirements. Cường has had a long career in both government and corporate sectors. His ten-year career with the RVN government began in June 1965. He was promoted to the post of vice minister for trade in 1970 and minister of trade and industry in 1973. He resigned from this position in November 1974. After April 1975, he settled in the United States and began a career in finance with Exxon Corporation, headquartered in New York. After twenty-nine years of service with Exxon Mobil Corporation and its affiliates, he retired and opened a Vietnamese restaurant in the Silicon Valley area, serving in particular phở, his favorite food.

I returned to Saigon in the summer of 1965, after six years of college and graduate studies in electrical engineering in the United States. I started out as a project engineer at the Industrial Development Center and was transferred to the Ministry of Economy a year later. I waved goodbye to engineering and said hello to economics and finance, a field in which I never had any formal training. But I never looked back.

As I was learning my way in economics and finance, I found that my engineering training, which was highly quantitative and problem-solving oriented, was very useful during my ten years of government service. More importantly, however, it was the people I met during this period, and a combination of fortuitous events, that helped me advance from staff specialist to assistant minister for commerce to minister of trade and industry in 1973.

During the first fifteen years of Republican Vietnam, from 1955 to 1970, we were mainly reacting to events and managing their impact on an ad-hoc basis. Military activity was increasing, and the influx of American troops and foreign aid put significant pressure on our meager domestic resources. The result was runaway inflation and a booming currency black market.

But by 1970, our ministry was in a position to take major initiatives of its own, establishing a new legal framework to develop the economy, especially in agriculture and natural resources. We took action to reform our exchange rates, interest rates, and taxation and developed new institutions while strengthening existing ones. Our objective was to build a market-based economy, relying on the private sector and the four pillars of legislation, institutions, policy, and good governance to meet the dual challenge of unrelenting war activities and dwindling foreign aid.

This chapter aims to provide a broad overview of economic development in the Republic of Vietnam (RVN) under both republics. The long-term perspective is useful to gain a sense of the republic's achievements and failures over two decades. Some of the major activities recounted below will be told in greater detail in the next chapters by my colleagues who were primarily responsible. I will also dwell at some length on the activities I was personally involved in since the mid-1960s.

Economic Development in the RVN

The republican era began with high hopes and expectations after eighty years of French colonial rule. Initial difficulties were to be expected; they included questionable loyalty from the armed forces, an empty treasury, internal political infighting, rural insurrection, and over eight hundred thousand Northern refugees requiring resettlement. Under the steadfast guidance of new prime minister Ngô Đình Diệm, and with a significant amount of American aid, these difficulties were overcome.

Vũ Quốc Thúc successfully negotiated the smooth transfer of monetary and financial authority from the French government to our new nation (see chapter 2 in this volume). At the time our country was impoverished by years of warfare and colonial rule, and income per capita was estimated at just $75 in 1955. Agriculture accounted for 25 percent of the economy, followed by a government military and civilian service sector of 35 percent. Our industrial base was negligible. Exports consisted mainly of rubber and rice, amounting to $80 million, while we consumed over $250 million of imported goods. This trade imbalance continued to swell as the war intensified.

Military activities dominated the entire republican experience, from guerrilla skirmishes to all-out conventional war, eventually involving over 1.5 million South Vietnamese troops alone. Without foreign aid, this was an impossible burden for a poor country of seventeen million people to bear.

Nonetheless, we achieved a measure of economic stability and growth during the early years of the republic, in large part thanks to American assistance, which unquestionably played a very significant role during the state's two decades in existence. In the first fiscal year alone, aid from the United States amounted to $320 million, about 35 percent of our gross national product (GNP), much of which financed the settlement of the Northern refugees.

During the first decade (1955–65), American economic aid averaged $210 million per year, roughly 15 percent of our GNP. Average U.S. aid soared to $620 million annually, some 20 percent of GNP, as the war escalated in the decade that followed. The total value of American economic aid over two decades of war amounted to $8.5 billion.[1]

American military aid to South Vietnam was even more substantial. The United States spent some $1.5 billion supporting France in its war against the Việt Minh.[2] As the level of American combat troops swelled beginning in 1965, so too did the volume of military aid, which averaged the entire amount spent assisting France—$1.5 billion—every year between 1965 and 1975. In total, American military aid to South Vietnam reached $16.8 billion.

This generous foreign aid was designed to provide near-term economic stability in order to facilitate the implementation of our political and military plan. But little progress could be made weaning our country from foreign aid as long as fighting remained intense. Still, despite the ongoing conflict, our government undertook several significant initiatives to enable long-term investment and growth during the last five years of the war.

The First Decade, 1955–1965

From France, South Vietnam inherited an economy that was in reasonably good working order. There was no run on the banks, and no runaway inflation despite an empty treasury. The foreign exchange rate was fixed, and the government tightly controlled all transactions. Although the young republic started with an empty treasury, American aid soon began flowing, beginning with $320 million in the 1954 fiscal year—equivalent to 35 percent of our GNP.[3]

The government's first notable measure was to transfer monetary and financial authority from France to Vietnam. Vũ Quốc Thúc attended the Four-Party Conference in Paris in late 1954, where he negotiated outstanding issues between France and the other Indochinese states. Thúc's delegation issued its recommendations on December 30, and they were approved and implemented the following day. This smooth and efficient transition set the tone for economic and financial policy in the years to come, establishing respect for the rule of law, private ownership, and continuity during the transition.

To advance their economic interests, the French had introduced modern banking into Vietnam. But the system we inherited had become antiquated, based on old sets of rules and regulations. Everything was reported directly to the Ministry of Finance in Paris, and all the major private banks were foreign-owned. Banking services were concentrated in Saigon, leaving the countryside almost entirely neglected.

On January 1, 1955, the establishment of the National Bank of Vietnam opened a new banking era. Vũ Quốc Thúc served as its first governor, and he soon formed the Credit Commercial Bank of Vietnam (Việt Nam Thương Tín or VNTT), responsible for implementing the National Bank and Finance Ministry's credit and banking policies and for complying with the import procedures required by the American aid program. After all, the existing Saigon private banks were not equipped to deal with the intricacies of the U.S. foreign aid regime.

The VNTT grew in influence and stature under the able leadership of Director Nguyễn Hữu Hanh, a dynamic graduate of the Hautes-Études Commerciales in France. In time, he would head both the National Bank and the VNTT, with Phạm Kim Ngọc serving as deputy. The VNTT became the bank of choice for local importers, a leader in terms of cost, availability of financing, know-how, and quality of service. And thus, modern commercial banking in Vietnam was born. It would play a critical economic role in the years to come, accommodating the influx of American aid dollars.

Overvaluation of the local currency had always been an issue. This was never fully addressed because, politically, devaluation was always a very difficult decision, and no minister of economy or finance wished to bear the responsibility. But by 1962, however, the difference between the black market rate of eighty Đồng to the dollar and the official rate of thirty-five Đồng per dollar had become too significant to ignore. In order to avoid the negative connotations of the term "devaluation," an exchange rate adjustment was disguised as a per equation tax, effectively changing the official rate from thirty-five to sixty Đồng per dollar on all commercial transactions.

Meanwhile, a Directorate General of Planning (DGP) was established under the direct stewardship of the president, thus enhancing its authority and influence. Yet the DGP had no direct authority over government-owned enterprises inherited from the French, including the Hà Tiên Cement Company, the Sugar Cane Processing Company, the Newsprint Company, and the An Hòa-Nông Sơn Mining Company, among others. Some funding was allocated to upgrade these enterprises, but other matters were more pressing, and due to budget constraints, no significant investments were made.

On the other hand, we made substantial progress in human resources development, especially in higher education, technical expertise, and training future leaders. Several new institutes of higher learning were established and continually maintained (see chapters 8 and 9 in this volume). One example was Nông Lâm Súc in the village of Blao, a two-year agricultural school. Founded in 1955, it was routinely upgraded, becoming a full university in 1974. Other examples included the College of Commerce (Cao Đẳng Thương mại), the Phú Thọ Polytechnic School (Cao Đẳng Phú Thọ), the Faculty of Pedagogy (Cao Đẳng Sư phạm), or the National Institution of Administration (Học viên Quốc gia Hành chánh). Additionally, military academies were upgraded into four-year programs.

Scholarships from the Fulbright Program, Colombo Plan, Rockefeller Foundation, or the U.S. Agency for International Development (USAID) accelerated the training of future leaders at overseas universities. Indeed, many of the contributors to this volume were the beneficiaries of these programs. At least 350 students attended university in the United States, with most returning to become leaders in government or in the private sector.

Another challenge was the resettlement of over eight hundred thousand refugees—by all accounts an important success. This gave the South an immediate and significant source of productive manpower, equivalent to 8 percent of its total population at the time. By and large, there were no refugee camps and no idle manpower sitting around waiting for a handout.

The cost of this resettlement program was estimated at about $100 million, and it was financed by direct American aid, including $34 million allocated directly to the central bank to fund individual payments to each arriving family. My own family of five received $25 each after we disembarked in Saigon. The rest of the funding covered the expense of air and sea travel, which the United States government paid to a series of contractors.

Other challenges proved more difficult to address. The first attempt at land reform, in 1956, achieved limited success. Its implementation was too centralized, its administration was top-heavy, and most of the work was done manually, and was therefore very slow. Worse still, big landowners were allowed to keep 150 hectares each, and as a result, 80 percent of the best rice fields remained in their hands. Farmers could only afford land using long-term loans, and the delinquency rate was very high. And as President Diệm came under fire in 1963, the program ground to a halt. Still, we achieved real economic growth of 8.5 percent in 1958 and 9.6 percent in 1959, quite an achievement for a newly independent country facing an armed rebellion.

It is also worth noting that the Southern communists carried out a similar, concurrent land-reform program in the areas of South Vietnam under their control. By contrast, they distributed land free of charge to the farmers who worked it, albeit with limited documentation. This made matters quite complicated after our troops regained control and absentee landowners attempted to collect back rent. Eventually, we carried out a new land-reform campaign, the Land to the Tiller program, which revolutionized the countryside beginning in 1970 (see chapter 4 in this volume).

Meanwhile, in North Vietnam, the transition from French to communist administration was relatively smooth. Communist authorities already controlled most of the North, with French influence concentrated around the Hanoi–Red River Delta corridor. They had their own central bank, which began issuing currency in 1946. Residents were forced to exchange French piastres for "Hồ Chí Minh" Đồng, or throw away their "Hồ Chí Minh" Đồng on pain of arrest after they headed South.

North Vietnam's economy was in bad shape and essentially at a subsistence level. Agricultural production was in shambles due to the disastrous agrarian reforms of 1954–56, which led to the persecution and deaths of thousands of innocent farmers. The state carried out a sweeping economic agenda, replacing the market system with a centrally planned economy and the collectivization or elimination of private business. By the end of the 1960s, the state controlled most of the trade in most agricultural and industrial goods. According to one expert, the end result brought "agricultural decline, economic stagnation and chronic hunger to North Vietnamese for the following two decades."[4] All the while, the Hanoi government was making plans to expand its communist revolution to the South, supported by substantial economic and military aid from China and the Soviet Union.

Turning back to the South, our first decade can be characterized as a transitional phase, from colonialism to a potentially vibrant independent economy. During this time, South Vietnam had enjoyed several years of relative peace and prosperity and achieved decent economic growth at 6 percent per annum between 1955 and 1962.[5] Our first group of engineers, educators, scientists, and economists returned home from overseas training full of fervor and hope. And despite the instability after the deposal of President Diệm, there was still reason to believe that we could follow in the footsteps of South Korea, Taiwan, or Singapore.

THE SECOND DECADE, 1965–1975

Our second decade, on the other hand, was characterized by our struggle to manage constant change, often due to factors or events beyond our control or even understanding. The first three thousand U.S. marines landed in Đà Nẵng in March 1965, paving the way for more than half a million American troops to follow. Our country was simply not equipped to cope with this sudden and massive influx of men and material. Almost immediately, we faced a number of serious challenges, including inflation of up to 63 percent by 1966, chronic congestion at our ports, shortages of essential goods like rice and construction materials, and rampant profiteering in currency and commodities on the emerging black market.

Congestion at the port of Saigon figured prominently in many of U.S. ambassador Ellsworth Bunker's reports to the president. Saigon was our major port of entry, and it was designed to clear a total trade volume of around $330 million per year. By 1966, this figure had doubled, owing to the rapid increase in American commercial aid. In terms of tonnage, it could handle one hundred thousand tons of imports every year, yet "by 1967, a million tons of supplies a month were pouring in to sustain the US force."[6] Clearly its capacity was totally inadequate.

Port congestion severely constrained the flow of goods into the country, resulting in serious shortages and spiraling price inflation. It also contributed to the image of an inept South Vietnamese administration, where corruption flourished at the ports and where tax-free luxury goods—imported for the exclusive use of American soldiers—inevitably found their way to the Saigon black market.

We had to alleviate port congestion, at any cost. Virtually overnight, the U.S. Army Corps of Engineers began dredging rivers and building roads, bridges, and even new deep-draft harbors, among them massive new ports in Saigon and Cam Ranh Bay. They erected fuel depots, warehouses, helicopter landing pads, and airfields scattered throughout the provinces to accommodate jets. Even remote parts of the country were connected with a state-of-the-art communications grid.

Even then, it took more than three years for the port congestion situation to be resolved. Built to very high military standards with little heed paid to the cost, this infrastructure would eventually prove very valuable during the postwar reconstruction.

At the Ministry of Economy, we soon faced a significant backlog of import license applications. This was no small matter: we depended on a smooth flow of imports to alleviate the shortages driving inflation and to reduce our budget deficits via the use of the counterpart fund, which resulted from the purchase of dollars to fund the import of goods.

The backlog at the licensing stage was created by the significant increase in foreign aid and our unfamiliarity with American procedures. Our importers, accustomed to the European Brussels Tariff Code, had no knowledge of the American Commodity Import Program Tariff Codes. As a staff specialist at the Ministry of Economy Directorate of Foreign Aid, I was on hand to witness the chaos in the summer of 1967. I was able to make myself useful simply because I knew the English language. In the process, I learned about the difficulties posed by importing such a large volume of aid, as well as the intricacies imposed by the U.S. Congress. The USAID mission also assigned a full-time staff just to assist us with moving through the paperwork and ensuring we complied with the regulations and procedures of the USAID program.

But the import license bottleneck was symptomatic of a deeper problem. In keeping with the French traditions of economic and financial management, licensing control in Vietnam had always been a tool of the Ministry of Economy. But in an environment of overvalued currency and limited foreign exchange availability exacerbated by soaring inflation, consumer demand was driven by a combination of speculation and inappropriate policies.

Government officials at the Ministry of Economy administered access to foreign exchange at the official rate. This job could become difficult, or even controversial, when there was a significant difference between the official rate and the black market rate. The lucky importers in effect were guaranteed a windfall profit when their application for the official foreign exchange rate was granted. There were three ways to deal with this imbalance situation: to tax away the windfall profit, an unrealistic scenario; to bring the official rate to be in line with the market rate by devaluation, a politically risky move; or to impose price control on the imported goods, a measure consistent with the traditions inherited from the French bureaucracy, therefore politically safe but ineffective.

Despite one round of devaluation in October 1961, the black market dollar rate continued to grow. So Finance Minister Âu Trường Thanh attempted another unpopular devaluation in October 1966, disguised as a per equation tax on imports. From then on, there would be no further action in the foreign exchange market until 1971, when the National Assembly granted the president the authority to set the tax, interest, and exchange rates. It took us until 1973 to liberalize the import licensing process via delegation to commercial banks, and by then, the official exchange rate was essentially in line with the market rate.

The birth of the Second Republic in October 1967 opened up new opportunities for our country after four years of political uncertainty. The new constitution allowed us to create a new legal framework to attract foreign capital and management know-how, and to update laws and regulations related to land reform, monetary and fiscal policy, foreign exchange, and in particular, exploration for petroleum and natural resources.

Two prime ministers came and went during the period between 1967 and 1969, with little accomplishments in the field of economy and finance. Inflation was still out of control, and the U.S. dollar black market was still thriving. This phenomenon was somewhat counterintuitive since foreign exchange was plentiful. Total American aid combined with money spent by U.S. troops averaged about $700 million per year between 1966 and 1968, triple the amount in the previous three years. The underlying cause of this black market was a significantly overvalued local currency.

A new cabinet was installed in October 1969 under the leadership of Prime Minister Trần Thiện Khiêm, a four-star general who would serve as head of government for the next five and a half years. This provided much-needed continuity and stability in order for us to take action on the economy, our finances, and long-term investment. The government was under tremendous pressure to attack galloping inflation and the growing budget deficit.

However, any monetary, fiscal, or foreign-exchange measures needed to be approved by the Senate and the House of Representatives. Working with the legislature became part of our responsibilities at the ministry. The result was innumerable and exhausting meetings between staff at the National Bank, the Ministries of Economy and Finance, and the various legislative committees.

To deal with inflation and reduce the deficit, we announced an austerity program in October 1969, following a series of meetings with the legislature where we discussed and agreed on new import duty rates. This was a time-consuming exercise, held behind closed doors in the House of Representatives Assembly Hall. In practice, the talks were not a well-kept secret, and the new rates were not effective in raising revenues. The end result was a disaster. According to Minister of Economy Phạm Kim Ngọc, little revenue was raised despite import prices shooting up significantly (see chapter 3 in this volume). The solution should have been an outright currency devaluation, but the president was not authorized to enact this under the new constitution.

Devaluation, rising interest rates, and increasing taxes were politically unpopular. And even though legislators claimed to support fighting inflation, none of them were in the mood to do so through taxes, interest rates, or devaluation. Finally, the president and the legislature reached a compromise in the form of the 1970 Program Law.

The Program Law authorized the president to take action on fixing of exchange rates, interest rates, or tax rates within a certain period of time. As a result, managing the deficit was now under his purview, a responsibility that the legislature did not truly want to assume. In essence, the budget deficit was out of control due to the salaries paid to over 1.4 million government employees and soldiers, which at one point consumed 80 percent of the total budget. To meet this fiscal challenge we needed to address three issues: the exchange rate that determined the level of foreign aid via the use of the counterpart fund; the interest rate determining the level of savings by the private sector to mop up excess liquidity; and our tax collection rates.

When we adopted a floating exchange rate in July 1971, political factors were pretty much taken out of consideration. Small exchange-rate adjustments were announced by the National Bank every few days, depending on market conditions and inflation. But the exchange rate stayed fairly stable, holding up rather well until the last few weeks of the republic. Likewise, a floating interest rate reflecting market conditions was also implemented. This provided an incentive for the private sector to save or buy government bonds, mopping up excess liquidity. By 1974, bond purchases by the private sector accounted for 12 percent of the national budget.

Finally, to tackle our fiscal challenge, we had to increase domestic tax revenues. We needed new taxes, along with strong programs to improve tax administration and collection rates. On the other hand, it was unrealistic to expect South Vietnam to carry the full burden of the war without a decent transitional period, allowing foreign aid to be phased out.

We took a big political risk when we introduced the value-added tax (VAT). It had two attractive features. First, the VAT could be established by presidential decree under the Program Law, without having to consult the legislature. Second, the VAT by definition is broad-based. Most importantly, according to Ministry of Finance calculations, the budget deficit could be meaningfully reduced by small adjustments to the VAT rate.

We were probably the only country in Asia with a VAT at that time. It had been introduced in just a few European countries. France experimented with the VAT on a limited basis beginning in 1954, but did not extend it to the retail level until 1968. Denmark was the first European country to introduce it fully, with a single rate in 1967. In the United States, the VAT was not well known.

VAT compliance and enforcement would also prove relatively simple. Businesses were required to keep records of purchases and sales, and taxes paid or collected, while retailers needed only to document their purchases and taxes paid. After computerizing license sales data, fraud detection would become much more straightforward, and the VAT was also useful in improving business tax compliance.

VAT initial implementation was somewhat hasty. It caused a significant political uproar and might have cost a minister his job. However, over time, it proved to be a significant source of tax revenue.

Eventually, we were able to overhaul the domestic tax system. New laws were promulgated in 1972, and by 1974, our domestic tax structure was almost completely modernized. By 1973, we were collecting 70 percent more in tax than we had the previous year, albeit only a 17 percent increase when adjusted for inflation.

Nonetheless, we also faced several different types of price crisis during this decade, notably in connection with the rice trade and the supply of petroleum products. Rice price crises in particular were recurring, due to a range of factors, including artificial shortages caused by speculative hoarding, hindered distribution stemming from constant military activity, shipping delays as a result of port congestion, or enemy crop destruction. The standard way to deal with rice crises was to dispatch inspectors to investigate and issue penalties. But this approach was plagued by corruption and abuses and never very effective at the best of times. We knew we needed to tackle the problem head on with a radical new approach: removing checkpoints, eliminating price controls, and establishing a strategic rice reserve in food-deficit regions. By 1975, we were prepared to begin exporting rice, after twelve years of net imports.

Meanwhile, regarding petroleum, we faced a crisis in 1973 created by the confluence of two events. Enemy rockets had destroyed almost 50 percent of our oil reserves in storage at the Nhà Bè petroleum deposit, just as oil prices quadrupled after OPEC's response to the Yom Kippur War. To keep our military fully supplied, we had to immediately and drastically reduce civilian consumption, resulting in the highest prices for gasoline and kerosene in the world. Yet the option of issuing ration cards was never under consideration.

Finally, we were worried about the threat of a bank run, which would have harmed our reputation as a reliable place to conduct business. Since the risk of a bank run was always high during wartime, steps must be taken to prevent it from happening. Just in case, the National Bank of Vietnam maintained a full set of brand-new Vietnamese Đồng stocked in the vaults in order to circulate or bail out the banks in the event of a run.

Our worst fears were realized in early 1975, as masses of civilians fled the communist advance through central Vietnam on the way to Saigon. We knew the communist strategy was to sow financial panic, perhaps even precipitating our government's collapse before the first shots were fired. In any case, the sight of thousands of refugees arriving in Saigon and withdrawing funds led to frenzy in the capital, resulting in long queues building up at every Saigon bank branch.

Because no single bank could survive the withdrawal of all its deposits, we needed the full intervention of the National Bank, our lender of last resort. Backed by the new uncirculated banknotes in the vaults, National Bank governor Lê Quang Uyển issued unlimited credit lines to all commercial banks, instructing them to cash out all customer demands without interference or red tape. After several days of unimpeded cash withdrawal, bank customers were faced with a new problem: how to protect their mountains of bills in the context of an ongoing war. And thus, most of the withdrawn cash was redeposited after the first week. We had avoided a potentially devastating banking collapse without much effort, and in the end, the National Bank did not even need to tap its banknote reserves.

Beyond grappling with perpetual crises, we also worked to set the foundation for future growth, based on a realistic assessment of our long-term strengths, limitations, and opportunities. Our long-term development goals were based on attributes like a solid legal framework, strong institutions, sound policies, and transparent processes. We worked to overcome challenges such as a lack of investment incentives, high war-risk premiums, limited technical expertise, and a shortage of manpower during wartime.

Two successful projects stand out to me: the Land to the Tiller land-reform program, and the search for offshore oil reserves. The Land to the Tiller program, promulgated in 1970, had four factors in its favor (see chapter 4 in this volume). First was farmers' pride of ownership, after we granted them the land their ancestors had worked for generations free of charge (up to three hectares in the Mekong Delta, and one hectare in central Vietnam). Next was the introduction of miracle rice, a technological breakthrough in food production that could increase rice yields by up to 400 percent. The third factor was the introduction of market pricing, which eliminated price controls and liberalized the flow of rice around the country. And finally, we benefitted from the farmers' own local expertise—nobody was better at assessing the risks to the harvest than they were. By 1974, we had achieved self-sufficiency in rice and were preparing to resume exports the following year.

As for the oil, there was no question that an element of luck played a role in our search. It is rare to strike oil after just the first few wells, but within a year of signing the first exploration and concession agreements, we had already unveiled a massive "Elephant" field. Credit must be given to Minister of the Economy Phạm Kim Ngọc, National Petroleum Administration general manager Trần Văn Khởi, and the members of the National Petroleum Board. Backed by a strong National Petroleum Law passed in 1970, they made a series of wise decisions, including the use of technical experts from Iran, the implementation of a well-balanced concession agreement, a transparent auctioning process that attracted the biggest and most reliable international firms, and the prudent choice to refrain from setting up a national oil exploration company. It would have cost us greatly, in terms of time and money, had we attempted to extract the oil on our own, and there was always the risk of coming up empty-handed. Ultimately, the sale of oil rights offshore—where the risks from the war were low—resulted in an immediate foreign exchange boost of $47 million, after just two rounds of auctioning.

Finally, I want to acknowledge the impact of American aid contributions to our long-term development opportunities. Financing for projects such the National Economic Development Fund, the Land to the Tiller program, and the strategic rice reserve was essential. Additionally, the value of infrastructure built by the Army Corps of Engineers should not be overlooked. I would estimate that the cost of these initiatives in order to facilitate the participation of U.S. troops amounted to roughly $3.2 billion, some 20 percent of total American military assistance during this period.

Postwar development programs also received much attention at the highest level of both our governments. During the 1966 Manila Summit, President Lyndon Johnson and Prime Minister Nguyễn Cao Kỳ determined that "effort should be made, by Vietnamese and American working together, to examine the probable problems and opportunities of the postwar period, and to establish policies and programs for the rapid restoration and development of the Vietnamese economy whenever that might be and however it should come about."[7]

As a result of the summit, a U.S.-Vietnamese Joint Development Group was established, which produced the Thúc-Lilienthal Postwar Development Report. Unfortunately, the report was left collecting dust on the shelves of our Ministry of Planning, likely because of insufficient time to review the recommendations. The assumption of an imminent postwar scenario was also premature and unrealistic.

With the benefit of hindsight, one recommendation from the report, on agricultural development, strikes me as particularly unrealistic and totally disconnected from the realities on the ground. It argued that

> the fragmentation of large holdings, irrespective of the consequences on production and farm income is undesirable. Many crops cannot be grown economically and competitively other than on a large scale, and land reforms should not be carried out so far as to make such profitable enterprises and potential employers of labor impossible. The solution to rural poverty in some areas may be found in an efficient farm labor force rather than in small tenant holdings.[8]

The goal of our land-reform efforts was completely the opposite; we had always aimed to create a class of small farm owners by granting them the land they had farmed for generations, free of charge. The Thúc-Lilienthal proposal would instead not only render them landless, but jobless as well. No doubt they would be compensated under this scheme, but what amount of money could justify enduring such upheavals?

Looking Back

In retrospect, we had no capital to squander on big government projects. We had no manpower or organizations to develop an expertise in any specific field. And we had sometimes tried to interfere with the markets, on the erroneous assumption that we could control prices, prevent speculation, and deprive the enemy of food supplies. More often, we strove to convince our leaders to let the market do its work, however imperfect it might be. Our task was simply to establish solid legal foundations, foster strong institutions, implement sound policies, and practice good governance.

We learned from the experience of other countries with similar forms of economy and government. We also saw how a combination of a market-based economy, reliance on the private sector, and sound government policies had done wonders in small Asian countries like Hong Kong, Singapore, Taiwan, and South Korea. And we believed that even in a wartime environment, the same policy measures could work in Vietnam.

Notes

1. Douglas C. Dacy, *Foreign Aid, War, and Economic Development, South Vietnam, 1955–1975* (New York: Cambridge University Press, 1986), 200.
2. Hugues Tertrais, *La piastre et le fusil, le cout de la guerre d'Indochine, 1945–1954* (Paris: Comité pour l'histoire économique et financière de la France, 2002).
3. Dacy, *Foreign Aid*, 200.
4. Tuong Vu, *Vietnam's Communist Revolution: The Power and Limits of Ideology* (New York: Cambridge University Press, 2017), 148.
5. Dacy, *Foreign Aid*, 40, table 3.1.
6. Stanley Karnov, *Vietnam: A History* (New York: Viking Press, 1983), 436.
7. Cited in Vũ Quốc Thúc and David Lilienthal, *The Postwar Development of the Republic of Vietnam: Policies and Programs* (Saigon: Joint Development Group, Postwar Planning Group, Development and Resources Corp., 1969), 2:ix–x.
8. Thúc and Lilienthal, *The Postwar Development of the Republic of Vietnam*, 2:30.

CHAPTER TWO

THE BIRTH OF CENTRAL BANKING, 1955–1956

Vũ Quốc Thúc

Vũ Quốc Thúc was born in 1920 in Nam Định, and graduated with a master's degree in economics in 1952 and a doctorate in law in 1953 from the University of Paris. He was dean of the Law Faculty at the University of Hanoi from 1951 until 1954 when it moved to Saigon. He served briefly as minister of education and youth under Prime Minister Bửu Lộc (1953–54). In October 1954, new prime minister Ngô Đình Diệm appointed Thúc to be a member of the Vietnamese delegation to participate in the Four-Party Conference and negotiate with the French government on various issues related to sovereignty transfer. After the National Bank of Vietnam was established in January 1955, Thúc was appointed deputy governor, then governor six months later. After leaving his position, he went back to teaching as dean of the Faculty of Law at the University of Saigon in 1957. He was called into government service again during 1969–71 as deputy prime minister in charge of reconstruction and development. In this capacity, he coauthored the Thúc-Lilienthal report (1968). Thúc stayed behind after April 1975. Raymond Barre, formerly his classmate at the University of Paris and then prime minister of France, intervened with the Hanoi government to let him go to France in 1978. He went back to teaching at the University of Paris until retirement in 1988.

THE FOUR-PARTY CONFERENCE

The July 1954 Geneva Accords divided Vietnam along the seventeenth parallel. I was then dean of the School of Law at the University of Hanoi. Like thousands of other families in the North, we uprooted ourselves and headed South to start a new life. There was a transition period of ten months to complete the move. I settled my family in Saigon during the summer of 1954. The entire School of Law had also moved South, and classes had already started for the academic year 1954–55 in Saigon.

Then, in October, I was unexpectedly called to the office of Prime Minister Ngô Đình Diệm in Saigon. I had never met him before. Prime Minister Diệm asked me to join the South Vietnamese delegation to the Four-Party Conference in Paris, where unresolved monetary, banking, and transportation issues would be negotiated between France and its former colonies, the State of Vietnam, Laos, and Cambodia. I gladly accepted the assignment.

I felt confident that I was qualified. I had graduated from the University of Paris with a master's degree in economics and a doctorate in law. And I was not unfamiliar with government service, or in dealing with the French government. I had served as minister of education and youth under former prime minister Nguyễn Phúc Bửu Lộc, Ngô Đình Diệm's predecessor. In that role, Prime Minister Bửu Lộc appointed me as a member of the delegation that had negotiated South Vietnam's transition to independence. In fact, I was in Paris with the delegation when Bửu Lộc resigned, forcing us to return to Saigon. Little did I know that just four months later, I would be back in Paris to once again negotiate with the French government.

As I prepared for the talks, the turbulence of the past six months weighed heavily on my mind. Vietnam was in great turmoil, politically, socially, and financially. Political observers did not give Prime Minister Diệm much of a chance; after all, he had assumed office barely two weeks before the Geneva Accords were signed. Over eight hundred thousand Northern refugees had already settled in the South. More challenging still, the commander of the armed forces, General Nguyễn Văn Hinh, had made clear his intention to topple Ngô Đình Diệm in a palace coup. The Bình Xuyên armed faction wanted to do the same thing with guns in the streets of Saigon. There was no money in the national treasury, and the business community's confidence was in tatters—what reason was there for them to feel optimistic about the future of the country? While the communist government was busy consolidating in Hanoi, Saigon's political infighting threatened to destabilize the entire South, with potential dire consequences.

External events were also moving quickly that summer. At the Geneva Accords conference, the five superpowers—the United States, Britain, China, the Soviet Union, and France—had gathered to discuss the conflicts in Korea and Indochina. France's defeat at Điện Biên Phủ pushed Vietnam to the top of the agenda. France also had a newly selected prime minister, Pierre Mendès France, who had pledged to resign if an agreement on Vietnam was not reached within his first thirty days. In fact, the talks went past the midnight deadline, but the final draft was dated to the previous day in order for Mendès France to claim he had kept his promise. In any event, it was clear that the Geneva Accords had been negotiated without much attention paid to the interests of Vietnam. The head of the State of Vietnam's delegation, Trần Văn Đỗ, refused to sign the final document in protest, but in practice, we had little choice but to accept it as a fait accompli.

Naturally, uncertainty in Saigon and the disappointment from Geneva were on my mind as I headed to Paris for the Four-Party Conference. The purpose of this conference was to resolve pending issues between France and its three former colonies, based on a structure established by the Treaty of Pau since 1950. Under the Pau Treaty, the plan was for France to grant independence to Vietnam, Laos, and Cambodia, while still maintaining influence through various agreements establishing partnerships in defense, foreign relations, and monetary and customs arrangements. But the Geneva Accords had rendered the terms of the Pau Treaty obsolete, and France was now prepared to walk away from the region altogether.

The Four-Party Conference dragged on for almost three months, from mid-October to December 29, 1954. The terms of France's departure were complex, and challenging, given that the French had ruled Indochina for almost one hundred years. In essence, the task before us was determining how to split up the balance sheet of the Institut d'Emission des Etats Associes (Institute of Currency Issuance of the Associated States), an organization set up in 1950 to effectively operate as the Indochina central bank. On the surface, the conference seemed like a simple accounting exercise, but it was in fact a highly complex technical issue due to several key factors.

First, while there was one common currency for Indochina, expenditures had been kept separate among the four states. We therefore had to agree on how to divide outstanding debt between the four parties. Using its so-called Trésor Indochinois (Indochinese State Treasury), France had spent heavily on our military efforts against the communist Việt Minh, and it now clearly wanted the State of Vietnam to assume these debts.

Second, our common currency had been backed by French francs kept in reserve accounts, and it amounted to about 30 percent of the total currency in circulation. Because the three former colonies now wished to establish their own currencies, we needed to determine the total amount of old currency in circulation for each state. Only then could we recall the old denominations and replace them with new bills. This exercise would require several months of careful preparation and implementation.

Third, we had inherited a number of crisscrossing arrangements between the three Indochinese states and France, which needed to be disentangled. Vietnam had collected custom duties on behalf of Cambodia, for example, while Laos owed collected duties to the other two states. Even more complicated was the port of Saigon, which had been jointly owned by all three colonies, and where imports to Cambodia had been taxed and cleared. We needed to determine how to resolve ownership of Saigon's port and to draft new navigational agreements on the heavily trafficked Mekong River.

Finally, French investors in Indochina had suffered a serious loss of confidence as a result of the war. Deep down, they must have suspected that the end was coming. The French Empire had been crumbling since the beginning of World War II, from which France came out victorious but very much impoverished. These investors now wanted to liquidate their Indochinese assets and repatriate their capital while the authority to approve these transactions still resided with the Ministry of Finance in Paris. But the process of withdrawing their resources required bipartisan cooperation and would take some time to complete.

From our point of view, establishing sovereign Vietnamese authority over monetary, banking, and financial matters was of paramount importance in restoring business confidence. Creating an immediate perception that our new government would survive was essential to the long-term financial viability of the country. After the first few meetings, I realized time was of the essence and that consensus on overall principles should not be sidetracked by haggling over details such as ownership percentages and the specific debt figures between the three new states.

My objective was to reach an agreement on these issues quickly, so I could return home and report to Prime Minister Diệm for his assent. To hasten the process, we agreed to assume 95 percent of the outstanding debt—aware that we would have to bear the entire burden, given that the North obviously wanted nothing to do with it. After the conference wrapped up in December, we went back to Saigon and proceeded directly to the prime minister's office, where our recommendations were all approved. It was now time to focus on implementation.

Our first and most significant action upon returning from the Four-Party Conference was to establish the new National Bank of Vietnam, as stipulated by Prime Ministerial Decree no. 48. Dương Tấn Tài, the head of the recent delegation to Paris, became the first governor of the National Bank, while I was appointed deputy governor and director of the new Directorate General of Exchange. At last, sovereignty over our own monetary and banking policies was established, albeit during probably the most difficult period our country had faced.

The first six months of 1955 would prove critical for Prime Minister Diệm, who was completely absorbed in a life-and-death struggle with his enemies at home and abroad. His most pressing task was the fight against the Bình Xuyên rebels, now raging on the streets of Saigon.[1] Beyond clashing with the Bình Xuyên, the head of state, former emperor Bảo Đại, was angling for a move against Diệm, hoping to lure him on a trip to Paris where he would be isolated from his supporters and his power could be stripped. We Northern refugees at times wondered whether we had made the right choice.

But fortunately for our young country, Prime Minister Diệm did not go to Paris as ordered. Instead, he fought valiantly, relying on the sheer strength of his personality and conviction. After crushing the Bình Xuyên and other rebellious religious sects in the Mekong Delta, Diệm then made his move against Bảo Đại, calling for a referendum in which he would contest the former emperor for the new position of president. On October 23, 1955, he won with 98 percent of the vote and three days later proclaimed the establishment of a new republic—the Republic of Vietnam.

The National Bank of Vietnam

Compared with this high political drama, my work at the central bank seemed rather mundane. My first responsibility was to lead both the Directorate General of Exchange and the Directorate General of Currency Issuance.

The most significant and politically sensitive issue that I faced was the takeover of the French colonial Office of Exchange, which had been managed until then by a French director reporting directly to the Ministry of Finance in Paris. There was a significant backlog of French investors and plantation owners desperate to withdraw their capital, but I had no means of determining the validity of their claims. These investors were alarmed by the anticipated cessation of French authority.

Yet rapid capital flight would have a serious impact on our foreign exchange reserves, causing the value of our new currency to collapse—with potentially explosive consequences. I knew I needed a concrete plan before meeting with the outgoing French director. The wrong approach could provoke an immediate crisis of confidence in the business community, which might spill over into politics and military affairs. In the meantime, I was acutely aware that the security situation around Saigon was precarious at best. Although American aid to help settle Northern refugees had started to flow in, our treasury was essentially bare.

I decided to begin by taking one step backward, in order to take two steps forward later on. Although allowing French capital to leave would hurt our foreign exchange reserves, I felt it was better to honor all of these applications, in order to demonstrate to investors that our new government could be trusted. This was also consistent with the basic principle in international law that incoming governments should guarantee continuity and respect prior commitments.

So before taking office, I made it clear that I would accept all existing applications to withdraw funds. The French director of exchange and the employees at the Office of Exchange welcomed this choice with great relief, and the minister of finance in Paris was delighted. From my perspective, this approach meant we could avoid creating yet another enemy in our struggle for survival.

After explaining the pros and cons to Prime Minister Diệm, I won his full backing on the foreign exchange issue. Diệm also sent over one of his young lieutenants,

Huỳnh Văn Lang, to serve as my deputy, and after I was promoted to governor of the National Bank, he served as my replacement at the Directorate General of Exchange.

With the foreign exchange crisis behind us, I turned my attention to our new currency, the Vietnamese Đồng. The first step was to recall the old colonial Bank of Indochina bills and coins and replace them with the new Đồng notes issued by the National Bank of Vietnam. In practice, this meant painstakingly counting banknotes by hand. This manual task was routine for commercial banks, but it was far more serious at the national level, given the sheer volume of notes and the fact that basic trust in the new government hinged on an accurate and transparent accounting process.

As it turned out, my caution had been warranted. I was right to have been apprehensive about the integrity of the counting process, for it was this that would ultimately cost me my job in just a few months' time—but more on that story later.

First, in order to achieve a smooth transfer from old to new bills, I placed the operation under the authority of the National Bank on an interim basis. Fortunately, the money counters were a most well-organized group with many years of experience in counting notes manually. To build a spirit of comradeship and solidarity, and to ensure that the highest standard of accountability was maintained, I made sure that they worked together, lived together in the same dormitory, and even went to work on the same company bus. They were also thoroughly searched upon arrival and before leaving work. For some reason, the staff consisted entirely of young women of Chinese origin, and the division head was also Chinese.

Next, I decided we needed to replace the staff of the colonial Bank of Indochina with new National Bank of Vietnam employees of our own. Why? Despite functioning as the effective central bank of France's colonies, the Bank of Indochina was in fact a privately owned French bank, established in Paris in 1875. The French government had granted it the authority to issue banknotes, not just in French colonies but also even in China. It was also permitted to conduct regular banking activities, such as taking deposits, providing letters of credit to importers, investing in real estate, and trading securities. As a result, the liberal media in France was constantly criticizing the special status it enjoyed. Although it had lost the right to issue currency at the 1950 Pau Treaty, the Bank of Indochina nonetheless wielded enormous influence in Vietnam, and it remained an important symbol of French empire and financial clout.

Given these imperial connotations, and my desire to develop an independent and truly Vietnamese central bank—the National Bank of Vietnam—I felt that replacing the old Bank of Indochina staff was unavoidable, even if it was certain to be seen as politically motivated. Having taken one step back by conceding on the capital withdrawal applications, I was ready now to go two steps forward by asserting the authority of the new National Bank of Vietnam.

To that end, I met with Mr. Ngô Trọng Hiếu, the head of the Directorate General of National Treasury. His unit was responsible for counting and safekeeping government banknotes and sending them to branches across the country as required. I worked quietly with him to begin hiring new staff and training them to replace the Bank of Indochina employees. Needless to say, friction and resentment from the old staff were unavoidable, though we minimized this with generous compensation packages.

Next, I prepared another symbolic and politically sensitive move: evicting the Bank of Indochina from its long-standing headquarters and installing the National Bank of Vietnam in its place. Given the political uncertainty of the day, this was, needless to say, a very delicate maneuver. I knew I needed complete support from Prime Minister Diệm. I presented my ideas to him, emphasizing that replacing the Bank of

Indochina staff and assuming their headquarters would signal that our country had taken full control of its economic destiny, establishing our legitimacy in the field of banking and finance. If successful, this meant a significant boost to Mr. Diệm and the nation's stature, both domestically and overseas. Seemingly convinced, the Prime Minister gave me carte blanche to approach the Bank of Indochina in order to negotiate the takeover.

Commensurate with its stature, the Bank of Indochina was headquartered in one of the most prestigious buildings in a glamorous quarter in Saigon, overlooking the river. This area was our equivalent of Downing Street in London or Wall Street in New York City. Eager to bring about a change of direction, I wanted the National Bank of Vietnam to take over this location, with its large vaults for deposits and stylish offices for entertaining high-profile visitors.

At the time, the Bank of Indochina was still only a branch of its parent company in France, and given the political situation, it was beginning to reduce its presence in the region. The director general, Mr. Louis de Champeaux, was an old-timer, well respected in Saigon financial circles. Luckily, when I broached the subject of transferring the headquarters with him, he responded very positively. My hunch had been correct: with France's accelerating departure from Indochina, the bank could no longer play as prominent a role as it had before. Selling the prestigious headquarters would generate much-needed cash for the bank to expand and invest elsewhere.

Since the headquarters and the three Bank of Indochina branches in Huế, Đà Lạt, and Đà Nẵng were long since fully amortized, we only needed to agree on three outstanding issues: the value of the headquarters and the three branch offices; the capital gains taxes on the sale; and the exchange rate for converting our Vietnamese Đồng into French francs.

After consulting with several real estate specialists, we settled on a price of 98 million Vietnamese Đồng. Our finance minister agreed to waive the capital gains tax, and I set the exchange rate at ten French francs per Vietnamese Đồng. At this rate, the sale returned some $2.8 million to the Bank of Indochina parent company.

With the deal settled so quickly, I was even able to push for two clauses, of little financial impact but important symbolic value. First, I insisted that the National Bank of Vietnam assume the Bank of Indochina's monopoly on the An Hòa-Nông Sơn coal mining project, on which they had yet to invest any serious capital. And I also persuaded Mr. de Champeaux that the "Bank of Indochina" name was now outdated, and he helped convince the parent company to break with the colonial past by changing the name to the Banque Française d'Asie (French Bank of Asia). On good terms with the new government thanks to the smooth resolution of these negotiations, the Banque Française d'Asie continued to play a constructive role in financing our economic development for years to come.

The Americans Arrive

Let us remember that we had inherited from the French government an empty treasury, a disheartened French business community, and a bureaucracy entrenched in antiquated colonial methods. It was against this gloomy backdrop that American aid began to arrive, first to help Northerners resettle in their new land, and later, to fund the import of American consumer goods for general public consumption, an initiative known as the Commercial Import Program. In practical terms, both endeavors meant we had to adapt rapidly to successfully manage the evolving situation. Learning

English, coming to terms with the American way of business, and coping with the influx of American consumerism—all of these were challenges thrust upon our government and our business community virtually overnight.

I played a relatively minor role administering refugee assistance, which was managed primarily by the minister of social affairs. The Commercial Import Program (CIP), on the other hand, meant opening a whole new horizon for us. We simply did not have any established mechanisms for dealing with the challenge. Our business and financial sector had barely understood what it meant, while our banking system was totally unequipped to implement it. But it was already clear that the program would be here to stay for the long term. I scrambled to learn everything I could about how it worked, making sure that we could comply with all the complicated U.S. government regulations and procedures.

At the National Bank of Vietnam, we were working closely with the Federal Reserve Bank of New York, our American counterpart at that time. My American contact and advisor on monetary and financial matters was one Mr. Dean. His job was to help us implement sound banking policies and to make sure that our private sector took the lead in importing American commodities for general sale.

Of course, there were a number of familiar problems. As usual during this time, our commercial sector—both French and Vietnamese—suffered from a serious lack of confidence in the country's future, which naturally tempered their willingness to invest. Having inherited French practices and traditions, we also understood little about American markets and products, or regulations and procedures. And we confronted a serious language barrier during the early days.

At a time when our troops were at war with the Bình Xuyên on the streets of the capital, and political and religious factions clashed with security forces and one another, time was of the absolute essence. If we couldn't find a way of absorbing the influx of much-needed American dollars, inflation would soar, destroying the government's financial and political credibility.

I proposed to Mr. Dean that the National Bank establish a commercial unit, to manage to inflow of U.S. dollars via the CIP, and to see that the funds reached the private sector, where they could be used to purchase American imports for sale among the general population. At first, Mr. Dean was reluctant—such a prominent government role was anathema to American free-market orthodoxy. But I patiently explained the scale of the challenge, and the ongoing political uncertainty, eventually persuading him to consider our approach more seriously. Several weeks later, he stopped by my office to report that he had secured official approval for our proposal. It was a pleasant surprise. I immediately contacted Prime Minister Diệm and got the go-ahead for a commercial unit in the National Bank, to operate autonomously with its own board of directors and offices. This became known as the Việt Nam Thương Tín Ngân Hàng (VNTT), or Credit Commercial Bank of Vietnam.

Next, eager to draw on whatever sources of expertise were at my disposal, I reached out again to Mr. de Champeaux at the Bank of Indochina. I hoped to acquire some of their specialists in letters of credit, accounting, and international finance, particularly those who were familiar with American banking methods. Eager to slim down their operations, Mr. de Champeaux readily agreed. I also managed to persuade him to permit their chief accountant to join us as a financial advisor on an interim basis.

And with that, housed on a separate floor of our new National Bank of Vietnam head office, the Credit Commercial Bank of Vietnam was born. Its official birth certificate was not issued until December 13, 1955, by Presidential Decree no. 35-TC. By this time, the political situation in South Vietnam had fairly stabilized. The Republic of Vietnam was officially declared on October 26, 1955, under an interim constitution, and Ngô Đình Diệm assumed the office of president of the republic.

Within two months, I was able to acquire a headquarters for the National Bank of Vietnam, set up the VNTT as a commercial arm of the National Bank to implement the American CIP, and hire adequate staff from the Bank of Indochina to operate it as an on-going concern. I appointed Nguyễn Hữu Hanh, a recent graduate of the London School of Economics, to direct the new Credit Commercial Bank. Another young graduate from the London School of Economics, who had worked at Standard Chartered Bank prior, showed up in my office one day in August 1955 asking for a job. I was happy to see him and offered him the job of chief of the Import Section at the VNTT. This was Phạm Kim Ngọc, who became Hanh's second-in-command; later, both men would play prominent roles in economic policy-making during the Second Republic (see chapter 3 in this volume).

Recruiting capable people to manage our transition during this difficult period was a top priority for me—I certainly did not want to be seen as having the sole authority to make decisions on banking and monetary matters. To help share the burden and expand our accountability, I established the National Council on Monetary Policy and Credit, a discussion forum that included the ministers of finance, economy, communication, and transport, along with the director of budget planning and the treasury. The deputy prime minister (later the vice president) served as the chairman, while the director of the National Bank acted as secretary general. The council met the test of time, meeting regularly to discuss matters of banking and finance for the next twenty years.

Looking back, it was a respectable series of accomplishments during an enormously challenging and turbulent first two months. How well did we do? Well, one year later, I ran into Mr. de Champeaux by chance on my way home from a conference in Oxford. I was shocked to learn that he had lost his position at the Bank of Indochina and had been demoted to a small regional branch instead. He confided that his bosses felt he had undervalued the Bank of Indochina headquarters and been far too pessimistic on our economic and political prospects overall. It was true—by then, we had turned things around considerably.

But de Champeaux was hardly alone in his bleak assessment of the situation in Vietnam at the time of our transaction in April 1955. Few political observers had given Ngô Đình Diệm much of a chance, not least of whom were both the French and U.S. governments. I now know from declassified cables that neither the French nor American ambassadors in Saigon had expected us to survive more than a few weeks, and possible replacements as prime minister had been openly discussed. But then Ngô Đình Diệm crushed the Bình Xuyên rebels, and American aid began to flow through our new banking structure. Confidence had been restored, as demonstrated by the 98 percent approval for Prime Minster Diệm in the autumn referendum.

Comparing the market price of the headquarters that April with its hypothetical value six months later was an exercise in hindsight and futility—and I was at pains to reassure Mr. de Champeaux that he had obtained the best value possible given the circumstances.

The Banknote Exchange Scandal

And yet, as I have hinted, it was not all smooth sailing. I had been worried all along that the temptation to manipulate, for personal gain, the conversion of old Bank of Indochina banknotes to new Vietnamese Đồng would be too great for some to overcome. It turned out that my fears would be confirmed.

The Banknote Exchange Scandal, also known as the Vũ Đình Đa Affair, happened on my watch in the summer of 1956. Vũ Đình Đa was head of the Recall and Exchange of Banknotes section at the National Bank. As I had mentioned earlier, counting banknotes was a manual process, fraught with the risk of theft and corruption regardless of how many safeguards were imposed on the process. This was exactly what happened. Caught in the act, Vũ Đình Đa admitted to the investigating committee tasked with getting to the bottom of the scandal that he—and he alone—had cheated the government out of some two million Bank of Indochina piastres during the process of exchanging them for new Vietnamese Đồng.

One afternoon in October 1956, I was summoned to the presidential palace and asked point blank about the scandal: How had I let it happen, and how much money had been lost? President Diệm was furious, worried that the scandal would deal a significant blow to the integrity and credibility of his government. I acknowledged full responsibility as governor of the National Bank for the miscounting of banknotes on my watch, but I rejected any suggestion of personal benefit or any political motive behind the scandal. To demonstrate my innocence, I proposed my own resignation then and there.

The president asked me to hold off on such drastic action—he would need time to find a replacement. Then he asked the investigating committee, waiting outside in the hallway, to enter and present him with their findings. It occurred to me that I would be arrested on the spot if there was even a hint that I had been involved. But after the committee cleared me of any wrongdoing, the president changed his tune, asking me to stay on for at least another month so that I could attend an upcoming meeting of the International Monetary Fund. In time, Trần Hữu Phương, then the minister of finance, would replace me, and I served instead as an advisor to the president on investment.

From my perspective, the period between October 1954 and October 1956 had been packed with significant historical events. I was very fortunate to have been given the opportunity to contribute. Today, over sixty years later, I am likewise grateful for the opportunity to share my side of the story with you.

I was not a politician and had never belonged to any political party. My guide throughout this challenging period was always a strong respect for the rule of law and for the value of private property and enterprise. These were the very foundation of my education and my beliefs as our country went through the wrenching revolutionary change from colony to republic.

Note

1 Bình Xuyên refers to a militia with origins in criminal gangs in the suburbs of Saigon. In the early 1950s, with permission by the French authorities this group controlled the gambling dens and the illicit narcotic trade in Saigon. Christopher Goscha, *Vietnam: A New History* (New York: Basic Books, 2016), 288.

CHAPTER THREE

REFORM OR COLLAPSE: ECONOMIC CHALLENGES DURING VIETNAMIZATION

Phạm Kim Ngọc

Phạm Kim Ngọc was born in Hanoi in 1928. He earned a bachelor's degree in economics with honors from Southampton University in 1952, and another degree in money, banking, and international finance from the London School of Economics. He left London for Saigon in August 1955 to run the Import Department of Credit Commercial Bank of Vietnam as it was opening for business. Ngọc worked in banking for the next eleven years and went into government service for a brief stint of six months under Prime Minister Nguyễn Cao Kỳ as deputy minister for economics in mid-1966. He finally left Credit Commercial Bank of Vietnam in 1967 to set up an investment company with a business associate. In October 1969, he became minister of economy in the government of President Nguyễn Văn Thiệu. Ngọc returned to banking, his lifelong interest, in March 1974 to set up an innovative agricultural bank called Ngân Hàng Nông Doanh, but this project was cut short in April 1975.

The Americanization of the war started in earnest in March 1965, with the landing of about three thousand American marines in Đà Nẵng. U.S. troops gradually took on more of the fighting as troop levels continued to climb significantly over the next three years. By mid-1969, they peaked at some 550,000 soldiers.

The Tết Offensive of 1968 drastically changed the political landscape in the United States. The American public was shocked when they realized that over half a million U.S. troops could not prevent the enemy from staging such a spectacular military offensive. In March, President Lyndon Johnson announced he would not seek reelection, and Richard Nixon was later elected as his successor on a platform of restoring peace in Vietnam. Weeks later, the Paris peace talks between Washington, Hanoi, and Saigon got started.

Meanwhile, the "Vietnamization" of the war—U.S. troop withdrawal—began. This was a difficult and painful process, militarily, politically, and economically. A major readjustment of thinking on the part of the Republic of Vietnam was required. Likewise, in the United States, the antiwar movement became more vocal and influential.

In order to replace the departing American troops, the Army of the Republic of Vietnam (ARVN) started to increase correspondingly. We aimed for nine hundred thousand soldiers, roughly 4.7 percent of the South Vietnamese population. In order to accommodate the growing defense burden, President Nguyễn Văn Thiệu reshuffled the cabinet in September 1969. He approached Nguyễn Hữu Hanh, the former head of the central bank, to serve as minister of economy, responsible for the transition from dependence on American assistance to self-sufficiency.

By tradition, and under normal circumstances, the minister of economy position was much sought after. It always had high visibility and prestige, but also carried heavy responsibility. All previous ministers had lasted no more than a year. Unbeknown to me, however, Nguyễn Hữu Hanh proposed my candidature instead, which was immediately accepted by President Thiệu and Prime Minister Trần Thiện Khiêm.

That same day, I was transported by helicopter to the presidential retreat in Vũng Tàu and ordered by Thiệu and Prime Minister Khiêm to appear on television to announce a new government austerity program. I pled clumsiness in public speaking, hoping to avoid the TV announcement, but my superiors quickly dismissed my lame excuse. Unwittingly, I thus became the center of controversy right at the start of my public career.

The 1969 Austerity Tax

That evening, totally unprepared, I delivered the speech on austerity. My deputy minister, Trần Cự Uông, had written the announcement for me on very short notice. But my mentor Nguyễn Hữu Hanh had already agreed in principle with this belt-tightening program, in consultation with American officials.

I was aware of the political risks connected with the minister of economy post; many friends advised against it. After all, I came to the ministry as a lone cowboy, with no staff of my own, no support from any political party, and no military background. Despite over a decade of work in banking, I had had barely six months' experience in government affairs. But I felt that addressing the challenges our country faced outweighed my own personal risks, so I decided in favor of the opportunity.

My position entailed working closely with the Ministry of Finance and the U.S. Agency for International Development (USAID). The immediate task was determining how to transfer privately held resources to the government in order to finance the war efforts. But this objective was stymied by certain laws, relics of the French system, requiring National Assembly approval of all fiscal proposals.

In order to raise funds for the war effort, we proposed implementing austerity taxes (*thuế kiệm ước*) on imports, which I outlined in my inauguration speech. Subsequently Deputy Minister Trần Cự Uông and I collaborated with Finance Minister Nguyễn Bích Huệ to prepare taxes on over two hundred categories of imports, from necessities like gasoline and diesel to luxuries like wine and brandy. We aimed to increase government revenue by 40 billion piastres. A large staff from both ministries handled the tedious job of fine-tuning the list of tax rates.

Next, Finance Minister Nguyễn Bích Huệ and I appeared before the assembly to negotiate and defend the austerity taxes. I'll always remember one elected representative demanding a lower tax rate on imported scooters—and then publicly criticizing me, after I agreed, for "doing a favor" for the scooter company. This was the moment when I lost my innocence in the world of Saigon politics.

In another instance, I was called to the presidential palace and instructed to remove newsprint import subsidies. But the local press, with a strong vested interest, was fiercely against the removal of these subsidies, which would result in higher newsprint prices. They condemned my pronouncement as "another government attempt to muzzle the free press."

A subsidy of newsprint imports made no sense to me—there was already a local producer of newsprint—but it created windfall profits for the newspaper companies. So the local newspapers went on strike, and the foreign press took notice. In response, I was ordered to restore this "fundamental privilege of democracy" after the minister of press and information declared the press to be "essential defenders of democracy."

Despite these quarrels, the austerity tax program was duly announced. The prices of luxuries but also basic necessities went up immediately. Old inventories were also illegally sold at the new prices. So even though our tax preparation had involved many principals and had been debated in public, critics pointed at me as the "partner" of profiteers.

But despite public indignation over my alleged misconduct and incompetence, the gain in revenue for the government was abysmal. The business community, from importers to retailers, made a killing because it was both impractical and beyond the capacity of Ministry of Economy officials to keep track of private-sector inventories, separating sales of old stock at the old prices from the sale of new stock at the new prices. In practice, the application of a myriad of tax rates—over two hundred different import tax rates, as I recall—was a nightmare. It only enabled smart importers to conspire with corrupt bureaucrats in order to evade taxes for personal gains.

We had hoped the austerity taxes would raise 40 billion Đồng; instead, they brought in only 4 billion Đồng of additional revenue, just 10 percent of what we had hoped for, while generating inflation and public outrage. Meanwhile, the 1969 budget deficit swelled to 50 billion Đồng. The black market rate for the dollar reached four hundred piastres. The 1970 national budget was forecasted to increase by 50 percent, from 131 billion piastres to 200 billion piastres in the first year of Vietnamization. U.S. domestic politics put pressure on the embassy and USAID to seek devaluation of the piastre, which had been kept at 118 piastres per U.S. dollar since the 1966 reforms.

In hindsight, the austerity tax fiasco enacted in October 1969 was due to poor timing, as much as ineptitude in implementation on my part. We imposed such heavy import taxes at a time when the import-based economy was severely shaken up by the prospect of price inflation at 50 percent and the simultaneous cutbacks of American aid. Hoarding and speculation were the order of the day.

The foreign press, which thought I had acted "courageously," reported that I had been overwhelmed by "vested interests." The local press was even worse, charging me with misconduct, with being in cahoots with profiteers and speculators, and with professional incompetence. They asked President Thiệu "for my head." Somehow, just by the skin of my teeth, I survived this fiasco. I believe I owed it to the president's confidence in me.

Working with the United States

The problem was that fighting a war the American way was not cheap—and definitely beyond our means. Between 1956 and 1975, total U.S. economic and military assistance amounted to $25.3 billion, or an average of $1.2 billion annually. At the peak, it was about $3.9 billion in 1973. The gross national product of South Vietnam was estimated at about $3.2 billion in 1972, so the peak year, 1973, saw American aid that was more than South Vietnam's entire gross national product.

Replacing expensive U.S. troops with South Vietnamese forces would be a real challenge. Our target was for the ARVN to expand to nine hundred thousand soldiers in two years. The U.S. government, however, looked at Vietnamization quite differently from the way that we understood it. The American economic counselor Robert Harlan demanded concrete evidence of our efforts toward self-help. He wanted major reforms and was anxious to see immediate action and results, such as increased tax revenues and stabilized prices. In other words, he wanted "shock therapy" and he wanted it immediately. Vietnamese leaders, on the other hand, were concerned about both the immediate survival and the long-term viability of the country.

Deep down, I had the feeling that the United States was trying to foist the Vietnamization program on unsuspecting Vietnam leaders without necessary increases in foreign aid, given the mood of the American public and in Congress before the looming presidential election in 1972. Mr. Harlan did not appreciate the travails we would have to endure in a new, democratic Vietnam. Nor did he take into account the limited capacity of our private sector to finance Vietnamization. I had the impression of being lectured, with much self-righteousness, on the political management of an economy in transition. Our government faced outright hostility from both the South Vietnamese and American public, while Mr. Harlan and my mentor Nguyễn Hữu Hanh goaded me with suggestions from the sidelines. We were in uncharted territory, since we had no historical data whatsoever with which to assess the impact and effectiveness of our revenue measures. I needed more time, and I needed more support for a slow and soft approach.

In the meantime, as a result of Vietnamization, the national budget deficit seemed to increase daily. Inflation soared, as the black market rate for the U.S. dollar hit the ceiling. To the foreign press, it seemed "immoral" for a country at war to demand American aid without increasing domestic taxes, when the streets of Saigon were swamped with luxuries and conspicuous consumption.

We were seen as a society detached from the reality of war and corrupted at all levels. Our inability to control our customs checkpoints was described as "an open scandal" by the American ambassador in his report to the president. In simple economic terms, we seemed to want both guns and butter, paid for by the American taxpayer. This did not conjure up a positive image, and it became a serious political issue, always high on the agenda each time officials from the two governments met. U.S. assistance to South Vietnam came to be seen by the American public as misguided at best, and squandered away by corruption at worst.

Already caught between a rock and a hard place, I was informed out of the blue by an American security official that my capable deputy minister, Trần Cự Uông, had some sort of secret relationship with the communists. I replied that that this was a matter for the higher-ups, since we had both been appointed by President Thiệu. Eventually, Thiệu dismissed Trần Cự Uông, and he went to work in the private sector.

Still, out of this unfortunate incident came the unexpected opportunity to work closely with another Ministry of Economy official, Nguyễn Đức Cường (see chapter 1 in this volume). We had known each other since 1967, when Cường was working as a specialist in the Directorate of Commercial Aid at the ministry. He was then drafted by the army and had reached the final stage of military training when he was discharged by special exemption from the Ministry of Defense. Indeed, many of our most talented technocrats were conscripted, and we had to allow them to serve at least nine weeks in the military before we could request them back. After Trần Cự Uông's departure, Cường took over the daily grind of the trade portfolio and eventually rose to become my deputy. Meanwhile, I was increasingly forced to negotiate with American officials and to market our government's policies to them, an unexpected role that I dreaded and was not always well-prepared for.

My first confrontation was with Mr. Harlan and his group of economists, who pushed for a "reform blitz" in an economy nurtured by American aid for over fifteen years. They dreaded the antiwar mood in the U.S. Congress and suspected their Vietnamese counterparts of harboring a dilatory demeanor.

The Americans wanted to withdraw "on schedule and with honor," and the fundamental question was whether or not South Vietnam would be in a position to take over the fighting without increased U.S. aid to soften the economic and social upheaval of Vietnamization. They all self-righteously believed that we could. Yet from my perspective, they misunderstood the reality of our challenging circumstances.

I had many meetings with officials at the highest levels of the U.S. government, and they were all very talented and capable. But the data clearly indicated that our defense spending was unsustainably high, and the American policymakers refused to grapple with the inability of our impoverished country to carry the full weight of Vietnamization in the long run.

Instead, the main American concern was that South Vietnam's economic woes did not threaten U.S. withdrawal or jeopardize Nixon's reelection prospects in 1972. Visiting American officials wanted to look at me straight in the eyes and hear me reaffirm the various measures we had planned, so as to prove our commitment to shouldering the burden of the war.

Still, not all Americans were unsympathetic. In April 1970, Vũ Quốc Thúc (see chapter 2) and I met with Deputy U.S. Ambassador Samuel Berger, and after a long conversation, I believe he came around to supporting our view.

Floating Exchange and Interest Rates

As a consequence of the austerity tax fiasco, I realized that we had no choice but to completely overhaul our entire economic and financial structure and to face head-on the challenges of devaluing the currency to reflect market conditions, adopting a realistic interest rate to combat inflation and modernizing the tax code to increase government revenue. But the first and most politically sensitive problem was tackling the black market in foreign exchange.

Of course, our proposed reforms required consent from the National Assembly, and I knew the ensuing debates would be just as debilitating as the struggle to impose austerity taxes. Grandstanding legislators enjoyed attributing the nation's misery to my personal incompetence, and I made sure to return the favor. They never forgave me for calling their intelligence into question. But then, fortunately, the president's legal assistant Vũ Ngọc Trân initiated what was called the Program Law, which bypassed the assembly and permitted President Thiệu to impose economic reforms by decree for a period of five months.

Of course, the assembly opposed this measure, and some elected representatives demanded my resignation in exchange for their support. After four months of dithering, they finally agreed to back just one of the Program Law's provisions: reforming the Đồng-to-U.S. dollar exchange rate. Henceforth, devaluation of the currency was now in the purview of the executive and could be implemented by presidential decree.

In order to soften the impact of currency devaluation on the economy, and to minimize political backlash, we decided to implement a crawling peg system, starting in October 1970. The National Bank of Vietnam would devalue the exchange rate only gradually, by a small percentage each time in order to meet our annual target. This floating rate also increased the purchasing power of U.S. aid. I want to emphasize here that what we did was revolutionary at the time; the world was still on a fixed exchange rate system, and the U.S. dollar did not leave the gold standard until August 1971.

Following the innovative crawling peg exchange rate reform, our next move was to address the problem of low interest rates—otherwise known as "cheap money." In the face of continuing currency devaluation and soaring inflation, cheap money was clearly a macroeconomic anomaly that needed to be dealt with. With budget expenses growing by another 30 percent in 1971, inflation was clearly unsustainable and intolerable, resulting in a catastrophic impact on consumer prices. The National Bank of Vietnam saw the need to rapidly reduce the amount of money in circulation.

The private Bankers' Association, on the other hand, had little or no incentive to change. They benefited from cheap money by fixing deposit rates at 2–4 percent, and loan rates at 7–9 percent, which were effectively "negative" compared with an inflation rate between of 30 and 60 percent. They claimed to keep deposit rates low due to "lack of employment of loanable funds" outside traditional commercial businesses.

As with the currency devaluations, we decided to adopt a floating rate system. In this system, the National Bank of Vietnam would adjust interest rates gradually, in small increments following a large initial adjustment. As a result, interest rates rose to 22 percent on one-year deposits, a level unheard of in Vietnam, and possibly in the world at that time.

Some American officials were wary about our innovative approach. I recall one meeting with a high-level U.S. Treasury official in 1970, who suggested issuing gold-backed treasury bonds to encourage the private sector to make loans to the government. Indeed, we certainly had an urgent need to sterilize the massive amounts of cash in circulation. But having been a banker for over a decade, I believed that private savers would be far more responsive to higher interest rates than to what they would see as the government's treasury bond bluff.

Sure enough, the public responded positively to the rising interest rates. Apart from its salutary effect on hoarding and speculation, "expensive" money increased private deposits in the third quarter of 1970 by 8 billion piastres, almost equal to our annual domestic taxes. For the first time, commercial banks began to invest significant amounts in treasury bills, with 90 billion Đồng—12 percent of the national budget—in 1974 alone. As a banker myself, I understood their financial conservatism and their historic preference for foreign borrowers. But now, to finance Vietnamization, we were finally able to employ sovereign borrowing in addition to taxation and the printing press.

In summary, the gradual adoption of both floating exchange rates and increased interest rates, with frequent small adjustments, had become the norm. As a result, for the first time since the establishment of the Second Republic in 1967, the banking system started to play an important role in the implementation of the government's monetary and exchange rate policies.

Toward Effective Tax Collection

The next challenge confronting us was to collect taxes from the general public more efficiently, without a repeat of the 1969 social upheaval and political uproar, least especially given the upcoming 1971 South Vietnamese presidential election.

Previously, our massive increases in defense spending to prosecute the war had been financed through a combination of American aid and deficit spending. But with U.S. aid scaled back and the ARVN forced to compensate for departing American troops, our budget deficit exploded. We simply could not cope with this double whammy.

While negotiating with the United States, I insisted that American aid should be phased out gradually and that our budget deficit could not be balanced right away. I did not dispute Mr. Harlan's insistence that we needed to increase our tax revenues, but taking into account the already agitated South Vietnamese public, I asked for time and patience, in light of these political sensitivities. My concern was to observe the art of the possible in a young democracy.

But the Americans had other ideas, self-righteously demanding a rapid response that ignored the reality of our political circumstances. On the tax issue, Mr. Harlan and I parted company from the very beginning. Concerned about antiwar sentiment in the United States, he insisted on immediate tax increases. I agreed that this might have produced some extra revenues, but it was not worth the cost—enormous protests on our streets. Given our tax collectors' impotence and corruption, and the determination of wealthy individuals to avoid paying their share, the burden was sure to fall on lawyers, doctors, teachers, and civil servants, and the political fallout would be untenable.

I tried to explain that harsh fiscal measures would result in disastrous consequences, even worse than the 1969 austerity tax protests. But Harlan insisted that both parties share the fiscal burden of Vietnamization. His approach amounted to a political time bomb, in the face of growing Buddhist and student unrest on the streets of Saigon.

To build support for my soft approach, I began courting foreign journalists, using an ARVN plane to take them and their spouses for weekend beach vacations. This provided a forum where I could state my case for the record without embarrassing my government.

Sure enough, the American press began to report that "Minister Ngọc says America needs to decide between troop withdrawal and economic assistance, because South Vietnam cannot cope with both demands at the same time." They also gave me the benefit of the doubt that I could deliver, if given sufficient time and support.

Next, I directed my public campaign toward our own journalists, and to the National Assembly. Nobody disputed the pressing need for us to take responsibility for our own defense against the communists. Yet there was no agreement on how to assume the enormous tax burden this would entail. Instead, the public was certain that the departing Americans would give us the wherewithal to replace them. And our minister of economy had already botched the austerity taxes, hadn't he, without punishment to boot? Journalists could not sell newspapers by supporting us, and in the face of public opinion, elected politicians refused to cooperate.

Thus, I knew I would also need support from the U.S. embassy. Fortunately, I was able to win over the ambassador, Ellsworth Bunker, in my struggle for political pragmatism over economic orthodoxy. In 1970, Bunker replaced Harlan with Charles Cooper, a former economic counselor whom I had known for several years. Charles Cooper and I began by reviewing our total domestic tax receipts. We both knew we needed to expand the tax base, from taxing imports to taxing domestic activity as well, in order to increase revenues. And we agreed to push ahead with a series of structural reforms, starting with monetary measures, which had attracted less opposition than tax increases.

Fortunately, Cooper did not see my reluctance to carry out the fiscal measures immediately as the usual South Vietnamese procrastination but, rather, as a wise delay. Mutual trust was a prerequisite to success, and we could not afford to lose precious time on fruitless discussion or confrontation. Backed by Cooper's influence, Harlan's two-year plan, which tilted the financial burden heavily toward South Vietnam, was shelved. I also pushed against American plans for price controls and rationing. At times, I could not help but feel that we were being accused of profligacy and untrustworthiness, and that it was the destiny of small countries to be pilloried on the altar of fiscal discipline by their duplicitous donors.

In fact, we had inherited our weak tax structure from French colonial times. Back then, failure to file and pay income tax was not a crime, and income tax debt owed to the government was only enforceable through civil courts. The government's tax revenue base had always been narrow, and other than customs duties, business licensing fees, and taxes on alcohol, tobacco, or liquor, the income tax was the only broad-based source of revenue.

Worse still, previous administration of income tax had long been ineffective and was generally seen as arbitrary if not corrupt by taxpayers. Beyond withholding taxes at the source on wages and salaries, we faced an uphill battle collecting from small unincorporated business and the public at large. Most kept no reliable accounting records, so tax collectors were forced to impose arbitrary negotiated settlements, often relying solely on visible evidence of wealth. The upshot was that tax assessments were often far lower than what taxpayers actually owed, even as they felt that our collectors were arbitrary and unfair.

Another challenging hurdle was our entrenched bureaucracy. But we simply had to work with them. We had to explain the fiscal predicament to our tax administration and devise a tax structure that was simple to administer, leaving little room for arbitrary improvisation by tax collectors.

Finally, there was the National Assembly, which refused to approve fiscal measures designed to transfer resources from the private sector to the public sector. They mostly belonged to the Saigon elite and, like me, were well sheltered in the capital city. On the other hand, our paltry collection of income taxes to finance the war was deemed offensive by foreign journalists and the American Congress alike, which further alienated the American public. There was no doubt that a quantum leap in internal tax revenues was imperative to reducing deficit financing, controlling inflation, and alleviating our dependence on foreign aid, which we knew would decline sharply in the near future.

Our team had decided early on that while a properly enforced progressive income tax had to be at the core of any fair domestic tax system, we also needed a broad-based tax on consumption to achieve our fiscal goal. The only question was which kind of tax would be optimal, given the context of the South Vietnam economy at the time. To achieve this goal, the Ministry of Finance fiscal team adopted a two-pronged approach. First, we sought to broaden the domestic tax base in a manner that would not inhibit future economic growth and development. And second, we worked to improve the efficiency and integrity of domestic tax administration. In pursuit of these objectives, we eventually settled on a value-added tax (VAT), since it was structurally more consistent with the goal of fostering economic development and exports, and the administration of this type of tax could provide more objective data for income tax assessment.

Conceptually, the VAT was a tax on the value added at each stage of the supply, production, and distribution chain, hence its name. In practice, it was a tax paid by the buyer at point of purchase and collected by the seller on behalf of the government. Failure to remit the tax to the government became a crime under Vietnamese law: taxpayers subject to the VAT could face criminal prosecution if they failed to comply. And by forcing business to record their purchases and sales, our tax collectors could obtain more accurate data. But the most attractive feature of the VAT was its broad base. It amounted to a tax on the largest component of gross domestic product, private consumption. And our calculations showed that the budget deficit could be meaningfully reduced merely by small adjustments to the tax rate.

Still, introducing the VAT was a leap of faith. At that time, it had only been attempted in a few European countries. We had no help from USAID, because the United States had no experience with the VAT, and it was not well understood even in academic circles. Little did we know that eventually the VAT would be recognized as a good revenue-raising measure and applied across Europe, Asia, and Latin America, with the United States still the exception.

The problem was the public had never heard of this type of tax—and was in no mood to learn, especially coming from young technocrats like us, who had little life experience. Worse still, when we translated "value-added tax" into Vietnamese, the result was a tongue-twister: "thuế trị giá gia tăng." With little public support for the measure, we had to bypass the National Assembly and impose the tax through presidential decree under the Program Law—a short-term solution to the weak existing legal framework. The initial rate was 10 percent, with an exemption on essential goods and services.

By 1974, our domestic tax structure resembled that of a modern nation, and we were able to increase tax revenues by 70 percent. Better still, despite the constant threat of cutbacks, American aid also increased moderately in 1971.

A Bold Initiative in Đà Nẵng

Having implemented major reforms including the flexible exchange rate, raised interest rates, and the value-added tax, we then continued structural reforms in favor of sustainable growth. We reduced the number of tax codes on imports from over two hundred to just four: 0 percent, 25 percent, 50 percent, and 200 percent. And we began to phase out protection of domestic industries in favor of a more free-market approach.

Through it all, the public and the press built me up as the front man, a lightning rod for the government's economic agenda. In reality, it was teamwork, with Charles Cooper and I leading a joint U.S.-Vietnamese team of experts. Charles and I set the plan, and colleagues at the Ministries of Economy and Finance, and the National Bank, carried it out. None of them enjoyed publicity, so I ended up being the group's spokesman to the outside world.

Of course, this meant that I became the bearer of bad news. It felt like I was the most controversial minister in the whole cabinet. But I was proud of our team, whose accomplishments were often lost amid the grandstanding and criticism. President Thiệu supported me behind the scenes, and Prime Minister Trần Thiện Khiêm did not interfere. This was more than I could have hoped for.

Looking back, I regard 1970 as the turning point in my tenure. It was then that the economy gradually began to stabilize. Inflation was brought back under 20 percent, and our floating exchange rate helped to tackle currency speculation. Banks began to buy government bonds, helping to raise much-needed revenue for the state.

Washington also seemed convinced that we were making progress, reallocating an additional $80 million in aid from other recipient countries in order to bypass the need for congressional approval. True, our structural reforms did not bring about change quickly enough to turn things around. Nevertheless, given the challenge posed by the ongoing war and American withdrawal, I believe that our team's achievements in 1970 and 1971 were significant.

But then, the war heated up again, and our reforms were overtaken by the 1972 "Fiery Summer"—another massive communist attack across the border. Economic policy, however innovative or pragmatic, suddenly felt irrelevant. Deficits hit the stratosphere, and inflation soared to 60 percent. Somehow our economic team managed to avoid retribution. For my part, I appealed to the business community to stand behind our armed forces. The Saigon Chamber of Commerce rallied behind me, visiting our troops at the front lines and giving away hundreds of millions of Đồng for the cause.

Nonetheless, I remained a lightning rod for controversy. In central Vietnam, long a hotbed of street demonstrations by Buddhists and students, I had abolished rice rationing in pursuit of my commitment to free-market principles. When President Thiệu arrived to visit, one province chief tried to disguise rice shortages by staging a "Potemkin" storage center. When it was revealed that his bounty of "rice" was actually no more than plastic bits and the remnants of shopping bags, my opponents were quick to hold me responsible.

Still, I remained committed to my ideals. During my trip to Đà Nẵng, now overwhelmed by refugees fleeing the violence, I rejected the standard view that humanitarian calamities are best solved by massive government relief. Instead, the maverick in me saw the refugee crisis as a problem of temporary unemployment. I was sure the dislocated farmers preferred to work rather than remain on the dole. So I set up a special agency alongside the relief camps, giving refugees the choice to work instead of accepting handouts.

The agency, known as the Agency for the Development of the Da Nang Area was managed by an executive from Shell Oil Saigon. And we were eventually able to secure funding and support from Charles Cooper and USAID. I hoped the project, which we called "the poor helping the poor," would serve as a model for other war-torn provinces.

And by all accounts, it was a success, given the circumstances. Refugees were put to work cleaning up sewers, digging irrigation canals, and contributing to public works in poor areas of Đà Nẵng. Later, it was expanded to Saigon and the other military regions, employing some thirty-two thousand people.

Looking Back

As the year 1973 began, things seemed to have settled somewhat. The Paris Peace Agreement was signed on January 23, and the last remaining American combat troops left sixty days later. That April, President Thiệu flew to California to meet with President Nixon. Our entire economic team was allowed to join, to help negotiate post-cease-fire aid with the American experts. We had been hard at work on a Keynesian model for developing the economy in a peace environment. But in the end, peace proved just as elusive as American aid.

In this conflict, there were two administrations and two armies at war in South Vietnam. This made our task of enforcing fiscal discipline, fighting inflation, and economic restructuring enormously challenging. We were asked to assume the financial costs of the war, though they were clearly well beyond our means. This endangered the very existence of our young democracy. In the face of this economic conundrum, both parties—the Republic of Vietnam and the United States—saw things through their own perspectives. Our American advisors moralized that "it was time for Vietnam to stand on its own feet" and complained that our inflation was compounded by the fact that South Vietnam's "haves" paid no taxes. Foreign observers saw conspicuous wealth in a country at war: motorbikes, televisions, and every kind of luxury. Economists criticized what they saw as a country that "consumes much, but produces little." Meanwhile, our politicians kept approving more expensive budgets but shied away from unpopular revenue-collecting measures, instead blaming the situation on incompetent ministers. For too long, we had avoided the political taboos of currency devaluation and taxation whenever confronted with the structural imbalances of our economy.

Still, looking back, I believe our reforms, carried out despite significant factors beyond our control, withstood the test of time.

CHAPTER FOUR

LAND REFORM AND AGRICULTURAL DEVELOPMENT, 1968–1975

Cao Văn Thân

Cao Văn Thân grew up in Saigon, attended French schools, and did his undergraduate and graduate studies in philosophy, law, and economics at French and American universities. After a tour of mandatory military service in the Army of the Republic of Vietnam for ten years, he worked as a lawyer, a judge at the Saigon Tribunal of First Instance, and an executive at Shell Petroleum of Vietnam, before beginning his teaching career in economics at different universities. From 1967 to 1974, he served the government of the RVN, first on President Nguyễn Văn Thiệu's staff, then as minister of land reform and agricultural development, concurrently minister of rural development, responsible for implementing the Land to the Tiller program. In 1974, he resumed his academic career and moved to the Sorbonne in Paris. After the fall of Saigon, he moved to the University of Arizona. When he retired, he was professor and chair of the Department of Economics, Montana State University. He now lives in Montreal.

This chapter focuses on major policies under President Nguyễn Văn Thiệu that transformed the countryside and contributed significantly to the economic development of South Vietnam in the last years of the war. These policies include land reform, an agricultural development program, price liberalization, and market stabilization. The policies practically eradicated land tenancy, reduced rural inequality by creating a large class of landowners, rapidly expanded production toward achieving food self-sufficiency, and stabilized market and consumption. This took place in the middle of a savage war and amounted to a successful rural revolution that has not been adequately acknowledged in the scholarship on the war. Rather than coercion and class struggle, our revolution was carried out based on a combination of economic incentives and new technologies that appealed to and benefited the majority of South Vietnamese farmers.

THE LAND TO THE TILLER PROGRAM

Shortly after the 1968 communist Tết Offensive, President Nguyễn Văn Thiệu appointed me minister of land reform and agricultural development, and later, concurrently, minister of rural development. I began accompanying Mr. Thiệu on his frequent tours of the countryside, talking to the farmers and trying to understand and address the issues they faced. In early 1969, I was given responsibility for designing and implementing a new land-reform project to solve our deeply unpopular land tenancy situation.

The Republic of Vietnam, about the size of Missouri, was a poor country, ravaged by violence since the end of World War II. In 1954, peasants accounted for about 90 percent of the total population. This percentage decreased very slowly over time—by 1968, the population of 17.4 million was still 80 percent rural. Very few people in the countryside owned their own land, especially in the Mekong Delta, where 70 percent of all farmers had to pay rent.

We realized that land reform was of utmost urgency and importance. Indeed, Article 19 of the 1967 constitution enshrined an official policy of "making the people property owners" and provided that the state compensate landowners in a speedy and just manner at the market rate in case of expropriation for public purposes.[1] We were convinced we could craft a good land-reform program to faithfully adhere to Article 19 while benefiting our dirt-poor rural population.

Although some people assume this was an American idea, the land-reform initiative, known as Land to the Tiller (LTTT), was in fact conceived and implemented by Vietnamese alone. As U.S. ambassador Ellsworth Bunker wrote to President Richard Nixon, "the basic concept of land distribution was done entirely by the Vietnamese on their own. The idea did not come from us, it came from President Thieu's new, young and dynamic Minister of Land Reform and Agriculture, Cao Van Than."[2]

I shared French journalist Bernard Fall's analysis that land reform in South Vietnam was "as essential a factor to success in the Vietnam war as ammunition for howitzers."[3] Although I am a strong believer in free markets and private enterprise, I was also convinced that redistribution to the poor and landless was the best way to redress the inequity of the agrarian system that we inherited from the past. History, I thought, would prove that this investment in our farmers would bring about significant returns in the near future, if free markets and private enterprise were allowed to operate.

I was determined that our new land-reform program would succeed. I felt I had to design an initiative that would meet the needs and desires of our landless peasants, and that was superior to the communists' previous land reforms in the South, or in North Vietnam for that matter. Our program must be easily understood by the farmers and readily accepted by them. I must be able to explain to them our program. I would offer them new ideas. Of course, new ideas often meet resistance. But new, good ideas and fresh eyes can also make a big difference.

To prepare, I spent months visiting villages in central Vietnam and the Mekong Delta, talking with hundreds of farmers, listening to their hopes and grievances, and collecting as much information as possible about North Vietnamese and Việt Cộng land reform. I wanted to "carry the war to the enemy," as Colonel Roger Trinquier, my unit commander in the French war against the Việt Minh, had advised. But I had to be realistic in estimating our ability to mobilize the necessary resources to finance our land-reform program.

Some members of the House of Representatives took issue with the name Land to the Tiller (or Người Cày Có Ruộng, NCCR), because the enemy had already used the same motto. I was happy to compromise on minor issues, but I insisted we keep the name, as it was a purely Vietnamese phrase rather than the Chinese-based name "Cải Cách Điền Địa" (land reform), which they preferred. It is worth mentioning that it was not the Việt Cộng who had invented the term NCCR. My reading of Lenin's works indicated that Vladimir Lenin had frequently talked about the tillers who must have the land. Several other countries had also chosen Land to the Tiller. I was finally able to persuade National Assembly members to accept the term.

The House of Representatives also disagreed with our proposed law because it called for the free distribution of arable land. Of course, the communists had already, if only verbally, granted free land to the rural poor, and I argued that we could hardly come up with any less if we were to compete against them. Our current approach was to sell expropriated land to farmers in installments, but I had learned that the delinquency rate on payments was close to 90 percent. Instead, I proposed free land for tenant farmers and, unlike the communists, land titles to guarantee their ownership.

Some House representatives were also strongly opposed to provisions issuing legal titles for land granted to farmers by the communists. The standing policy was that after our forces regained control of communist villages, communist land reform was immediately overturned. Farmers were forcibly evicted from their fields, and the land was turned back over to absentee landlords. Aware of the resentment this engendered, I pushed to discontinue the practice of reinstating absentee landlords, instead permitting farmers to remain on their communist-distributed land. We also froze land occupancy and rents in villages under temporary communist control while the new legislation was being drafted. Obviously, farmers would not be willing to pay distant landowners for fields that the communists had already promised belonged to them.

By June 1969, I had completed my proposal and presented it to President Thiệu, who submitted it to the National Assembly on July 1, 1969. After seven months of arduous deliberations, the National Assembly finally approved the proposal, now known as the LTTT program. President Thiệu signed it into law on March 26, 1970.

The final draft was five pages long, with twenty-two articles. Its objective was the elimination of land tenancy through the expropriation of land not directly cultivated by its owner. Expropriated land was to be delivered free of charge to the famers themselves, with a maximum of three hectares per family in the Mekong Delta and one hectare in central Vietnam. Farmers who received the distributed land were required to cultivate it themselves and prohibited from transferring ownership for the first fifteen years. They were also exempted from registration fees and taxes on the land for the first year.

Of course, the landlords whose property was to be expropriated had to be fairly compensated. We developed the following formula: 20 percent of the expropriated land value was paid up front, in cash, and the remainder paid in eight-year bonds bearing 10 percent annual interest. In order to resolve disputes, we also established a special land court with jurisdiction over cases involving the LTTT law. The law also detailed punitive measures for anyone charged with preventing the implementation of our reforms.

Although the American media welcomed our endeavor, U.S. officials in South Vietnam had mixed feelings. The U.S. Agency for International Development (USAID) staff were not enthusiastic, and they doubted we could carry it out successfully. Our plans were totally different than any land-reform program they had seen before. Furthermore, they worried that compensating landlords would create a huge budget gap for the South Vietnamese government and that USAID would have to help fill the gap with even more financial aid. And indeed, the ten-year cost of the program was estimated at $400 million.

However, the reception among the U.S. embassy personnel was favorable. Though they, too, were aware of the financial cost, they balanced this against the potential political benefits. They were also more willing to take a chance on good ideas. U.S. ambassador Ellsworth Bunker met with me many times during the LTTT implementation phase and always offered congratulations and encouragement: "keep doing an excellent job." He also invited me to meet with visiting American congressional delegations, so they could learn firsthand about our progress.

These efforts helped persuade the American government to help with funding. In 1969, Ambassador Bunker signed an agreement whereby the United States would cover 10 percent of the estimated cost, beginning with an initial grant of $10 million. These American funds were not to be paid to the landlords directly; instead, they would help finance the cost of imports from the United States. In 1970, another $30 million was awarded, pending continued progress on implementation, and by 1973, the United States had contributed almost its full $40 million share. The South Vietnamese government, on the other hand, had expended just over $200 million worth of contributions.

Although the scale of American assistance was modest, it produced an important psychological effect. Most landlords doubted that we could deliver compensation without American financial backing (though few of them knew how little the United States was actually providing). U.S. support certainly helped reduce landlord opposition during the four years of the land-reform process.

It was generally agreed that the land problem was at the root of the conflict in Vietnam. In a March 31, 1968, editorial calling for land reform in South Vietnam, the *New York Times* projected that "virtually overnight, South Vietnam's landless peasants would be given a stake to defend in their society. The Việt Cộng would be deprived of a gut issue. No military victory or political achievement would be more likely to move Hanoi toward the peace table than evidence of a substantial shift in peasant loyalty."[4] Then, two weeks after our LTTT law was promulgated, on April 9, 1970, the same *New York Times* declared that our new land-reform program was "probably the most ambitious and progressive non-Communist land reform of the twentieth century."[5]

The LTTT program included roughly one million hectares of land and involved some one million landless families. Given that the average family has six members, we can assume that roughly six million people stood to benefit. The success of the program depended on its swift implementation. In order to achieve this, we also adopted an entirely new set of revolutionary procedures, decentralizing the government and devolving authority onto elected officials in over two thousand rural villages.

We started with a massive training program beginning in early 1969 to instruct village officials on their new duties. Next, we embraced aerial photography in order to delineate plots of land, replacing the obsolete land register that had not been updated since the 1930s. This accelerated the process at least twentyfold. We also employed over fifty thousand armed Ministry of Rural Development cadres to identify farmers and assign land down to the hamlet level. These cadres played a critical role in implementing the LTTT program. Trained at the Vũng Tàu National Training Center, they were our civilian shock troops in the battle for hearts and minds. They lived in the areas where they were assigned and strove to form connections with the locals. Beyond land reform, they also assisted elected officials in the countryside with security, health care, education, and agricultural development.

To ease the burdens of paperwork, our team also established a series of special legal and administrative organs designed to bypass the usual bureaucratic backlog, with officials at the local, regional, and national level. Ours was an immense undertaking, and its complicated implementation required close and constant monitoring at all levels. President Thiệu himself took a keen interest, reviewing our progress at monthly meetings and tasking each of four regional military commanders with responsibility for meeting implementation targets. Military cooperation was necessary, as rural security was essential if the program was to succeed. The Prime Minister's Office also appointed a top-ranking general to supervise the proceedings and to resolve any administrative bottlenecks.

With the full weight of government support behind the program, we were able to award title to over two hundred thousand hectares in the first year alone—equal to almost the entire hectarage distributed by previous South Vietnamese governments over the past twenty years. By the end of 1973, we had completed some 1.1 million hectares, almost 40 percent of the total cultivated land in South Vietnam.[6]

By 1974, land tenancy had practically disappeared in South Vietnam, and farmers' standard of living had significantly increased compared to the pre-land-reform period, thanks to a 30 percent increase in the value of agricultural output between 1968 and 1971.[7] Developments in agriculture—accounting for roughly one third of the gross national product—contributed to South Vietnam's overall economic growth, which averaged 8.6 percent between 1969 and 1971.

In short, our land-reform program had created among rural people a very large class of small landowners. Combined with agricultural modernization, landownership significantly reduced the degree of poverty and inequality in rural South Vietnam.

The Green Revolution

I believe President Thiệu deep down was a farmer at heart. In addition to land reform, he also ordered me to launch an ambitious agricultural development program to jumpstart the agriculture-based economy and to consolidate the transformative gains that the long-deprived segment of our population had just obtained.

South Vietnam was an agrarian society since time immemorial, with abundant unexploited natural resources. Unlike the bloody agrarian reforms of the North, where tens of thousands of innocent people lost their property or even their lives, ours was a peaceful revolution—not a single landowner died as a result of the LTTT program. No other undertaking in the history of our country has ever brought about such a drastic change in rural landownership, or so improved the livelihood of farmers, by far the majority of our people.

I directed a massive five-year agricultural development plan, encompassing nine agricultural sectors and including some three dozen crop programs, as well as livestock, fisheries, and timber production. The plan was formally announced in 1970 by President Thiệu, in a landmark proclamation to the nation delivered in Long Xuyên Province. Mr. Thiệu announced that his administration would launch the five-year program to achieve three main objectives: satisfying the national demand for essential commodities; increasing rural standards of living; and expanding exports while reducing our dependence on imports in order to boost the local economy and generate foreign exchange.

Of the more than three dozen components of the first five-year plan, I considered the Accelerated Miracle Rice Production Program (AMRPP) to be the centerpiece. Rice production is of course an integral part of Vietnamese culture. More than just a staple of our diet, it lies at the center of our culture and our way of life. And in the annals of economic development of Vietnam there has never been any agricultural development program that is grander in scope, more complex in implementation, more remarkable in impact, and more successful in outcome than the AMRPP.

One of the most significant developments in the history of food production was the discovery by the International Rice Research Institute (IRRI) of new high-yield rice varieties in the 1960s. This innovation was at the heart of the global "Green Revolution," which helped make the problem of starvation a thing of the past. The international scientists working at the IRRI learned how to hybridize several new varieties of high-yield and short-maturation rice. This doubled, then tripled, and then even quadrupled the normal yield of existing native local varieties of rice, revolutionizing the world's most important crop almost overnight. By shortening rice maturation times from between 120 and 140 days to between just 90 and 100 days, they allowed for multiple harvests within the two traditional growing seasons. These scientists also developed short, sturdy rice plants, less susceptible to damage from the wind and rain. The new rice also absorbed more fertilizer, allowing it to grow faster and produce more grain. They also invented long-stem varieties, capable of accommodating more deeply flooded fields, and even produced pest- and disease-resistant strains, and plants capable of withstanding high levels of salt or acidity, a major problem in estuaries like the Mekong Delta.

South Vietnam was fortunate to have been given the opportunity to participate in the field trials of these varieties on a national scale, beginning in 1967. In a land disrupted by a destructive insurgency fomented by international communism, which wreaked havoc on its food production, rapid large-scale agricultural changes were urgent indeed, especially with American aid for food imports beginning to taper.

To emphasize his determination to launch the Green Revolution, and to signal its importance to rank-and-file administrators, President Thiệu made sure he was seen wading knee deep in the mud, planting miracle rice, and showing off new portable harvesting machines. He also personally distributed land titles across the country. Miracle rice production was added to his list of overall pacification and development goals, and he took care to personally monitor its progress. At monthly meetings at different military regions of the country where the highest military and civilian authorities were gathered, he paid keen attention to land distribution to farmers and to acreage of miracle rice production as much as the number of enemy soldiers killed and villages secured or villagers liberated.

Nothing was more effective at delivering change than the direct support of the president. I accompanied him on monthly high-level inspection tours and enlisted the help of the provincial and regional military authorities to clear administrative bottlenecks wherever we faced impediments to reform. Military security was often the most intractable problem, especially in far-flung corners of the country, and Mr. Thiệu's direct orders to regional commanders helped ensure that these challenges were promptly confronted.

Beyond even LTTT, the AMRPP was indeed the biggest and most ambitious civilian effort undertaken by the government. All key government organizations were involved, although the Ministry for Land Reform and Agricultural Development took the lead. Eight out of nine agricultural directorates were involved, and at its height, the program occupied eighteen thousand out of twenty thousand agricultural directorate employees—this was the biggest civilian branch in the entire government.

Rice, especially the new high-yield varieties, is a very tedious and demanding crop to produce because of the exacting requirements of many factors involved in the processes. These include proper land preparation, selecting the appropriate seeds for each particular field, nurturing the seedlings, correctly timing insecticide and herbicide application, managing water levels, applying suitable fertilizers for each type of soil, forecasting the weather, managing animal and human labor, investing in machinery, and, finally, harvesting, transporting, storing, processing, and selling the rice, all of which requires ready credit and military security.

At the height of this program, tens of thousands of the Ministry of Land Reform and Agricultural Development technocrats of all levels—central, provincial, and regional—along with rural development cadres in every province, were intricately involved in a multitude of daily tasks. We made plans, implemented our ideas, trained cadres and farmers, carried out research, supervised support workers, conducted inspections, corrected errors, and drafted and filed reports. My job was like conducting a symphony orchestra, with each step of the process requiring precision timing given the demands of the rice-growing cycle. It was a feat rarely seen in the history of agriculture due to the unpredictable nature of the weather, our limited financial resources, and the paucity of manpower of an underdeveloped country at war.

Other ministries and government agencies provided varying degrees of assistance. The Ministry of Economy prioritized its scarce foreign exchange for the import of vital goods such as fertilizer, insecticides and herbicides, farm equipment, and machinery. It was also responsible for rice-marketing policies that would incentivize farmers to increase production. This marked a change from years of disastrous policy, which had reduced peasants to subsistence farming and resulted in food shortages, hoarding, inflation, speculation, the disruption of traditional rural and urban life, and plummeting military and civilian morale.

In 1973, a cabinet reshuffling resulted in a new rice-marketing approach that favored rural producers over urban consumers. To understand why this new marketing policy was important one just needs to look at the Philippines where miracle rice originated and where the Green Revolution first started but whose rice-marketing policy has favored urban consumers. To this day the Philippines still imports large quantities of rice annually to feed its urban population. The rice-marketing policy we implemented in 1973 in South Vietnam brought about an upsurge in the production of commercial high-yield varieties of rice throughout the land and moved us closer toward the goal of self-sufficiency. So desirable was our rice that communist insurgents began smuggling seeds to the North in order to bolster their own poor food production rates.

Meanwhile, to help farmers fund their investments, the central bank and Ministry of Finance oversaw a program whereby rural banks awarded small loans, averaging $50, to purchase high-yield seeds, farm equipment, pumps and motors, and fertilizers, herbicides, and insecticides. This expansion of rural credit had an immediate transformational effect on the countryside as many farmers were able to move from subsistence to commercial rice farming. The sight of small wooden boats, powered by imported shrimp tail motors, crisscrossing the canals carrying goods to the markets was most uplifting.

It began in earnest when the Agricultural Development Bank of Vietnam (ADBV) started the Rural Bank program in 1969, opening and cosponsoring four rural banks along with private investors. The aim was to provide banking services and credit down to the hamlet level in rural areas where there had never been a commercial bank presence. Nguyễn Đăng Hải served as the general manager of the project, and by 1974 he had increased the number of rural banks to eighty-six.

Each rural bank was a separate entity, just like any other commercial bank, and under the control of the National Bank of Vietnam. It has its own board of directors elected by shareholders and had to apply to the National Bank to obtain a license. As a special sponsor and co-owner of the rural banks, the ADBV held training courses for the employees and boards of directors of each branch, to ensure that the rural banks upheld shareholder interests and abided by the law. The ADBV also conducted routine surprise audits to monitor compliance.

Meanwhile, the Ministries of Defense and the Interior played an important role by providing rural security. They launched military operations timed to accompany the harvest, and allowed for deferments for conscripted agronomists during the most critical stages of the growing season. Some fifty thousand rural development cadres also stepped up to help ease chronic manpower shortages stemming from the military draft.

South Vietnam was one of the first few countries to test these new varieties of miracle rice, and because there were more than half a dozen varieties, we had to plant them on a trial-and-error basis to determine the most appropriate strain for each region. It was a time-consuming proposition at best, fraught with difficulties and frequent failures. On top of this, our seeds came from the Philippines, which forbade the export of the new varieties, severely inhibiting our efforts. It took direct intervention by President Lyndon Johnson before we received our first batch, which meant working overtime at our research stations to proliferate this initial sample. But our team was determined, and fortunately, we were blessed by clement weather during the first few harvests.

Even before miracle rice, Vietnam already had almost nine hundred varieties of rice, some of them very unique and precious. Persuading conservative farmers to abandon their time-tested favorites for our new experimental seeds took some doing. One of our favorite schemes to entice farmers was to order rural development cadres to sleep outdoors, next to the miracle rice plots. Convinced that anything so closely guarded must be very valuable, farmers began stealing the miracle seeds to test on their own, whereupon they were quickly won over. They would steal some of these seeds for use at their land for seed multiplication for the next planting season. The ploy succeeded well beyond our expectations.

A more transparent approach was simply to show by example. When farmers saw their neighbors growing wealthy practically overnight, their resistance crumbled. A farmer in the Mekong Delta with three hectares of land after two harvests of miracle rice would produce about twenty-four tons of paddy a year.[8] Selling at 10,000 Đồng per one hundred kilograms of rice and assuming that one hundred kilograms of paddy produces seventy-five kilograms of rice, this would provide the farmer a significant profit usually equal to 30 percent of gross income.

The impact of this massive agricultural development was far-reaching. It helped lift the peasant majority out of abject poverty almost overnight, turning society's most disenfranchised into a fledgling rural middle class. Our estimates suggested that income in the countryside doubled and in some cases quadrupled following the advent of miracle rice.

As a result of these initiatives, we recorded a surge in miracle rice acreage to nine hundred thousand hectares by 1973, a total that did not include the no-doubt significant adaptation beyond our official program. Expanding paddy production and processing activities also contributed to a surge in meat, poultry, and fish production as well. It was by any account a tremendous accomplishment at a time of ongoing warfare. A thriving middle class began to emerge just a couple of years after completion of the LTTT program. It brought South Vietnam back to rice self-sufficiency as early as 1975 after almost a decade of rice imports that amounted to as much as six hundred thousand metric tons a year.

Price Liberalization and Market Stabilization

Production was only half of the challenge. The other half, just as critical to the success of the program, was financing, collection, storage, and distribution. Rice would not move from the farmer to the consumer in the cities at competitive prices unless we could resolve satisfactorily these critical issues of the second half. Responsibility for marketing rice fell within the purview of the Ministry of Economy, later known as the Ministry of Trade and Industry.[9]

The rice trade had traditionally been controlled by a small handful of rice merchants. Over the years, they had developed a network of collection, transportation, financing, and storage. But partly due to the war, this network began to erode, to the detriment of farmers and urban consumers alike. The rice supply was constantly disrupted by military activities and enemy sabotage, and hindered by checkpoints intended to withhold rice from enemy hands. Hoarding and price speculation were rampant.

By 1973, the situation was in crisis. That summer, Vice Minister of Agriculture Trần Quang Minh was summoned to the presidential palace for breakfast. Over a bowl of phở, he was told in no uncertain terms by the president himself that the problem had to be resolved immediately. His solution was the establishment of strategic rice reserves in rice-deficit regions, similar to the strategic petroleum reserve in the United States, which was at that time dealing with the shortage of oil due to the oil embargo imposed by OPEC following the Yom Kippur War.

Following the meeting, Trần Quang Minh was transferred to the Ministry of Trade and Industry, where he was to head the newly established National Food Administration tasked with solving the recurring rice crisis. In addition to the strategic reserve concept, the National Food Administration considered a number of options, from lifting price controls and removing military checkpoints, to increasing access to finance for farmers and merchants.

The first two measures were politically risky, given the ongoing war, and the winners and losers of liberalized pricing were unclear. But the status quo was not working, and we decided to take a chance on all four measures. To that end, we waived price controls, removed the checkpoints, encouraged commercial banks to invest in the countryside, and set up a three hundred thousand ton rice reserve in chronically deficient central Vietnam. This helped reduce annual shipments from the South from forty thousand to just seven thousand tons. By late 1974, we had managed to stabilize the situation.

In Reflection

Looking back, I believe that the Second Republic succeeded in delivering a complete rural revolution in the space of just five years. It was achieved without bloodshed, during a period of the most intense warfare. Credit for this spectacular accomplishment undoubtedly belongs to the visionary leadership of President Nguyễn Văn Thiệu.

Notes

1. Tổng Bộ Thông Tin Chiêu Hồi, *Hiến Pháp Việt Nam Cộng Hòa ban hành ngày 1 tháng 4 năm 1967* [The constitution of the Republic of Vietnam issued on April 1st, 1967] (Saigon, 1967), 17.
2. Douglas Pike, ed., *The Bunker Papers* (Berkeley: Institute of East Asian Studies, University of California–Berkeley, 1990), 3:667.
3. Bernard Fall, "Viet Nam in the Balance," *Foreign Affairs* 45, no. 1 (October 1966): 5.
4. "Muddling through in Vietnam," *New York Times*, March 31, 1968, E12.
5. Editorial, *New York Times*, April 9, 1970, 40.
6. See Douglas C. Dacy, *Foreign Aid, War, and Economic Development, South Vietnam, 1955–1975* (New York: Cambridge University Press, 1986), 113.
7. Ibid., table 3-2, 41 and 58.
8. This assumes that the yield was four tons per hectare per harvest.
9. This section was written in consultation with Dr. Trần Quang Minh, former vice minister of agriculture, and Nguyễn Đức Cường, former minister of trade and industry (see chapter 1 in this volume).

CHAPTER FIVE

STRIVING FOR A LASTING PEACE: THE PARIS ACCORDS AND AFTERMATH

Hoàng Đức Nhã

Hoàng Đức Nhã served in the government of the RVN soon after returning from his studies in the United States in January 1965 with a bachelor's degree in electrical engineering. He was a telecommunications engineer at the Ministry of Interior, then a project engineer at the Industrial Development Bank of Vietnam. He joined President Nguyễn Văn Thiệu's staff in October 1967 soon after the latter was inaugurated as president, first serving as policy analyst—when he developed the framework of the land-reform undertaking—and later as private secretary (chief of staff) and concurrently press secretary to the president. As private secretary Nhã was also a main advisor to President Thiệu in the Paris negotiations. After the peace agreement was signed in January 1973, Nhã joined the cabinet as minister of mass mobilization and open arms and coordinating minister for nation building. He resigned in November 1974 over policy differences with the prime minister. From 1975 to 2003, Nhã worked at three major companies, General Electric, FMC Corporation, and Monsanto Company. In mid-2004 he cofounded and served as CEO of a company specializing in big data analytics serving Fortune 100 companies and various U.S. government agencies. He retired in 2012 and now lives in Chicago.

I returned to Saigon in early January 1965 after three and half years of study in the United States, where I had obtained a bachelor of science degree in electrical engineering. I had great expectations to be an active participant in the nascent industrialization of the South Vietnamese economy.

As a scholarship recipient trained abroad, I had agreed to work for the government upon graduation. I first spent a year as a telecommunications engineer, followed by another year as a project engineer at the Industrial Development Bank. But the majority of my time was spent being seconded to work as a staffer to the minister of economy.

It was in that assignment that I got to understand the importance of sound macroeconomic planning and vigorous implementation of practical plans, in order to avoid the pitfalls of centralized planning and white elephant projects that developing nations usually fell in love with. Upon returning from an additional four months of specialized training in the United States on the management of development projects, I found myself back at the Industrial Development Bank ready to put into practice what I had learned. Shortly after that, in early September 1967 South Vietnam held the first presidential and National Assembly elections of the Second Republic, a momentous development for the country, and a turning point in my career.

How I Got into Politics

Nothing in my studies or training had prepared me for what I would be asked to do shortly after Mr. Nguyễn Văn Thiệu was inaugurated as the first president of the Second Republic. Soon after assuming office, President Thiệu created a kind of brain trust, formally designated the Office of Experts, to assist him in policy and issues analysis and crisis management for all nonmilitary issues. I was invited to join and promptly left the Industrial Development Bank.

There were ten of us in the brain trust; nine were graduates of French and Vietnamese universities, and I was the only one trained in the United States. I took over the portfolio of agricultural reform, and within three months submitted a framework for both narrowing the social divide in the rural areas between landowners and tenant farmers, and increasing rice production for self-sufficiency. This later formed the basis of our Land to the Tiller land-reform program (see chapter 4 in this volume).

Shortly after the 1968 Tết Offensive, I was promoted to personal secretary to the president, a kind of sounding board and analyst to the president on key issues. This was a highly political job, normally reserved for a much more senior person with knowledge and experience in the political workings of the country. I was twenty-five at the time.

As personal secretary I participated in all the major decisions the president made, and as the pressure grew to achieve a peaceful solution to the war, I was front and center in all the discussions, at first as a behind-the-scenes strategist. Then, starting in early 1972, I burst onto the scene at the side of the president, much to the surprise and then consternation of the Americans. Few political observers in Vietnam knew who I was or why the president had given me such an important position.

I was soon thrust into the heat of the battle, so to speak, and became a key witness to history, and a participant in the tumultuous relationship between President Thiệu and President Richard Nixon and his national security advisor Henry Kissinger.

The Meandering Road to Peace

During his inauguration as the first president of the Second Republic in early October 1967, President Thiệu swore to defend the constitution promulgated a few months earlier, to safeguard the territorial integrity of South Vietnam, and "to open the door and leave it open" to a lasting peace, in order to implement programs for the betterment of the South Vietnamese people. This promise was indeed a tall order, considering that the country had just come out of a tumultuous phase of its political evolution and was dealing with an ally who, after having Americanized the war, now wanted to Americanize a solution to end it.

President Thiệu inherited a country at war, wracked by political turmoil and instability and a sagging morale in the population. The bloody coup that ended the First Republic on November 1, 1963, was followed by an interregnum period when the generals jostled for power and not much progress was made. The ensuing domestic turmoil and lack of leadership within the military junta emboldened politicized Buddhist monks and other political and religious groups to clamor for change.

President Thiệu realized that the country needed a broader political base to offset the negative consequences of the last years of the First Republic and the chaos during the interregnum years. He also realized that in order make the people of South Vietnam more engaged in the fight to protect and develop the homeland, he needed to win their hearts and minds. This meant bringing the war to a peaceful end as soon as possible and leveraging that peace to build a stronger nation in South Vietnam. The daunting task facing him was further compounded, on the one hand, by a relentless war of aggression waged by North Vietnam in violation of the 1954 Geneva Accords and, on the other hand, by an ally, the United States, that began to unilaterally implement an exit strategy.

President Thiệu realized that the march to American disengagement was irreversible. Even before he was elected president on September 3, 1967, he became aware of U.S. intentions when, in March 1965, President Lyndon Johnson declared that he was "ready to go anywhere, at any time, and meet with anyone whenever there is a promise of progress toward an honorable peace." One month later, President Johnson stated that he was ready for unconditional discussions and promised aid to Southeast Asia, including North Vietnam. Johnson further hinted that the United States would not oppose a coalition government in South Vietnam and that he was willing to stop all aerial bombardment of the North.

At the December 1967 Canberra Conference, Johnson increased the pressure by "suggesting" to newly elected President Thiệu that he engage in direct talks with the National Liberation Front (NLF), Hanoi's proxy in the South. President Thiệu was worried that the United States was slowly Americanizing the peace process. However, he agreed to negotiate with North Vietnam when, on March 31, 1968, President Johnson shocked the world by announcing the halt of bombing in North Vietnam to facilitate negotiations with Hanoi and his decision not to seek a second term in office.

President Thiệu approved this peace process but also cautioned the Johnson administration that the roles and responsibilities between the United States and South Vietnam in the peace negotiations should be clearly delineated before talks began. He was understandably worried that Washington would negotiate over South Vietnam's head, similar to what had occurred during the 1954 Geneva Accords. Fortunately, the success of South Vietnam's armed forces in defeating the 1968 communist Tết Offensive gave us a position of strength going into the negotiations.

MOUNTING PRESSURE TO NEGOTIATE FAST

At the July 1968 Honolulu Summit between the United States and the Republic of Vietnam (RVN), the two sides agreed to require North Vietnam to withdraw its forces from South Vietnam before the United States began to depart. The United States also promised not to support the imposition of a coalition government in South Vietnam. Two weeks prior to arriving in Honolulu, President Thiệu said in a press conference that the RVN was willing to shoulder a bigger burden of the war starting in 1969, so that the United States could begin withdrawing troops while at the same time increasing its economic and military support to South Vietnam.

The Paris negotiations between the United States and North Vietnam that began soon after March 1968 produced no results, while Hanoi continued massive infiltration to make up for losses incurred during the Tết Offensive. Nevertheless, the United States continued to show flexibility pursuing a settlement, and the upcoming American presidential elections further increased the pressure on us to engage in direct talks with the NLF while Washington negotiated with Hanoi in a separate forum.

But President Thiệu refused to meet with the NLF, because we had still not agreed with the United States on our common objectives in Paris, let alone the issues that the talks would cover, or their procedures. For us, these negotiation procedures were of paramount importance.

Our refusal to send a delegation to the Paris meeting infuriated the American side, especially Defense Secretary Clark Clifford and Ambassador William Harriman, the head of the U.S. delegation. The Johnson administration, and most of the American media, thought that South Vietnam had been influenced by Mrs. Anna Chennault, apparently on behalf of the Nixon campaign, who had asked us not to attend the Paris talks until after the election. Even President Johnson, in his memoir, alludes to this rumor.

Mrs. Chennault indeed met with two South Vietnamese officials, our ambassadors to the United States and to Taiwan (the latter was President Thiệu's older brother). The information she gave them was passed on to President Thiệu, who then conferred with some of his inner circle. I took note of her message, but insisted that before we sent our team to Paris, we needed to have our strategies and plans clearly defined and developed, as well as a joint modus operandi with the American delegation.

Furthermore, after Tết, South Vietnam was winning on the battlefield, and we believed that we should negotiate in a position of strength. The RVN government was further incensed when Secretary Clifford, in a December 1968 interview, stated that the United States need not work out common positions with the Vietnamese allies. It was not until mid-January 1969 that North Vietnam, under pressure from Moscow, caved on the important procedural issues for the talks. We then sent our delegation to the Paris talks in January, now expanded to include both the RVN government and the NLF. The October 1968 skirmish with the United States on negotiation strategies and tactics was a harbinger of the many more disputes to come.

Building the Nation while Bracing for the Negotiations

After the 1968 Tết Offensive, the South Vietnamese government and people were very encouraged by the successes of our military campaigns and by the initiatives launched by the president in his quest to strengthen the nation. We repaired infrastructure that was destroyed by the fighting and also developed other capabilities that were essential to our nation-building efforts. Among the most challenging tasks were the building of a democratic system as prescribed by the 1967 constitution based on the respect of basic human rights and the rule of law, and the implementation of plans for developing both a market economy and our agriculture in order to increase productivity, create a new middle class, and improve living standards.

South Vietnam has abundant resources, and a population blessed with entrepreneurial spirit and hard work. Our education system, along with scholarships for gifted students to be trained at overseas universities, had produced a class of well-trained technocrats who were critical to the success of our nation-building efforts (see chapter 8 and chapter 9 in this volume about developments in South Vietnam's education system).

The South Vietnamese government at that time was in a unique and challenging situation. On the one hand, we had to defend our territorial integrity and defeat the communist invasion, and on the other hand, we had to create transformational change for the betterment of the entire population. We did all that while cooperating with the Nixon administration to restore peace to the two parts of Vietnam.

It was quite a daunting task. But little could we predict that our so-called unified negotiating position with the United States was being constantly frayed by secret exchanges and communications with Hanoi. Relations gradually took a turn for the worse when we realized that President Nixon and Dr. Kissinger wanted to end the war their way, South Vietnamese opinions or objections be damned.

Rocky Journey to a Peace Accord

The peace negotiations were conducted by the White House. President Nixon and Dr. Kissinger had effectively sidelined the State Department under Secretary William Rogers. It was also clear to us that the White House rarely updated the leadership of the House and Senate, if at all, except for a few selected representatives and senators, and some friendly commentators and reporters.

On the South Vietnamese side, President Thiệu consulted with the leadership of our own House and Senate. He also relied on a well-coordinated National Security Council composed of Vice President Trần Văn Hương, Prime Minister Trần Thiện Khiêm, Chairman of the Joint General Staff general Cao Văn Viên, Minister for Foreign Affairs Trần Văn Lắm and Vice Minister for Foreign Affairs Trần Kim Phượng, Special Assistant to the President for Foreign Affairs Dr. Nguyễn Phú Đức, and myself, as personal secretary to the president and spokesperson.

Not once had we thought that the American side, in its haste to arrive at a solution, would run the negotiations by themselves without consulting us. The first skirmish happened on May 14, 1969, when President Nixon, without first confirming with President Thiệu, publicly advocated the simultaneous withdrawal of American and North Vietnamese forces from South Vietnam. This was a clear departure from an agreement, adopted by all troop-contributing countries in 1966, that allied forces would only withdraw six months after the North had pulled out of the South.

President Nixon also advocated the participation in political life by all political elements in South Vietnam, including the National Liberation Front—without giving credit to a similar proposal that President Thiệu had already made the previous month. After we communicated our dismay to the U.S. embassy in Saigon, the White House quickly moved to reassure President Thiệu by proposing a June 1969 meeting between the two presidents at Midway Island in the Pacific, half way between Washington D.C. and Saigon.

The communiqué from this one-day summit meeting reiterated the American view that only the South Vietnamese people could determine their political future and that there would be no coalition government in South Vietnam—another promise that was to be tossed away years later without prior consultation. In turn, we reiterated our offer to begin replacing American forces with South Vietnamese troops, beginning with the withdrawal of twenty-five thousand U.S. soldiers.

Most galling at Midway was that the Americans did not bother informing us that in order to fast-track the negotiations, it was already laying the foundation for secret talks between Dr. Kissinger and the leaders of the North Vietnamese delegation, Xuân Thủy and later Lê Đức Thọ. Declassified materials show that the first secret talk between Dr. Kissinger and Xuân Thủy took place on August 4, 1969, at the Paris apartment of Jean Sainteny, the former French delegate general in Hanoi. These materials also show that at the meetings, Dr. Kissinger made many important concessions, especially on the political issues in South Vietnam that should have been the purview of our government and the NLF.

We followed the Midway meeting by proposing free and fair nationwide elections, but Hanoi rejected our proposal. Meanwhile, the phased withdrawals of American troops continued. On July 25, 1969, President Nixon introduced the "Nixon Doctrine," and thus launched the "Vietnamization" program. A few days later during a visit to Saigon, he pledged his steadfast support for South Vietnam and promised not to make any further concession to Hanoi. The next two years were marked by a series of proposals from the United States and the RVN aimed at breaking the diplomatic stalemate, but Hanoi continued to stonewall, believing that Nixon would eventually abandon South Vietnam to get U.S. troops and POWs back home in order to secure reelection.

North Vietnam's Fight Fight/Talk Talk Approach

After years of stalled negotiations, 1972 was a year of tectonic political and military changes, the results of which in many ways sealed the fate of South Vietnam. The year began with the January 9 revelation by President Nixon that Dr. Kissinger had been conducting secret talks with Hanoi since August 1969. The talks had been conducted without consulting with or informing South Vietnam. This shocking turn of events was followed by Nixon's dramatic February visit to China. He and Dr. Kissinger hoped to implement triangular diplomacy, using China as leverage against Russia, Russia as leverage against China, and both of them as leverage against North Vietnam.

However, Hanoi broke off the Paris talks, opting to end the war militarily with a decisive victory. In April, the communists launched a three-pronged offensive against us: across the northernmost provinces of Quảng Trị and Thừa Thiên; through the Central Highlands; and past the town of An Lộc, a mere sixty miles from Saigon. The Easter Offensive, or, as we called it, the "Fiery Summer" (*Mùa hè Đỏ lửa*), saw North Vietnam deploy thirteen combat divisions, leaving only one division in the North as a reserve.

After some initial setbacks, our forces regrouped, and with the help of massive American air and naval bombardment, we slowly repelled the invaders, retaking most of the captured territory by the middle of July. President Nixon decided to bring North Vietnam back to the negotiation table, and in a May 9 address to the nation, he announced Operation Linebacker—the massive bombing of the North, and the mining of Haiphong harbor.

A Decent Interval

One of my responsibilities as personal secretary to the president and presidential spokesperson was to monitor and analyze American and international media, in order to detect clues about what was being floated concerning a potential settlement. We knew that the Americans liked leaking information on the negotiations, through deep backgrounders or quotes attributed to "sources close to the administration."

And by that time, through American press coverage and talks with journalists, key members of the U.S. National Security Council, and staffers in the U.S. Congress as well as members of Congress and senators on visit, I had begun to pick up on a balloon being floated in Washington about a "decent interval" concept for ending the war. According to this concept, the United States would settle for the fall of South

Vietnam—provided it occurred only after a "decent interval" had passed following the final withdrawal of American troops.

Having launched Operation Linebacker, Nixon then headed to Moscow for a summit meeting with Leonid Brezhnev, the leader of the Soviet Union, and his foreign affairs minister Andrei Gromyko. Here too, Dr. Kissinger tossed around the concept of a decent interval, using such words as "a degree of time," "eighteen months," or "a year or two." Soon after the meeting, Gromyko informed Hanoi that the United States favored a political solution that did not guarantee a communist victory—but did not exclude it.

Then, in July, Kissinger returned to China. Here, he apparently reassured his host that after the implementation of a cease-fire in Vietnam, the United States would withdraw all its remaining troops and POWs and, after a decent interval, refrain from intervening in the political situation in the South. This time, he did not attempt to quantify the decent interval, instead using words like "sufficient" or "reasonable" to describe his intentions. After Kissinger left Beijing, Hanoi's chief negotiator Lê Đức Thọ also paid China a visit, where he was apparently instructed by Prime Minister Zhou Enlai to drop his insistence on President Thiệu's removal.

While all these high-stake maneuvers were being played out in secret between Nixon and Kissinger, Brezhnev and Gromyko, and Mao Zedong and Zhou, the Paris talks remained stalled. Dr. Kissinger told us only that there was little movement in the secret negotiations and that Hanoi was still being intransigent.

Our side showed good will and made many more concessions on key points in order to quickly reach a negotiated settlement. But when we asked whether our proposals had been passed on to the North Vietnamese, the Americans replied only that "the other side will not accept it." Still, although we were miffed at not having direct contact with the North, our leadership always assumed that the United States would have our interests in mind in their dealings with Hanoi.

Showdown in Saigon

Shortly after Dr. Kissinger's June trip to Beijing, the Paris negotiations seemed to have taken on new life—much of it hatched behind the backs of President Thiệu and his government. Reality literally barged in when the American ambassador Ellsworth Bunker informed us that Dr. Kissinger would visit Saigon on October 19 to review our mutual position on the political settlement. We had no inkling that during this visit, he would present us with a near-complete ready-to-be-initialed agreement between the United States and North Vietnam.

I had, however, received a tip about what Dr. Kissinger planned to discuss with us. Two days before Kissinger's arrival, the chief of Quảng Tín (a small province south of Đà Nẵng) called me with a serious report about a document found on a dead North Vietnamese soldier. It contained instructions for North Vietnamese troops operating in the South on how to prepare for an impending cease-fire and the formation of a coalition government in South Vietnam.

I immediately went to see President Thiệu in his private quarters to report on this dramatic development. I recall telling him that something was being cooked up behind our backs and that Washington and Hanoi must have agreed on a deal. I then briefed him on the possible ramifications of such an agreement. He asked point blank whether I thought the Americans had "gone in the night with the communists," using a popular Vietnamese saying for when one party keeps another party in the dark about its intentions. I told him that with all this smoke, "there must be a fire somewhere," and that we had every reason to suspect foul play from our ally. We decided not to inform the rest of our national security team, as we wanted them to walk into the meeting with their eyes open and their minds not shrouded with suspicion.

On the morning of October 19, President Thiệu received Dr. Kissinger and his team in a calm and collected manner in the situation room next to his office. I was also present, serving as the National Security Council secretary and taking notes. Later, I would brief the rest of the cabinet and the leaders of the National Assembly on our deliberations with the American delegation. And then President Thiệu and I would have one-on-one discussions, conducting post mortems and planning our next moves.

President Thiệu kept the Americans waiting while we huddled in his office, making sense of a telephone conversation I had had with Arnaud de Borchgrave of *Newsweek*, who phoned just before Dr. Kissinger arrived at the palace. Arnaud told me that he had rushed in from Hanoi after interviewing North Vietnamese prime minister Phạm Văn Đồng about a deal Dr. Kissinger had apparently concluded with Hanoi a few days earlier. During the interview, Phạm Văn Đồng had mentioned a "transition coalition," and Arnaud had asked me if we planned to accept it. Needless to say, I was on high alert after the tip-off from Arnaud, just one day after finding the document on the dead North Vietnamese soldier.

Dr. Kissinger and his delegation were surprised to see me at the meeting, because my name had not yet featured in their profiles of President Thiệu's advisors. He proceeded to present what he described as a most comprehensive agreement to end the war and restore peace to Vietnam. He further claimed that the deal was a total collapse of the bargaining position that Hanoi had clung to for so many years. Incredulously, Dr. Kissinger even told us that the North Vietnamese leaders had cried after consenting to the provisions of the agreement!

After many more reassurances about the merits of the deal, and a message from President Nixon promising not to abandon South Vietnam, Dr. Kissinger asked us to review and approve the draft agreement so that he could take it to Hanoi to sign in three days' time. It was as if he was telling us, "Well gentlemen, this is the best deal we can hope for, and you are not going to have a better one!" It was so incredible that I could not help but shake my head after Dr. Kissinger finished his monologue.

We were shocked that the draft text of the agreement they gave us was in English, and we asked for a Vietnamese copy that arrived only four hours after the meeting ended. President Thiệu asked Dr. Kissinger for clarification on a few points, and I asked him about the timeline of his path forward. He replied that he intended to return to Hanoi by October 23 at the latest, in order to have them initial the draft. It was not lost on us that the deal was meant to be announced before the American elections. Not that President Nixon needed this development to secure his victory, with the polls showing him well ahead of George McGovern, the Democratic presidential candidate.

President Thiệu thanked Dr. Kissinger and told him we would have our comments ready the next day. He then instructed me, his special assistant for foreign affairs Nguyễn Phú Đức, our ambassador to the United States Trần Kim Phượng, and Phạm Đăng Lâm, our ambassador to France and concurrently chief of the South Vietnam delegation to the Paris talks, to analyze the agreement and report back.

The meeting adjourned with nary a smile on our side. The four of us analyzed the deal over lunch and immediately lost our appetites after reading through it.

Basically, we were being asked to end the war on Hanoi's terms. The United States had agreed to pull its troops from the South even as North Vietnamese forces stayed behind. All POWs were to be exchanged and repatriated, and a coalition government was to be imposed, disguised as an "administrative structure for national reconciliation and national concord" that would organize elections to determine the future of South Vietnam.

The four of us briefed the president, and all he said was that it was the first time we had even heard of such a deal and that all our proposals and counterproposals had evidently been tossed out by the Americans and North Vietnamese. He then instructed me to carefully analyze the Vietnamese text and report back. I spent almost three hours going through the Vietnamese version and identified sixty-five issues, a dozen of which we considered deal breakers. The deal was dramatically different from what we had been discussing with the United States for the past two years.

We were particularly shocked to see that the draft agreement referred to only three countries in Indochina—Vietnam, Cambodia, and Laos—instead of four, with South Vietnam included. There was no mention of the demilitarized border zone stipulated by the 1954 Geneva Accords on Vietnam. There was also a clause according to which North Vietnamese troops did not have to withdraw from South Vietnam, even though the Americans were compelled to depart. Most offensive to us, however, was the provision for a de facto coalition government in South Vietnam, composed of representatives from our government, the NLF (Hanoi's proxy), and the independent South Vietnamese opposition groups collectively known as the Third Force.

That evening, I met again with the president to discuss my analysis of the agreement. We both realized the Americans were getting out of South Vietnam on terms entirely advantageous to the United States and North Vietnam, leaving an uncertain future for the people of the South.

The next morning, the four of us along with Minister for Foreign Affairs Trần Văn Lắm met with Dr. Kissinger and his team at the foreign minister's private residence. President Thiệu meanwhile was consulting with our military commanders and province chiefs to discuss the battlefield situation, where the enemy was racing to capture as much land as possible before the anticipated cease-fire.

The session at the foreign minister's house only increased our apprehension about the draft agreement. We became even more suspicious after the American side tried to explain glaring mistakes in the document as mere typing errors, and new demands by Hanoi as minor points that the United States had unsuccessfully attempted to have removed.

The following day, October 21, President Thiệu and our national security team met with the Kissinger delegation, which was told that South Vietnam could not accept the agreement. The Americans responded, reiterating the same arguments they had already given the previous day. Then at Dr. Kissinger's request the general meeting adjourned for a private session format that included President Thiệu, myself, Dr. Kissinger, and U.S. ambassador Ellsworth Bunker.

October 22 saw two additional tense meetings among the four of us, with no substantial movement from either side. President Thiệu once again insisted that he could not accept the deal as currently proposed. By now, Dr. Kissinger was growing impatient, aware that the window to visit Hanoi was quickly fading.

He asked for another meeting with President Thiệu after a quick dash to Phnom Penh, apparently to reassure Prime Minister Lon Nol that the agreement was good for the people of Vietnam. This kind of outreach activity was also being conducted in Saigon, with American personnel promising various political groups that the deal meant an honorable and lasting peace and that President Thiệu had already approved.

Back from Phnom Penh that afternoon, Dr. Kissinger and Ambassador Bunker went straight to the presidential palace, again hoping to convince President Thiệu to sign. The meeting was quite tense, and I will never forget Dr. Kissinger's remark to me that my boss should not try to become a martyr!

When it became clear that he would have to return empty-handed, Dr. Kissinger asked President Thiệu for yet another meeting on October 23. When we asked why we should meet again, Kissinger explained that he wanted to leave the impression that there was still movement in our discussions.

Spinning a Debacle

On October 23, at 8 AM, we again received Dr. Kissinger and Ambassador Bunker. The president asked Dr. Kissinger to give President Nixon a personal letter explaining why he could not accept the deal as it stood. Before taking leave, Dr. Kissinger cautioned us not to reveal the details of our discussions over the past four days.

As I accompanied him out of the president's office, Dr. Kissinger remarked to me that the visit had been the worst failure of his political life and that he would not be returning to South Vietnam. I replied that he would be most welcome anytime. But all I got was a grumble!

President Thiệu and I immediately conferred on our next moves, agreeing not to reveal all the details of our meetings with Dr. Kissinger and Ambassador Bunker to the rest of the national security team. I said to President Thiệu that we should assume the Americans would spin the mini debacle in their own way and that we must avoid being portrayed as obstructing peace by refusing to cooperate. The Americans, I warned, were sure to use deep backgrounders and nonattributable quotes to explain their side of the story.

After debriefing the rest of the national security team, the president and I started to draft a nationwide televised address to be delivered that evening. Without describing the agreement in detail, we explained our position on a political settlement with the communists and insisted that on a number of critical issues, we would never surrender. The speech was very well received by the people and in our National Assembly.

Reaction came swiftly from Hanoi, however, which released the text of the deal the following day, forcing Dr. Kissinger to hold a press conference explaining the impasse, during which he declared that "peace is at hand." This earned a rejoinder from the North that "peace is at the end of the tip of the pen," while I merely opined to the press that as far as I knew, war was still around the corner.

Put Up . . . or Die

The next few months saw our exchanges with the Americans becoming angrier, with rather unusual diplomatic language. True to his word, Dr. Kissinger did not return to Saigon, instead appointing Ambassador Bunker to serve as his messenger. General Alexander Haig, Dr. Kissinger's deputy, did visit Saigon though, and in his meetings with President Thiệu and me, he tried to cajole and coerce us, threatening "brutal action" in order to force the president to accept the deal.

In the meantime, Hanoi refused to negotiate, continuing its military offensive throughout South Vietnam. It took the 1972 Christmas Bombing campaign to force them back to the table, where they eventually agreed to some of the key changes we had been requesting. Meanwhile President Nixon sent us many letters promising continued assistance to South Vietnam, while threatening to go it alone and cut off aid should we refuse.

We faced a situation where further American or North Vietnamese concessions were unlikely. But with assurances of continued U.S. assistance in the postsettlement period, and a commitment to a full-force U.S. response should Hanoi violate the treaty, we signed the deal on January 27, 1973.

Hard Times Ahead

The peace accords proved to be a Pyrrhic victory for South Vietnam. North Vietnam soon began to violate the agreement, which forced us to respond, leading to increasingly violent military confrontations combined with foot-dragging at the negotiating table over the implementation of the agreement.

Unfortunately for us, the U.S. Congress was now controlled by the Democratic Party, increasingly taking over foreign policy from the executive. The 1973 War Powers Act and Case-Church Amendment further tied President Nixon's hands. As a result, the Nixon administration did little to respond to North Vietnam's violations, despite the promises from President Nixon to President Thiệu. More ominously still, the American military did not even lift a finger when, in January 1974, the Chinese Navy attacked our forces and seized our Paracel Islands off the coast from Đà Nẵng.

Our challenge was further compounded after the Watergate scandal incapacitated President Nixon. Ironically though, until his resignation, he did his best to reassure us that the United States would continue providing aid so we could defend ourselves and would react strongly against communist violations of the Paris Accords. Concurrently, the U.S. embassy in Saigon and visiting White House officials all insisted that the United States would not waver in its promise to help South Vietnam.

Throughout all this I was practically the sole dissenter in the South Vietnamese government, arguing that we needed to chart a different course of action because there was no guarantee that the United States would honor its commitments, with or without President Nixon. I could not substantiate my hunch about a "decent interval" with any profound fact-based analysis. But from my unscientific gauging of the mood in America through radio and television reports, I could sense that we were rapidly losing the support and assistance we desperately needed.

Meanwhile, American military and economic assistance was shrinking by the day, and it looked to us like the Democratic Party was exacting revenge for our alleged role in defeating the Democratic nominee for president in 1968. Additionally, general amnesia in the American media and the indifference of key congressional leaders killed off any efforts to provide us with more aid.

Psychological Warfare

Against this backdrop, our government still had to defend against continued communist violations of the treaty terms. And President Thiệu also had a nation-building agenda to pursue. Of particular importance was the battle for the hearts and minds of the South Vietnamese people, so that they could contribute positively to the undertaking, ready for the new political reality of nationwide elections stipulated by the Peace Accords.

One week before signing the peace deal, President Thiệu tasked me with preparing the country for psychological warfare with the communists in the South. I had to quickly formulate effective new strategies to enlist the population in this psychological struggle, while continuing the Open Arms program whereby we appealed to communist soldiers and cadres to join our side.

I drastically transformed our rather static approach to engaging with the population, urban civil society in particular, opting for a more dynamic and time-sensitive model. I hoped to explain to the people the government's plans and programs to build a democratic society based on the rule of law and respect for human rights, and to fast-track agricultural and industrial development to improve their livelihood.

I reorganized the existing Ministries of Information and Open Arms by formulating new strategies and developing correct plans to fulfill the mission of reaching out to the people. Those two ministries were traditionally staffed with members of whatever political party happened to run them, so cronyism and nepotism were rampant. I replaced them with well-trained personnel, graduates of our universities and the National Institute of Administration. I then integrated the two ministries into a single department, the Ministry of Mass Mobilization and Open Arms, which I managed for nearly two years after the peace deal.

At the same time, I initiated an aggressive global information and outreach campaign, setting up information centers in Washington D.C., Paris, London, and Tokyo. They were staffed with experienced bilingual diplomats and communications experts, capable of rapidly responding to new developments. We did all this with a very modest budget.

We faced an indifferent and often hostile media in the United States and received little attention from key leaders in a Congress that had deliberately turned against the Nixon administration, refusing to fulfill his promises to South Vietnam. The fact that the executive branch had not even sent the Paris Peace Accords for Congress to ratify made the situation more dire each day.

But we marched on and executed our programs enlisting international support, while countering similar efforts from Hanoi. We scored a few impressive public relations victories by exposing their treaty violations and their indiscriminate shelling that caused the deaths of innocent people, including in some cases young school children.

Aftermath

I had always worried that we were too reliant on American promises made in secret exchanges and confidential conversations rather than through concrete measures. Immediately after we signed the Peace Accords, I advocated a more self-reliant course of action. We needed this to cope with a violent war of Northern aggression, shaky morale among our own troops, dwindling aid from an ally we could no longer trust, and a foreboding sense of imminent U.S. abandonment once the decent interval had run its course.

But our commitment to nation building remained strong: on the one hand, defending the country and its people from the aggressors, and on the other hand, upholding the constitution and making the government smaller and more efficient in providing services to the people. We strove to rally the people, our soldiers, and even cadres from the other side to join us, while managing our dwindling resources to promote economic development.

Yet nobody in the cabinet, least of all Prime Minister Trần Thiện Khiêm, wanted to believe my concern that the decent interval could indeed transpire. With convincing assessments from my staff at the overseas information centers I had created, I now could build a stronger case, albeit with some anecdotal evidence, that the United States would not abide by its commitments and that we needed to chart our own course while publicly insisting that the Americans keep their promises.

Our biggest mistake had been continuing to believe that America would stand by us. Now, we had to respond to the new world order between Washington, Moscow, and Beijing, where American troops and POWs were on their way home to their families. Sadly, most of our cabinet and our generals continued to blissfully and unrealistically hope that Nixon's pledges would be kept. For advocating self-reliance and warning that we should not put too much faith in American promises, I became the bête noire of the Kissinger team in Washington and the new U.S. ambassador in Saigon, Graham Martin.

I sensed that President Thiệu was torn between soothing assurances of support from the American leadership and his fears that the decent interval would indeed come to pass. Even key members of his staff put their faith in American promises, and pressure mounted on him to fire me—so I made his decision easier by offering to resign late in October 1974.

The president did not want to appear as though he had caved on American demands to dismiss me, so he disguised the move as a change in cabinet, replacing three additional ministers at the same time. I felt terrible that Minister of Trade and Industry Nguyễn Đức Cường, Minister of Finance Châu Kim Nhân, and Minister of Agriculture Tôn Thất Trình had become collateral damage in my removal.

I watched helplessly and very painfully as South Vietnam spiraled downward, fast and furious. I felt no gratification assisting President Thiệu in writing his resignation speech, when he told me that I had been right not to trust the United States.

Like most South Vietnamese who love their country, I still nurse the pain and sorrow of my homeland's demise. And I still ponder what might have happened if our Churchillian plea to "give us the tools, and we will finish the job" had been answered.

Chapter Six

Public Security and the National Police

Trần Minh Công

Former colonel Trần Minh Công joined the South Vietnam Police Forces in 1963. He received military training at the Thủ Đức Infantry Officer School, served as police chief of Đà Nẵng City (1966–67) and police chief of the Second District, Saigon Metropolitan Area (1967–69). In 1969 he attended a Senior Officer Course at the International Police Academy in Washington, D.C. From 1969 to 1975 he served as commandant of the RVN's National Police Academy. After April 1975 he resettled in California and worked for the County of Orange as an urban planner for twenty-four years until his retirement in 2000. Công held a bachelor's degree in economics from the University of Western Australia (1962), took courses in postgraduate studies from Saigon University's Law School (1970–72), and earned a master's degree in public administration from California State University at Fullerton (1978). He now lives with his family in Huntington Beach, California.

The military historians of the Vietnam War commonly highlight the role of the U.S. military in big battles. Few pay attention to the Army of the Republic of Vietnam (ARVN), and even fewer do so for the National Police (Cảnh Sát Quốc Gia), which was responsible for the public security of the republic. Actually, the Vietnam War was not fought militarily but also politically and ideologically between a communist dictatorship and an aspiring democracy. In the midst of a savage war, South Vietnamese were also fighting for political stability, economic development, and democratic governance.

This chapter will consist of six parts. First, I will briefly outline the history of the National Police (NP) of the RVN. Next, I discuss police training to meet the two main objectives of protecting the people and providing domestic security. The third part focuses on outstanding security initiatives and programs in which the NP played an important role. Finally, I will recount the general security situation in South Vietnam and two particular events in 1966 and 1968 in which I was personally involved.

A Brief History of the National Police

The history and formation of the National Police can be divided into three main phases: the first phase of development under French rule until around 1950; the second phase after it was transferred from French to Vietnamese control until around 1960; and the third phase when the NP grew to meet the needs of South Vietnam during the war.

Modern public security as a government organization was first developed by the French who ruled Vietnam for nearly seventy years from 1884 to 1954. The organization was initially modeled after the French gendarmerie, whose main functions were to control the colony and collect taxes. By 1946 the French government had set up the Sûreté Nationale or National Security Service. This was the precursor of the Vietnamese police force. Under the Sûreté were public security offices in major towns and police offices in each locality.

These security and police offices operated independently. Security personnel dealt with political security, mainly tracking and capturing opponents of the French colonial administration. Police personnel kept order, prosecuted criminals, and arrested smugglers, especially of contraband alcohol, which was a monopoly of the French government at that time. In this period, both the security and police were led by French officers who had Vietnamese officers working under their command. By 1948, when negotiations for an independent government of Vietnam within the French Union took place, the two branches of security and police began to be transferred to Vietnamese control. This was the first phase in the development of the National Police.

Phase two started in 1950 when the Vietnamese government established a General Directorate of Security and Police to command and coordinate the individual police and police agencies in each province. After the Geneva Accords were signed in 1954, under the leadership of Prime Minister Ngô Đình Diệm in South Vietnam, the police force was gradually reformed and reorganized into a unified force composed of the police dealing with law and order and the public security dealing with security and intelligence. Through the U.S. Agency for International Development aid programs, the United States helped reorganize and build the National Police of the RVN. Advisors from Michigan State University were sent to help with administration, logistics, communication, and training. Several police training centers were built with U.S. aid. Thereafter, the Vietnamese police gradually moved away from the French model and became influenced by the American model of police organization, operation, and training.

In 1961, a new branch of the NP, the Central Commissariat for Intelligence (Phủ Đặc Ủy Trung Ương Tình Báo), was established and tasked with protecting domestic intelligence. By 1962, public security and police departments were merged under the collective name of the National Police. Since then, only one National Police Office existed in each province, covering security, public order, and the enforcement of national law.

In the early 1960s, North Vietnam began to send large military units to invade South Vietnam. In response to that situation and the increased need for security protection, the National Police created two new special branches in early 1965: the Antiriot Police (Cảnh Sát Dã Chiến, which can also be translated as Police Field Force) and the River Patrol Police (Giang Cảnh) to assist law enforcement personnel. At the same time the number of police officers gradually increased from twenty-two thousand to seventy-three thousand, thus requiring more commanding officers.

As war intensified, the General Directorate of Police was changed to the National Police Forces (modeled after the army), and the size of the force increased rapidly to thirteen thousand by the end of 1973. The organizational structure was also greatly specialized. The NP's central headquarters now housed the following departments: General Administration, Personnel Administration, Law Enforcement, Training, Logistics, Communications, and Special Police in charge of monitoring enemy activities inside the country, especially covert activities within the population in the areas under communist control. In addition, the Department of Military Operations (Khối Hành Quân) coordinated the operations of the various regional police organizations and the joint activities with the ARVN. The Department of Military Support administered the Antiriot Police, the River Patrol Police, and Provincial Reconnaissance Groups. Finally, the Pacification and Development Center (Trung Tâm Bình Định và Phát Triển) was in charge of the coordination between the military units in the Phoenix and Rural Development programs.

In terms of military command, the territory of South Vietnam was divided into four military regions and a capital region. For the convenience of coordination, the NP was also divided into four regions mirroring the four military regions, each of them comprising several provinces. The regional police commander was usually a colonel, and a provincial or city police chief usually held the rank of lieutenant colonel or major. In each province there were many districts, and each district had many hamlets (formerly called villages). By the end of 1975 South Vietnam had 44 provinces, 10 towns, 247 districts, and over 10,000 hamlets (10,944 in 1973). Unlike the military units that usually did not stay in permanent locations, the NP must always be present and provide security in all the hamlets under government control, including those in areas that were frequently harassed and threatened by the insurgents at night. The task of protecting the locality was therefore a very heavy responsibility of the NP, especially in the period between 1960 and 1975.

Besides maintaining national security and law enforcement, the NP had to deal with an insurgency orchestrated by Hanoi. It became more multifaceted and complex as a paramilitary force. Here lies the difference between the NP and other police forces around the world. The civilian and military mission required the NP to have a semiparamilitary structure, and the police training program added a military component in order to carry out the task according to the country's requirements and the needs of the time. Like police organizations in other countries, NP officers must patrol every day to keep order, to investigate and prevent crime, and to prosecute the offenders and criminals. The NP also must organize intelligence in the areas and villages to promptly uncover the enemy's illegal activities such as propaganda, assassinations, threats to the population, and the use of explosive devices. For that reason, the NP had a program of checking ID cards and the registry of each household every night to detect the presence of enemy infiltrators. These wartime activities required the NP to develop appropriate training programs for both security maintenance and law enforcement.

NP units sometimes had to fight as a military although that was not their main task. They were not trained to fight such combat either. In reality, they had to fight along the ARVN to protect the people throughout South Vietnam, especially in rural areas, whenever the need arose. In some provinces in central Vietnam, the Antiriot Police were involved in numerous military operations with the American military in its search and destroy campaigns.

It was because of these diverse activities that I think the NP had responsibilities unlike any professional police agencies in other peaceful countries. Many of our commanders were trained not only in police administration in the United States but also in counterinsurgency in Malaysia (Sir Robert Thompson's plan). Professional knowledge of organization and management were acquired in U.S. training schools and helped the NP's performance a great deal compared to other police agencies in Southeast Asia.

In the final years of the war, the focus of most government's civilian programs was on the rural areas. The NP was mobilized into rural areas to beef up security in support of the development programs (more on these below). In his commencement address to the graduating class of police officers in April 1972, President Nguyễn Văn Thiệu directed that all officer graduates be sent to serve in the countryside. He wanted to pacify the countryside, to promote democracy, and to protect farmers from the insidious propaganda and constant threats of the insurgency.

Police Training

In July 1965, the National Police Academy (Học Viện Cảnh Sát Quốc Gia) was established to recruit university students to serve in the police force. The academy was to train more than 1,500 officers a year and was considered one of the largest police academies in Southeast Asia. The training program at the academy lasted one year. After graduation, police officers would serve as investigators (*biên tập viên*) and inspectors (*thẩm sát viên*). Later, when the NP was militarized, these ranks were respectively changed to lieutenants and captains to be in line with military rankings, thus facilitating the coordination between the ARVN and the NP. After the 1968 Tết Offensive, the National Police grew rapidly to meet the needs of the government. From an agency dedicated to the maintenance of public order and law enforcement, the NP was now facing another war: the communist insurgency. The tasks of police became more complex and multifaceted. Police organizations as well as their training programs had to change as well, to meet the needs of the time.

Generally speaking, the training for noncommissioned officers and staff of the NP lasted from four to five months. There was a basic training center in each military region. Basic training focused on basic legal knowledge, security patrolling, and criminal investigations. After a period of service, these police officers may have been sent for additional training in specialized subjects such as judicial investigation, communications, supply, and intelligence. Since 1965, a one-year police training program was introduced, which consisted of military training for one third of the time, and specialized training for the remaining time.

The legal training program was considered the most important component of the program. About half the police officers' training program was in this area. Knowledge of civil and criminal laws was considered to be central to the duty of an NP law enforcement officer who was required to respect the law. The rule of law must always be upheld for the sake of fairness and the trust of the people. The police in a country at war like South Vietnam must be able to take measures to monitor the population to prevent communist infiltration while respecting the freedom of the people as stipulated and allowed by the law. Measures of social monitoring and control could easily lead to abuses of power and violations of the rule of law. The pursuit, arrest, interrogation, and prosecution of communist infiltrators were prone to abuses. Due to legal constraints such as the restriction of seventy-two hours maximum for detaining citizens for investigation (unless an exception was obtained from the prosecutor office), and the ban on threatening or torturing a suspect, police officers were somewhat hampered in the investigation and prosecution of those suspected of collaborating with the enemy.

Officers of the Antiriot Police also received specialized training in military operations to destroy communist infrastructure, to detect enemy infiltrations via waterways, and to prevent the smuggling or resupplying of enemy troops. These duties were part of the responsibility to control the resources and cut off supplies to the enemy in the sanctuary areas, and to detect the transport of mines, weapons, explosives, and other means of warfare to communist troops. The search, confiscation, and detention of suspects were always subject to the rule of law and thus were difficult for those on duty.

Another specialized training was in psychological warfare, that is, how to win the hearts and minds of the people, especially those in the rural areas. In an insurgency, winning the people over is essential. While the enemy used fraudulent propaganda and threat of force to coerce people, the government did not conduct such activities. Police officers' activities to inspect people and their vehicles in operation, to check family registries at night, and to prevent those protests led by communist agents— these activities could be easily misinterpreted by people and often condemned by Western media as violations of their human rights and freedom. The training was aimed at providing officers with knowledge and skills to act appropriately and within the law so as to minimize potentially negative impressions.

Pacification and Rural Development Program

The Civil Operations and Rural Development Support (CORDS) program, established in 1967, was a joint program between the U.S. and South Vietnamese governments. This program combined military and civilian activities on both sides to enlist public support, especially in the rural areas, for the government. U.S. deputy ambassador Robert Komer and General Creighton Abrams, commander of U.S. forces in Vietnam, were very supportive of this program. Komer believed that the success of this program depended on the maintenance of rural security to ensure that the communists could not enlist farmers to join their insurgency activities. Previously, the Ngô Đình Diệm government was quite effective in separating farmers from the insurgents with the establishment of strategic hamlets. Unfortunately, the strategic hamlet program was dissolved by the generals who overthrew President Diệm in 1963.

The National Police were involved in various aspects of CORDS. We teamed up with local defense militia (*nhân dân tự vệ*) and rural development forces (*xây dựng nông thôn*) to coordinate the elimination of communist cells in the countryside and to gain the support of farmers. Parallel to the launch of the Pacification program, the Open Arms (Chiêu Hồi) campaign was initiated, resulting in many communist troops deserting their ranks to join the RVN government. Through the Phoenix campaign, discussed below, we played a leading role in restoring security and destroying enemy infrastructure. The CORDS program was considered very successful. However, as conventional warfare intensified and the resources reserved for the program were no longer available, the program slowed down in the 1970s and was almost abandoned in 1973 when U.S. military and civilian personnel assigned to this program began to withdraw from South Vietnam.

A special component of the CORDS program was the Phoenix program, which was also successful although subject to misunderstanding and to significant domestic and international criticism. The Phoenix program was a joint intelligence program between several national security agencies, with the initial involvement of the American Central Intelligence Agency (CIA), to uncover and neutralize the enemy's regional infrastructure. Launched after the Tết Offensive, this joint military and civilian program offered incentives for people to provide information that helped to detect communist infiltrators. In 1968 alone, more than 13,000 communist cadres were detained, and 2,230 former enemy combatants were eventually persuaded to join the ranks of returnees under the Open Arms program. In less than four years, by the end of 1972, the total number of communist returnees had risen to 22,013 and no less than 70,000 of their troops had been deactivated. Overall, the program succeeded in disabling 81,740 people in the communist infrastructure with regard to intelligence, liaison, and supply.

In spite of its success, the Phoenix program suffered from much criticism. Hanoi and the National Liberation Front (NLF) misrepresented it as a campaign to destroy the political opposition by the South Vietnamese government. Some Western media portrayed the program as an "assassination campaign" of the RVN. And because the CIA was initially involved in this program, critics have charged it with training RVN units in various forms of terrorism such as assassination, torture, abduction, and intimidation of innocent people. Some Western media alleged that inhumane torture methods such as waterboarding or driving nails into a prisoner's ear were used by the program to extract intelligence.

Despite the criticisms that have been inevitably leveled, the program generally succeeded in effectively shutting down many communist structures, helping the ARVN maintain security in almost all its territories. As reported by the U.S. government, 91 percent of the hamlets (out of 10,944) were considered secure or relatively secure in late 1970; only 1.4 percent of total hamlets were controlled by the insurgency. After 1975, Hanoi admitted that the Phoenix program had weakened the base of the NLF, destroying 95 percent of its sleeper cells in some areas of South Vietnam. The Phoenix campaign clearly helped to secure South Vietnam. This suggests that the collapse of the RVN in 1975 was largely due to the lack of military resources on the battlefield when confronted with fully equipped North Vietnamese armed forces and not by a popular insurgency as claimed by communist propaganda.

General Security Situation from 1965 to 1975

In general, the security situation was relatively stable from 1954 to 1963, especially during 1954–60. Thanks to this stability, the South had the opportunity to organize the society and build the foundation for economic development facilitated by the large amount of financial aid from the United States. The reorganization of the young South Vietnamese police and, in particular, the increasing effectiveness of the special police force contributed to the security situation.

After the 1954 Geneva Accords, Hanoi ordered many of their cadres to stay behind in South Vietnam. Those communist cadres heading North in accordance with the terms of the Geneva Accords also left their families behind. Most of these families later formed the liaison and supply network for the insurgency. Subsequently, Hanoi sent back the rallied Southerners and other communist cadres to operate in the South. It also established the so-called National Liberation Front to cover its communist design for South Vietnam. By 1963, Hanoi had dispatched more armed units to the South, and the fighting had intensified. Many battles took place openly throughout the territory of South Vietnam. In mid-1965, when U.S. military units were brought into Vietnam to support the ARVN, the NLF's terrorist operations also increased, largely targeting American personnel and facilities.

In the years to come, the NP was tasked with preventing not only terrorist attacks against Americans, but also terrorist attacks and psychological intimidation against ordinary Vietnamese, especially those in remote rural areas. With over ten thousand hamlets in forty-four provinces, ensuring security protection against communist intrusion on a twenty-four-hour basis was very complex and difficult and required a relatively large number of troops. Thus, rural security was another headache for the NP.

In addition to the above-mentioned terrorist attacks, our enemy also tried to disrupt public order, such as instigating public demonstrations and protests. After the coup against President Ngô Đình Diệm in 1963, the military came to power and met with resistance from many opposition groups. Among these groups were several religious organizations, especially a Buddhist sect considered to be a key player in the coup. To all outward appearances these oppositions were just as legitimate as their demands for a new democratic constitution and democratic elections. The leaders of some factions were ambitious and difficult to satisfy.

The 1966 Upheaval in Central Vietnam

The 1966 upheaval was instigated by a Vietnamese Buddhist faction and led by Reverend Thích Trí Quang who had led protests against President Diệm in 1963 and whose picture appeared on the cover of a *Time* magazine issue at the time with the caption "the man who shook the United States." The excuses for the protest march of Thích Trí Quang and his followers in the two largest cities of central Vietnam, Huế and Đà Nẵng, were to protest Saigon's decision to replace General Nguyễn Chánh Thi, then commander of Military Region I (I Corps).

At that time, General Thi demanded that the new government under Prime Minister Nguyễn Cao Kỳ immediately elect a Constituent Assembly to draft a new constitution replacing the old one previously proclaimed by President Ngô Đình Diệm on October 10, 1956. The demand for a new Constituent Assembly and a new constitution was legitimate. Yet the ultimate goal of the protest, which sometimes became very violent, seemed to be to pressure the Kỳ government into sharing power with Thích Trí Quang's Buddhist faction.

The protest movements and demonstrations attracted idealistic students who became enthusiastic participants. During several months Huế and Đà Nẵng were almost paralyzed by the protests and strikes. After months of turmoil, security and order in the two cities were restored, but the police still had to face continuous protests from some Buddhist monks and temples for six months thereafter. During this event, the detention and prosecution of those who disrupted law and order rested on the very blurry line between the violation of national law and the right to free political action. Out of respect for the rule of law, the police in many cases did not prosecute these protestors and troublemakers. And so the rioters had free rein, causing difficulty to the police for many years to come. This was a difficult situation that perhaps few police departments in other countries had encountered.

The Tết Offensive of 1968

Another prominent event that shocked and left an indelible mark on both American and Vietnamese psyches was the 1968 Tết Offensive. It was both a military and political battle: military because North Vietnam wanted to incite South Vietnamese to revolt against their government; political because Hanoi wanted to prove to the world and especially to the American people that they really controlled the situation in the battlefields and even in the big cities of South Vietnam, including the capital Saigon.

I discuss this battle because it directly related to the NP at that time. A cease-fire truce during the three days of the Lunar New Year between the two sides was signed so that the Vietnamese people and soldiers could enjoy three days of peace during Tết. In spite of what they had signed, communist forces suddenly and simultaneously attacked most South Vietnamese cities. They selected the most prominent targets that were prone to create confusion and panic. In Saigon, they attacked the presidential palace, the American embassy, the national radio station, the Joint General Staff headquarters, and several other important sites. They specifically targeted densely populated areas and poor working neighborhoods with the belief that they might be able to incite civilians in these places to revolt against their government. The number of soldiers remaining at their post during the truce period was very small; so when the enemy suddenly attacked, the South Vietnamese side was somewhat in disarray though the troops guarding the capital put up a valiant fight.

Only NP units had to be on full alert, and thus a 100 percent readiness was maintained. It was meticulous planning and vigilance against any uncertainty that enabled the NP to react promptly and become the first line of defense against communist attacks at many sites in the capital city. The situation in the first few hours when communist sappers attacked the Independence Palace was dire as they overwhelmed the defenders, ran over an auxiliary defense post on Nguyễn Du Street, and brought a car containing explosives into the Independence Palace compound. Only when the police promptly responded were the intruders pushed out of the Independence Palace perimeter. They were destroyed one day later. A sapper team also tried to seize the national radio building, hoping to broadcast calls for a general uprising. Here they were pushed back by the NP's Antiriot Police.

The Tết Offensive was a surprise attack against South Vietnamese people and soldiers. With that element of surprise, the communists should have achieved a lot. Yet they failed, not able to hold onto any key position for long or to incite a popular uprising as they had hoped. In this battle, despite their military and political defeat, Hanoi achieved the propaganda victory in the world and especially in the United States thanks to the international news agencies with their ambiguous and negative reports as this battle was taking place.

It is instructive to recall a tragic incident in the 1968 Tết Offensive. It was a fact that General Nguyễn Ngọc Loan, the commander of the National Police at the time, executed a captured communist commando on the battlefield. Eddie Adams of NBC television captured the execution of this commando in a photo that was widely broadcast and shocked the American public. The South Vietnamese government was condemned for not respecting the UN prisoner-of-war convention. Eddie Adams was awarded a Pulitzer Prize in Media, and antiwar activists would never miss an occasion to showcase it as a cruel and repugnant reminder of the war in Vietnam. It is unfortunate that they forget to mention the more abominable acts perpetrated by the communists, like the massacre of nearly three thousand residents of Huế during the Tết Offensive or the case of a communist shelling of a primary school in Cai Lậy District, Định Tường Province, killing dozens of innocent school children. We should mention as well how the communists killed thousands of local government officials during the war.

When General Loan died in July 1998, Eddie Adams came to Washington D.C. for the funeral with a wreath that read "Tears are in my eyes" (for you). He sat next to me and was very upset about the picture that he took of General Loan in the Tết Offensive. He said he regretted very much that the picture told only half the truth. Half the truth is that General Loan shot the communist commando; the other half that the picture and its author did not tell was that just a few minutes before, the same commando killed in cold blood the entire family of a police officer nearby. He was arrested when he fled the scene and was handed over to General Loan on the battlefield. Eddie Adams said he regretted destroying the political career of an intrepid hero with a half-truth picture.

Missed Opportunity

The Vietnam War was not just a confrontation of the forces between North and South Vietnam but also a confrontation between communism and liberalism. The Communist Bloc wanted to expand into Southeast Asia and was opposed by the liberal world that America represented. South Vietnam eventually became an outpost to stem that red wave. Both North and South Vietnam respectively leaned on the assistance and arms supply by Russia and China on the one hand, and by the United States on the other. South Vietnam lost in 1975 when the U.S. government drastically reduced aid to us from $1 billion a year to about $300 million in 1975. The soldier, however good and valiant he was, could not win when he did not have enough arms and supplies.

There were certainly various other causes that led to the collapse of South Vietnam in April 1975. In addition to the military imbalance between North and South Vietnam that we all know, the scale had tipped in favor of the North when the United States withdrew its troops from and almost stopped the flow of aid to the RVN after 1973. In this last stage, the lives of people and society in South Vietnam were relatively stabilized thanks to the policies of economic development, education, and especially various rural pacification programs such as the Phoenix program in which the NP had actively participated.

In human terms we had won over North Vietnam, but we lost to them on the battlefield due to the shortage of weapons and ammunition. We also lost in the propaganda battle waged with antiwar campaigns in world opinion and relying on media biases in the United States. In 1975 we lost not in the battlefield but in America. With aid being cut off, the collapse of South Vietnam was a foregone conclusion.

During wartime the RVN had built a relatively secure and developed society both economically and democratically, albeit an economy that was only taking off and a relatively embryonic democracy compared with many Western nations of the time. Despite the war to defend South Vietnam, our government stayed on the path of building a democratic society that had grown through many programs supported by the United States such as land reform, health, education, and economic development. Since 1967 the president and National Assembly in the RVN had been directly elected by the people. In the final years of the war village councils in the countryside were also directly elected by villagers. Democratic institutions had been established and were being strengthened.

America had missed an opportunity to help build a good democratic model in South Vietnam.

Chapter Seven

Reflections of a Frontline Soldier

Bùi Quyền

Former lieutenant colonel Bùi Quyền was born in 1937 in Phủ Lý, Hà Nam. He was a student in the Mathematics Department at Saigon University College of Sciences prior to joining the armed forces of the RVN. After graduating first in his class from the Đà Lạt National Military Academy in 1959, Quyền served in the airborne infantry from 1962 until April 30, 1975, when he was a lieutenant colonel and deputy commander of the Third Airborne Brigade of the airborne division. During his military career, Quyền earned numerous medals for his valor in combat, including (from the RVN) National Merit Medal 4th-Class, National Merit Medal 5th-Class with palm, twelve Valor Crosses with palm, eight Valor Crosses with gold star, five Valor Crosses with silver star, one Valor Cross with bronze star, and (from the United States) one Silver Star, two Bronze Stars, both with "V" for valor, and one Army Commendation Medal with "V" for valor. After April 1975, Quyền spent thirteen years in reeducation camps. After coming to the United States thanks to direct intervention by President George H. W. Bush, Quyền worked as a correctional officer at the Santa Clara Department of Correction Programs Division from 1991 to 2009 and retired in San Jose.

I arrived in Saigon with my family around July 1954 at seventeen years old. I was completely perplexed by the sprawling houses, the unending streets, and the simple, gentle folks there. Life seemed relatively easy. There were plenty of amenities that were lacking in Hanoi at that time. One thing that stuck in my mind to this day was the weird practice of tearing the banknote in half to give customers as change, due to lack of smaller denominations. I think that of all places on earth this could only have happened in South Vietnam in those days. This unique feature testified to the easygoing, tolerant, and trusting nature of the South Vietnamese people.

At that time, the adults around me all said that Prime Minister Ngô Đình Diệm's government faced serious difficulties and would not last long. The South's many religious sects, once supported by the French, all ganged up against his government, intending to overthrow him. And the government was also busy transferring nearly a million Northerners to the South for resettlement. But following patient and persuasive negotiations, some of the sects rallied to the government side. Meanwhile, Mr. Diệm successfully reorganized the national armed forces despite resistance from Emperor Bảo Đại. One major challenged remained: the Bình Xuyên armed gang. In April 1955, Bình Xuyên forces attacked governmental facilities in Saigon.[1] The new army was ordered to put down the rebellion, and after two months of intense urban fighting, it prevailed—a major victory for the nascent Ngô Đình Diệm government. Subsequent military campaigns pacified regions controlled by other religious factions and challenged the communists' rural authority. Then, on October 23, 1955, Prime Minister Diệm staged a referendum to depose Emperor Bảo Đại, which he won with nearly 100 percent of the vote. Three days later, he declared South Vietnam a republic under a provisional constitution and assumed the office of the presidency.[2]

BUILDING THE ARMED FORCES OF THE REPUBLIC OF VIETNAM (ARVN)

In addition to political, economic, social, and educational reforms, President Diệm's nation-building project focused on transforming and developing the armed forces. First, to remove French influence, Vietnamese officers took full control of the Joint General Staff, and the Vietnamese language was mandated for all official correspondence.[3] Military strength increased from 150,000 troops, as stipulated by the Geneva Accords, to 220,000 by 1963, comprising army, navy, and air force. Additionally, the new Ministry of Defense drafted high school graduates with baccalaureate diplomas for reserve officer training in order to command the newly formed army units. A great number of officers were sent to the United States for further training. By 1963, the army included nine infantry divisions, one airborne brigade, one marine brigade, one airborne-ranger group, six ranger battalions, and a number of separate ranger companies.

Apart from these regular forces, the Ngô Đình Diệm government also created local territorial forces like the Regional Forces (RF) and Popular Forces (PF) under the control of the Ministry of Defense. Combat support troops like the armored cavalry, artillery, and other technical units like engineers, medical, transportation, signal corps, and logistics branches were also created.

In July 1955, Vietnamese naval personnel totaled 2,567, including 190 officers and 2,377 petty officers and seamen.[4] When the French withdrew from Vietnam on April 25, 1956, they left a total of twenty-one oceangoing ships and riverine boats. The navy's Lieutenant Commander Lê Quang Mỹ immediately reorganized the naval forces to be compatible with their new responsibility: the control and defense of the coastal regions, maritime islands, and inland waterways. To that end, the 1958 Naval Forces Plan added five thousand sailors, ninety-six river boats, and twenty-one oceangoing ships. Likewise, the new Nha Trang Naval Academy trained new officers with an entirely Vietnamese staff of professors and instructors, as did the Riverine Force headquartered in Cần Thơ. Personnel often came from experienced local fishermen. At the end of 1962, the Vietnamese Navy consisted of four deep-water flotillas and some thirty-six thousand sailors.

Finally, there was the air force. On July 1, 1955, France transferred the Nha Trang Air Force Training Center to the Vietnamese authorities. At the time, the total personnel of this service branch amounted to 1,345 men with four squadrons of fifty-eight aging planes. Air force officers were mostly army graduates from the Nam Định and Thủ Đức Reserve Officer Training Schools, transferred to the air force. As a result of President Diệm's reforms, the Vietnamese Air Force changed its command structure from the French to the American model and increased in size to eighteen squadrons, including six fighter squadrons, four observation squadrons, four helicopter squadrons, two transport squadrons, one training squadron, and one special mission squadron, with a total of 393 aircraft.[5]

These bold initiatives were critical in enabling President Diệm to consolidate his authority over a decentralized and divided society, and in allowing the new republic to withstand the many challenges confronting it from its very birth.

The ARVN during the Second Republic

With the fall of President Diệm in 1963, the Armed Forces of the Republic of Vietnam once again found itself facing a number of overlapping challenges. By 1965, with communist forces making rapid gains in the country, the ARVN once again embarked on a program of modernization. The first phase was spread out over a period of four years, from 1965 to 1969. The army added two infantry divisions (the Eighteenth in 1965 and the Third in 1971) and upgraded its general reserve forces, including the airborne division and the marine division.[6]

Ranger units, Regional and Popular Forces, and supporting and logistical units were also substantially expanded and better equipped. From the 1967 force level of 888 companies, the Regional Forces were expanded to 1,810 companies by the end of 1972. There were, in fact, RF battalions or even RF groups as well as mobile battalions and mobile groups in many provincial sectors.[7] Supporting and logistical units of the armed forces were also upgraded, both in quantity and in quality. M-41 tanks replaced M-24 tanks around February 1965. By July 1966, each infantry division had an armored cavalry squadron as its organic maneuver unit. At the end of 1967 the armor branch used the term "armored cavalry squadron" in lieu of armored regiment.[8]

Likewise, by July 1965 the Maritime Boat Force was regrouped into Littoral Flotilla and put under the command of various maritime tactical zones with a total 644 assault boats. The Maritime Assault Force was renamed Riverine Assault Force. Each of them had 150 men and 12 APC/M-113 (armored personnel carriers) and was used to support large operations.[9] These new riverine assault forces allowed the navy to expand operations in the Mekong Delta and beyond.

During the modernization phase, the air force acquired new Skyraider planes A-1H and A-1G and a few B-57s to cope with the burden of surveilling and targeting the Hồ Chí Minh trail. In 1967, the United States transferred to the South Vietnamese Air Force seventeen F-5A and two F-5B jet fighters to create the 522nd Jet Fighter Squadron, together with twenty-five A-37A jets to replace the A-1 Skyraiders, and a number of AC-119 and AC-47 armed cargo planes for the formation of an Attack Transportation Wing. Between 1969 and 1972 alone, the air force grew by some one thousand planes and thirty-six thousand pilots and auxiliary personnel. The helicopter branch was equipped with UH-1 and CH-47, while the transport branch was equipped with C-123 and C-130 cargo planes, and the observation branch was equipped with O-1 and O-2 observation planes.[10]

Pressure to expand and improve ARVN capacity was intensified by the concurrent withdrawal of American forces beginning in 1969. By 1972, with U.S. combat troops largely redeployed and only a relative handful of support personnel remaining, the ARVN ground forces had swelled to include eleven infantry divisions, two general reserve divisions (the airborne and marine divisions), and sixteen ranger groups, including the Border Defense Special Forces and the elite Eighty-First Airborne Ranger Group.[11]

The ARVN armor branch, meanwhile, comprised eighteen armored cavalry (tank) squadrons and three M-48 tank squadrons, while the artillery branch fielded five battalions of 175mm self-propelled guns and four air defense artillery battalions. The navy included some 84 oceangoing and 950 riverine ships staffed by 43,000 sailors, and the air force boasted 61,147 troops commanding 2,071 aircraft of all types.[12]

From modest beginnings supporting France in the First Indochina War, the ARVN had grown rapidly to become one of the world's largest and best-equipped militaries, playing a critical role in prolonging the republic's survival in the war against communist forces.

Reflections and Analysis as a Frontline ARVN Officer

Created to defend a new state facing formidable internal and external challenges, the ARVN was tasked with protecting the country and deterring its enemies. After almost a century of domination by France, our new leader Ngô Đình Diệm faced the daunting task of stabilizing complex political, economic, and social situations while also reorganizing and modernizing the armed forces.

The ARVN began with its commanding officers trained according to French tactics and systems. Its general strategy had been the purview of the French general commander-in-chief. Later on, with the advent of American assistance, commanding officers were instead trained in modern tactics and strategies at various military institutions in the United States. In my experience, there was not much difference between the French and the American military doctrines. In addition to Western models, our officers also analyzed Chinese warfare precepts and the Communist Bloc's military doctrine.

This task required much time and effort during a period of intense battlefield and ideological conflict, when both warring sides within the same country acted as the military proxies of the Cold War's two superpowers. At first, to the outside world, this complex type of war appeared like an internal conflict, an armed rebellion against the Saigon regime by native antigovernment elements. But this phase was quickly followed by the infiltration of armed forces from the North. In a very short time, the conflict became an all-out conventional war of aggression by the Northern communists.

In my view, the Second Indochina War was thus fully initiated by North Vietnam according to the People's Warfare strategic concept of Mao Zedong. This strategy involves the following stages: First, a guerrilla warfare phase, followed by a mobile maneuver warfare phase after recruiting a more substantial number of combatants. Next comes the fortified installations assault warfare phase, a form of escalating battleground warfare, concluding with a general offensive employing large-scale conventional warfare. Their entire offensive strategy was designed to achieve total control of South Vietnam.

When two countries are in conflict and cannot resolve their differences peacefully, armed confrontation is the likely outcome. Strategy is always the decisive factor. An inappropriate use of the armed forces during war always leads to defeat. Communist commanders' goals were ranked as follows: first and foremost was "winning the enemy's heart and mind" or psychological warfare; second, dismantling the enemy's logistical supplies; and third, destroying the enemy's forces. Drawing on theorists such as Sun Tzu, the enemy prioritized psychological warfare in order to achieve its objectives while minimizing casualties. For the RVN, on the other hand, the major difficulty was to battle an enemy that belonged to the same nation and shared the same culture and language but was subjugated by the communist ideology.

After eighty years of colonial rule, French forces returned to Vietnam in 1945, having earlier been swept from power by imperial Japan. They tried to reimpose their colonial regime, but the Vietnamese people were motivated to resist by memories of French colonialists destroying villages, murdering peasants, and raping women. In the eyes of simple-minded rural people, Hồ Chí Minh was a savior. He had cleverly captured the mantle of Vietnamese nationalism during the struggles against France, while the South Vietnamese leader Ngô Đình Diệm and his successors were tainted with a civil service and army structure inherited from French colonialism. As a result, the South Vietnamese government was considered by many as a puppet government of foreigners. To dissuade everyday citizens from accepting this distorted notion, Southern authorities had to wage a very time-consuming psy-war in order to win the hearts and minds of their own people, especially those living in the countryside.

A difficult task for our government's information and propaganda specialists was to explain clearly to the people that the communist ideology was a foreign import incompatible with our enduring heritage and traditional way of life. We believed that North Vietnam was just an extended arm of the Communist Bloc under the control of the Soviet Union and Red China. To succeed, our government needed to inculcate in the people's mind that fighting the communist insurgency was not just the job of the armed forces. Among the urban population in the South, we achieved some degree of success. After the 1968 communist Tết Offensive when forty-four provinces were attacked and innocent civilians massacred in Huế, many townspeople changed their attitude toward the communists, as demonstrated by the increased number of recruits volunteering to fight after Tết. So long as the people and the armed forces were united in their will to fight, victory was possible.

Due to our deficiencies on the propaganda front, the communists were able to infiltrate various segments of our society, causing severe political and social disruptions that adversely affected the performance of our armed forces. Overseas, our psychological warfare activities should have been carried out more much effectively by the Ministry of Information and our embassies, in order to raise awareness in the American Congress and among the left-leaning international community about communist atrocities, including the indiscriminate killing of schoolchildren by rocket attacks or the wanton massacre of thousands of innocent people in Huế during the Tết Offensive of 1968. Our inability to match the communists' skills in psychological warfare, both at home and abroad, proved incredibly costly indeed.

Next, turning to logistics, it is common knowledge that apart from a will to fight, any military unit must be adequately supplied with logistical support and weaponry. I agreed with U.S. Army General Bruce Palmer Jr., commander of the Second Field Force in Vietnam, when he said that if "cut off from substantial out-of-country support, the Viet Cong is bound to wither on the vine and gradually become easier for the South Vietnamese to defeat."[13] But communist supply bases were located in secret sanctuaries deep in Cambodia and Laos, or in hidden bases in South Vietnam, where all kinds of logistical supplies were stockpiled. These supplies were either trucked down the Hồ Chí Minh trail in Laos, or shipped to the port of Sihanoukville in Cambodia. And they were critical in enabling the North Vietnamese communists to carry out attacks ordered in Hanoi against Southern districts, province capitals, and cities.

In more than a decade of fighting, the American and South Vietnamese armed forces never succeeded in choking off the flow of North Vietnamese logistical support for their insurgency. Instead, we managed only to reduce it. American forces settled merely for bombing the scattered supply depots lying along the Hồ Chí Minh trail, while the ARVN attempted only one ground assault against enemy positions in Laos, with Operation Lam Sơn 719 in February 1971.

The communists also adopted Mao's strategy of "using the countryside to encircle the city" during the guerrilla warfare stage. They sought to destroy the government's rural presence, thereby isolating the cities. And they knew that without popular support, the Saigon government would eventually fall. Initially, the central government effectively controlled 20 percent of the population, concentrated primarily in cities; yet the remaining 80 percent of the people lived off the land in the countryside. To carry out this strategy, communist forces assassinated, kidnapped, or threatened local officials, political cadres, teachers, and their families, in order to exert their authority even if only after nightfall. This created what were known as insecure areas (usually far away from cities), where the government held authority only in the daytime, while the communists terrorized at night. In these areas, insurgents were able to collect food and medicine and to forcibly recruit teenagers as young as fourteen or fifteen.

Under the First Republic, our government attempted to contest this strategy with the Strategic Hamlet program, which it modeled after successful counterinsurgency methods employed in Malaysia. But there were a number of reasons why the Malaysia model proved unsuitable for Vietnam. First, Malaysian villages were much more tightly concentrated, whereas in South Vietnam, villages were strung out along canals and other natural waterways. Our villagers had a strong traditional attachment to the lands where they were born and their ancestors were buried. Uprooting people from their ancestral homes and moving them into these strategic hamlets caused understandable resentment and inevitable resistance. Furthermore, in Malaysia there were easily recognizable ethnic differences between the Chinese communist insurgents and the local Malay population, whereas in Vietnam, there was no such distinction. A costly failure, this policy was abandoned after the fall of the First Republic.

Nonetheless, we were able to make progress during the Second Republic, which began in 1967. At times, the government was generally able to control the people living in cities, and in rural areas that bordered district towns and provincial cities. Looking back, the reorganization and development of the South Vietnamese armed forces by the Ministry of Defense was critical to protecting rural areas, the most vital segment of a predominantly agricultural country. This importance was reflected by new president Nguyễn Văn Thiệu prioritizing vigorous implementation of the Rural Development program starting from 1968 (see chapters 4 and 6 in this volume). The Rural Development program was mostly the responsibility of the local territorial forces, in close cooperation with the National Police, and funded by the United States. Its main objectives were to eliminate the communist insurgency infrastructure that operated surreptitiously in the villages, to protect the rural population from communist subversive activities, and to assist farmers in agricultural production with modern technology. The result was a measured success; according to American Civil Operations and Rural Development Support statistics, the rural population living under government control had increased from 47 percent in 1967 to 80 percent by 1972. Concurrently, the communist insurgency infrastructure decreased in number from eighty-five thousand in August 1967 to fifty-six thousand in February 1972.[14]

The success of the Rural Development program hinged on the local forces tasked with maintaining rural security: the RF and the PF. From some 300,000 troops at the beginning of 1967, their ranks swelled to 520,000 by the end of 1972.[15] These units were placed under the direct command of the provincial authorities and were organized and deployed as each province chief sector commander saw fit. Each sector usually had a few mobile and garrisoned RF battalions, only some of which had barracks. Those who did not have rear bases would instead camp out along provincial routes to rest while also providing security for rural transportation. The garrisoned units, meanwhile, were usually responsible for the security of designated localities, such as outposts, bridges, or highways. Because of their fixed nature, rural outposts were subject to the insurgents' constant monitoring and constituted the main target for the communists to attack when a propitious time came.

PF platoons, on the other hand, were in charge of protecting rural hamlets, as well as defending smaller outposts and watch towers. Unlike the RF, PF troops held regular jobs in the community and performed security duties, conducted night patrols, laid ambushes, and searched houses for arms caches. These tasks required great courage, and sadly, it was the RF and PF that suffered the greatest hardships and heaviest casualties during the early phases of the war due to inadequate equipment and weaponry compared to ARVN regulars. Their losses are estimated at 25 percent of the total losses incurred by the ARVN. It was as though the Saigon government almost did not pay attention to these essential units, which proved to be a serious mistake.

In my view, RF and PF units had many important attributes. Because they lived among the local populace, these units obtained valuable intelligence from their fellow villagers. They knew well the enemy's habitual movements and were especially familiar with the local terrain. As a result, their counterinsurgency potential was far greater than what could be achieved by other regular armed forces. After all, they were fighting to protect friends and relatives living in the areas they defended. There were many stories of wives helping crew-served weapons-operating husbands in these units. During a firefight the wife helped her husband with ammunition feeding and replaced him to operate the gun when he was wounded or killed. The people who lived peacefully in these hamlets were naturally loyal to the government who were protecting them. Besides the logistical warfare, securing the countryside also meant winning the psy-war.

Still, like the ARVN regulars, RF and PF forces faced a number of challenges and obstacles. As the first line of defense in the countryside, they were certain to be overrun by larger enemy forces, especially as they did not receive the same air and artillery support that regular forces enjoyed. Yet the countryside was the enemy's primary target for guerrilla warfare since it was the main source of his supplies and recruitment. On top of that, stationing troops at fixed locations predisposed them to easy scrutiny and infiltration. This helps explain why RF/PF forces were constantly targeted and suffered disproportional losses.

During both the First and Second Republics, I believe that the majority of the time, the ARVN performed admirably when it came to attacking the communist forces that controlled rural villages and hamlets. But the most important aspect of fighting insurgents in rural areas was winning the hearts and minds of the people living there. Unfortunately, the damage caused to houses and properties during these firefights was not always satisfactorily compensated by our government. After our forces clashed, the communists often withdrew, leaving behind utter devastation of which rural citizens bore the brunt. This tended to engender resentment for both sides of the conflict. Of course, this was on top of the noxious communist propaganda that fueled rural antigovernment sentiment. Even after encounters in remote unpopulated areas, government forces often simply disengaged, leaving the territory open for future communist reinfiltration. Our regular armed forces were never big enough to occupy the entire vast territory of South Vietnam.

I often recall the military doctrine that "a fighting force is valuable when it is well trained, not when it is numerous." In order to improve, armies must be forged through the crucible of battlefield experience, which requires time and opportunity. Armed forces are rarely effective in countries that live in peace for decades. Even when well equipped and numerically sufficient, an effective military also requires capable command. Before 1975, ARVN operations at the division or corps level were rare apart from cross-border incursions in 1970 and 1971, as well as during the summer 1972 offensive. In the spring of 1975, when we faced full conventional warfare, the disarray and incompetence displayed by our high command, compounded by shortages of fuel and ammunition, led to the ARVN's disastrous final debacle.

Finally, let us not forget that modern armed forces require an appropriate defense budget. During the Second Republic, the payroll of the military and public sector alone amounted to 47 percent of the national budget (see chapter 3 in this volume on financial and budgetary issues).[16] Without the assistance of the United States, we were not in a position to meet these obligations. Any country that relied so heavily on foreign aid was bound to encounter severe budgetary problems should such aid be reduced, and unless peace can be restored, defeat is a matter of course.

Reflections on American Military Performance and Command

Beginning with the first two U.S. Marine battalions in March 1965, the allied military gradually grew to a peak strength of 543,400 fighting troops by the end of April 1969, including the First, the Fourth, the Ninth, and the Twenty-Fifth Infantry Divisions, the 101st and a brigade of the Eighty-Second Airborne Divisions, the 173rd Airborne Brigade, and the First Air Cavalry. The forces from the Southeast Asian Treaty Organization countries included South Korea's Tiger, White Horse, and Blue Dragon Infantry Divisions numbering roughly fifty thousand; the Royal Thai's Black Leopard and King Cobra Divisions numbering some thirty-eight thousand fighters; and the Royal Australian Regiment and New Zealand forces numbering about eight thousand soldiers.

The Americans began to wage the Vietnam War according to their military doctrine. Their strategy at the outset was containment aimed at preventing the spread of international communism because the prevalent thinking at the time was that according to the domino theory, if Vietnam fell, the rest of Southeast Asia would follow. Because this was just a preventative posture, a defensive strategy with limited offensive tactics was appropriate. I believe the United States was afraid that a military response by the People's Republic of China (PRC) could lead to a conflict similar to the Korean War, if not World War III. Furthermore, the United States always weighed in the war cost that it would be willing to pay for such conflict versus the benefit it could gather from such a venture to decide on the time frame of involvement regardless of public opinion on such action.

The top American military commander in Vietnam, General William C. Westmoreland, viewed the Vietnam War as a war of insurgency. The strategy he chose, therefore, was a "counterinsurgency war" model. Once the rebellion was crushed, Westmoreland felt that the government of South Vietnam would be able to devote itself to building a constitutional democracy and, from there, economic development that would lead to a desirable society and a prosperous nation. To achieve this objective, Westmoreland aimed to deplete the enemy's forces by capitalizing on the military superiority that the Americans enjoyed. He used search and destroy tactics to annihilate the insurgents. Unfortunately, the American armed forces did not accomplish this objective. The body count statistics showed that although enemy losses were significant, they were always willing and able to suffer a high casualty rate. Moreover, the bulk of the enemy's forces were able to escape to their secret hideouts, only to reappear later and reoccupy the areas they fled from.

Westmoreland did not succeed because he failed to recognize that the guerrilla war fomented in Vietnam by the communists was just the first phase of Mao Zedong's People's War. The bulk of the communist fighters were North Vietnam regular soldiers who infiltrated into the South, and if this southward flow could not be curtailed, the attrition war could never succeed. Despite losses of over three hundred thousand men, including the seriously wounded personnel between 1965 and 1967, the total number of communist forces in the South kept increasing.

The geographical features of the South also precluded any prolonged search and destroy tactics. Enemy forces had to be quickly destroyed once located. But to completely neutralize the enemy required not only overwhelming them, but also blocking their escape routes. Given the mobility that America's airlift capability provided, this could have been accomplished had President Lyndon Johnson provided Westmoreland with sufficient ground troops. Unfortunately, for most of the conflict, Westmoreland's requests for additional troop deployments were met with inconsequential reinforcements by the White House. As a result, his hands were tied while waging a no-win war.

I do not know whether Westmoreland knew how much President Johnson was relying on Secretary of Defense Robert McNamara's advice. McNamara and his assistants conducted the war in Vietnam in an inept manner, as they relied on computer-generated data or statistical analyses that might be applicable to business activities, but not to military matters. Consequently the adoption of the limited warfare concept, in which gradual or flexible response tactics were employed, was in total contravention to long-established military doctrine.

After the 1968 Tết Offensive, General Creighton Abrams succeeded General Westmoreland as commander-in-chief in Vietnam. Having served as deputy commander, Abrams understood the shortcomings of search and destroy tactics, and he supplemented these with his own clear and hold approach. After Tết, communist forces were devastated and their underground infrastructure was discovered and seriously weakened. As a result, the communist insurgency was nearly paralyzed. With its Pacification and Rural Development and Land to the Tiller programs in full swing (see chapters 4 and 6 in this volume), the Saigon government was gradually winning back the allegiance of the rural population. Additionally, ARVN forces were now reequipped with more modern weaponry, comparable to what North Vietnamese forces enjoyed. This allowed our government to reassert its self-confidence and to go on the offensive with cross-border search and destroy operations against communist sanctuaries in Laos and Cambodia.

At the rank and file level, American forces had the following advantages. First, there were adequate men and material to rapidly replace battlefield losses. Second, the American systems of storage and logistics were modern and efficient—one could even say that their weapons and supplies were too abundant. American fighting troops were excessively supported from every aspect during engagement. Air and artillery support could be obtained at any time on demand. Wounded troops would receive rapid medical evacuation. Apart from field hospitals at major cities, which were well equipped and well staffed by competent doctors, there were also military hospitals on aircraft carriers stationed in the South China Sea. Severe cases would be airlifted to other U.S. territories.

But American forces also suffered from the following disadvantages: Their soldiers were not adequately taught about the customs, culture, and history of the natives. They were not well schooled in dealing with the local population, like the old folks and women they encountered. They were also poorly trained in responding to communist guerrilla warfare tactics, in particular booby traps. We could see the manifestation of these deficiencies during the first three months after their arrival in Vietnam; without having been conditioned to our tropical climate, and without any battlefield experience, American troops suffered substantial casualties. Six months later, having since undergone intense combat, American forces became overly cautious whenever there was an engagement with the enemy, seeking only to survive until the end of their tours of duty. Another common fault that I found with the American units was overconfidence, if not arrogance, in their belief in their own fighting ability. With modern, state-of-the-art weapons and equipment, they had a tendency to underestimate their adversaries, considering them as unworthy and even childish opponents. This led the Americans to become derisive or dismissive toward their tenacious enemies and to abandon tried-and-true military precepts.

I offer the following example: One time, my unit was coordinating with an American force for an operation just outside Saigon. The delineation between our respective outfits was a small stream. At the end of the day, as our two battalions were preparing to rest for the evening, I heard the crack of gunfire near the stream where some of my paratroopers were bathing. Recognizing at once the familiar sound, I immediately knew that it was friendly fire. And so, I asked my American adviser to call the American unit across the stream to find out what was going on. His response made me laugh: "Our friends over there thought your guys were Việt Cộng because they didn't wear helmets when while bathing in the stream!" Luckily, nobody was hurt by their fire.

Later, as the sun went down, I once again heard gunfire from the Americans across the stream, which made me think that the enemy was attacking. Strangely enough, I could not hear any communist weapons returning fire. After further inquiry, I found out that before camping for the night, American troops were trained to gather at the defensive frontline and adjust their gun sights by firing volleys into the dusk. This practice may have helped them become familiar with the terrain, but in terms of security and maintaining the element of surprise, it was dead wrong. They were practically telling the enemy, "Hello, VC! Gentlemen, we are over here! Come and hit us!" Once the enemy knew our precise position, at least one of three things was sure to follow: if we outnumbered them, they would pound us with mortar fire while avoiding direct engagement; if they were stronger than we were, they would attack; or, they might opt to ambush us later, at a time and place of their choosing.

Throughout the war years, there were abundant stories of American advisors who misinterpreted their role and overstepped their authority by trying to command rather than assist us, which led to untold friction. One American advisor incurred the wrath of Colonel Phan Trọng Chinh, commander of the ARVN Twenty-Fifth Infantry Division, by doing something that Col. Chinh found insulting to his unit—he used his finger to smear the grease from an ARVN soldier's dirty rifle on the poor man's face during a weapons inspection.

Another example is the story of John Paul Vann, who was the chief advisor to the ARVN Seventh Infantry Division in 1963. Vann then briefly retired and went home to write a book in which he claimed to know how to manage the war in order to win in Vietnam. The book was met with approval in Washington, and Vann was appointed chief advisor to Lieutenant General Ngô Dzu, the commander of the II Corps tactical zone in the Central Highlands. Vann was tasked with coordinating between American civil affairs staff and the ARVN military commanders in the region. Even though he was just a civilian at that time, he brashly attempted to command the South Vietnamese forces in II Corps, as though he, not Ngô Dzu, was their commanding general. Needless to say, his abrasive, heavy-handed, and impetuous style of leadership quickly alienated many ARVN commanders.

In my view, the lower-ranking American advisors were somewhat better. Most came to South Vietnam with a condescending attitude toward their Vietnamese counterparts. However, after time together on the battlefields, and from daily comradeship, they realized that there was much they could learn from their Vietnamese counterparts. These Vietnamese military leaders were forged in the crucible of armed conflict and hardened through long years of leading men into battle, while American advisors were mainly tasked with the all-important job of securing air support for friendly forces, for air strikes of hard enemy targets, and for evacuating wounded combatants, tasks that they performed with great effectiveness.

THE ARVN BEFORE AND AFTER ALLIED INTERVENTION

Before 1965, the ARVN essentially held an active offensive posture, the objective of which was the destruction of an antigovernment armed rebellion. We sought to defend national sovereignty against Northern aggression, to dismantle the Southern rebel forces, and to build a democratic republic.

When U.S. forces arrived in 1965, they immediately asserted the right to conduct the entire war effort, perhaps because they were financing everything. I believe they thought our command was still in its infancy. Because of this subordination to the United States, it is safe to say that the ARVN commanders did not formulate any specific strategy during the Americanization of the war.

Still, our morale was in general quite high, especially after our troop strength increased and our weaponry improved. Of course, the fact that we were fighting alongside a superpower in the face of the communist threat also helped. Our leaders and rank-and-file soldiers learned much about waging modern, conventional warfare with state-of-the-art weapons as a result of this experience. We used this knowledge to great effect during the communist Easter Offensive in 1972, at the battles of An Lộc, Kontum, and Quảng Trị.

However, we also suffered serious disadvantages. To conduct conventional warfare, as during the final Spring Offensive of 1975, the adequate and timely supply of ammunition is essential. Unfortunately, this was woefully lacking. The United States gave the South Vietnamese people a false hope that it would not abandon them. This led to a bad habit on the part of the South Vietnamese forces to overrely on the U.S. Air Force for assistance from B-52 bombing.

After the withdrawal of the American armed forces in 1973, the absence of a national policy was quite obvious. Additionally, South Vietnam found itself victimized by many detrimental stipulations of the Paris Peace Accords (see chapter 5 in this volume). We sensed even more misfortune would befall the RVN when the PRC invaded the Paracel Islands in 1974. Although the U.S. Seventh Fleet was cruising nearby, the Americans not only declined to intervene but did not even rescue the unfortunate South Vietnamese Navy sailors, who were bobbing along the high seas after abandoning their sinking ships. This was clear proof that we had been abandoned by our allies.

Our political leaders should have formulated a policy of self-reliance and self-preservation then, but they instead relied too much on the promises of President Richard Nixon, even when the North Vietnamese communists unleashed their entire armed forces in an all-out invasion in 1975. The lack of a prepared plan to resist or counter such massive aggression, the rapid depletion of ammunition and fuel, and our inability to deploy forces in order to take advantage of geography inexorably led to the final debacle, and the loss of South Vietnam.

Notes

1 Đoàn Thêm, *Việc từng ngày, 1945–1964* [Daily events, 1945–1964] (Taipei: Xuân Thu, 1989), 167.
2 Ibid., 184.
3 Phòng 5 Bộ Tổng Tham Mưu [Fifth Department, Joint Chiefs of Staff] (1972), "Quân Lực Việt Nam Cộng Hòa trong giai Đoạn hình thành, 1946–1955" [The ARVN in the formative stage, 1946–1955], 245.
4 Vũ Hữu San, *Lược sử Hải Quân Việt Nam Cộng Hòa* [A brief history of the Republic of Vietnam's navy] (San Jose, CA: Hương Quê, 2009), 22–23.
5 Liên Hội Không Quân Úc Châu [Association of Former Air Force Service Members in Australia], *Quân Sử Không Quân Việt Nam Cộng Hòa* [A history of the RVN air force] (Melbourne: Van Luong, 2005), 32, 42, 47.
6 Nguyễn Thu Lương, *Chiến sử Sư Đoàn Nhảy Dù* [History of the airborne division] (San Jose, CA: Hương Quê, 2009), 45, 58, 60; Ban Biên soạn Thủy Quân Lục Chiến [Editorial Committee of the Marine Division History], *Quân sử Thủy Quân Lục Chiến* [History of the marine division] (San Jose, CA: Hương Quê, 2011), 23, 24.
7 Spencer C. Tucker, *The Encyclopedia of the Vietnam War* (New York: Oxford University Press, 2000), 394.
8 Hà Mai Việt, *Thép và Máu* [Steel and blood] (San Jose, CA: Papyrus, 2005), 417, 418.
9 Vũ Hữu San, *Lược sử Hải Quân Việt Nam Cộng Hòa*, 124, 126, 134, 155, 182.
10 Liên Hội Không Quân Úc Châu, *Quân Sử Không Quân Việt Nam Cộng Hòa*, 62, 104, 109, 112, 118–20, 141–45, 147–50.
11 Trần Ngọc Thống, Lê Đình Thụy, and Hồ Đắc Huân, *Lược sử Quân Lực Việt Nam Cộng Hòa* [History of the armed forces of the RVN] (San Jose, CA: Hương Quê, 2011), 604; Nguyễn Đức Phương, *Chiến tranh Việt Nam Toàn Tập* [Battles of the Vietnam War] (Toronto: Làng Văn, 2001), 841.
12 Lê Văn Trang, *Kỷ Yếu Pháo Binh Việt Nam Cộng Hòa* [RVN artillery review] (Taipei: n.p., 2010), 136; *Nguyệt san KBC số 8/2016* [Monthly review KBC] (Westminster, CA, 2016), 14; Liên Hội Không Quân Úc Châu, *Quân Sử Không Quân Việt Nam Cộng Hòa*, 183.
13 Harry G. Summer Jr., *On Strategy* (New York: Bantam Doubleday Dell Publication Group, 1984), 172.
14 Tucker, *The Encyclopedia of the Vietnam War*, 315.
15 Ibid., 395.
16 Nguyễn Đức Cường, "Building a Market Economy during Wartime," in *Voices from the Second Republic of South Vietnam (1967–1975)*, ed. Keith W. Taylor (Ithaca: Cornell University, Southeast Asia Program, 2014), 96.

Chapter Eight

The Philosophies and Development of a Free Education

Nguyễn Hữu Phước

Nguyễn Hữu Phước received a bachelor's degree from the Saigon Faculty of Education and taught at Petrus Ký High School and Thủ Đức Demonstration High School. From 1969 to 1971 he served as a lecturer at the College of Education, dean of the Saigon Elementary Teacher Training College, and director of the Saigon Center of Training and In-Service for Elementary Teachers. After earning a PhD in education at the University of Southern California in 1974, Phước was promoted to be head of the Directory of Elementary Training and In-service Training, supervising all teacher training colleges and the Saigon In-service Training Center. After April 1975, Phước resettled in the United States. From 1991 until his retirement in 2000, he served as director of the Asian Child Protective Services Program of the Los Angeles Department of Children Services. During that time he also served as field instructor for California state universities of Los Angeles, Long Beach, and Pomona. He has written articles on American and Vietnamese education and has published two books on the Vietnamese language, one in 2004 and another in 2008.

Historical Background

For centuries until 1919, the Confucian educational system in Vietnam was characterized by the civil service examinations and by the use of Chinese writing (with Sino-Vietnamese pronunciation) in schooling. The French established their political and governmental system in Indochina in 1884. By 1917 the governor general of French Indochina ordered the promulgation of the French Public Instructions Codes, which was a transplant of the French educational system to Vietnamese society. The French system of education in Vietnam was characterized by a classical Western curriculum and a centralized national organization.

When the Republic of Vietnam (RVN) took over, the Ministry of Education (MOE) continued the French-style centralized educational system, while the 5-3-4 system was maintained. Other developments included an overwhelming preponderance of college-preparatory high schools and a dichotomy of one system for technical agricultural schools and another for university in higher education.

Philosophies of Education

During the early years of the RVN, our first educational guiding principle emerged, which was **nationalism**. However, education in general did not undergo significant changes for the newly formed republic, which faced multiple reorganizations and political realignments. The education system continued to be viewed as a legacy rather than a Vietnamese system that would serve the needs of Vietnamese society.[1]

In 1956 the minister of education concluded that Vietnamese education needed a reevaluation and reorientation. In light of these objectives, the 1958 National Conference on Education adopted the position that Vietnamese education should be "nationalistic," "humanistic," and "open mind for changes."[2]

> **Nationalism**: Vietnamese education must teach its citizens to respect the values of an independent country and assure its survival and its development as an independent nation of an independent people.
>
> **Humanism**: Vietnamese education must teach its citizens to respect the sacred value of all human beings, considering human beings as the most important value and therefore paying attention to developing all the best aspects of human life.
>
> **Open Mind for Changes**: Vietnamese education respects the cultural values of all other nations in the world and must use all possible scientific methods as the most important factors for the progress of the country, for the development of society, and for democratic attitudes toward accepting changes in all aspects of the Vietnamese education system.

In reality, we found that we could not easily realize the first two philosophies in the curriculum through natural science subjects such as physics and chemistry. The curriculum taught nationalism through history lessons about the historical struggles against Chinese and French domination of Vietnam. The civic education curriculum was used as a tool for teaching humanistic lessons.

The last philosophy, "open mind for changes," was the most concrete philosophy that fitted very well into the reform of the Vietnamese education system. Several factors affected the reform of Vietnamese education:

- The intensity of the war after 1959 between communist North Vietnam and republican South Vietnam.
- The continuing French efforts to perpetuate their cultural and educational influence in the RVN through cultural accords.
- U.S. economic assistance to South Vietnam with primary focus on projects, beginning with research on the RVN's education system followed by assistance programs.
- The efforts of Vietnamese educators who perceived the need for modernization to develop the country.
- The direct involvement of the U.S. Mission Operations (USOM) through various educational contracts with American universities such as Michigan State University for the reorganization of public administration; Southern Illinois University for elementary education and elementary teacher education development; Ohio University for comprehensive high school; and University of Wisconsin, Stevens Points for higher education development.

The 1964 National Educational Conference confirmed again that it supported the three positions of Vietnamese educational philosophy and emphasized the need for the development of technical education. They proposed an orientation program (guidance services) for youth in secondary education. The presidential message to Congress in 1969 strongly supported the promotion of practical education for the masses. Accordingly, the minister of education, at the Culture and Education Council in 1970, presented his plan to concentrate on the development of community elementary schools, comprehensive high schools, and polytechnic universities in the coming years.

THE COMPREHENSIVE HIGH SCHOOL

The comprehensive high school in Vietnam was called "trung học tổng hợp," which literally means "synthesized high school."

In the early 1960s, secondary high schools in Vietnam—most of them college-preparatory centers with a purely academic curriculum of general education—received criticism as being obsolete. In the climate of searching for a new type of secondary school curriculum, a contract between Ohio University and the U.S. Agency for International Development (USAID)/Vietnam brought an Ohio team of educators to Vietnam to assess and to provide technical assistance to the Vietnamese secondary education system beginning in 1962. The original assignment was to work with the Faculties of Education at the University of Saigon and the University of Huế for the purpose of upgrading the curriculum, materials, and facilities. In addition, a modern, experimental comprehensive high school was to be provided as an educational laboratory for each of the pedagogy faculties. The Ohio University team cooperated with the Vietnamese Faculties of Education and the Vietnamese Secondary Education Directorate in the following areas:

- initiating a modern comprehensive secondary program, utilizing three pilot schools under the direct supervision of the three Faculties of Education;
- introducing new courses of study to these schools, which included guidance counseling, comparative education, school administration, and science education;
- establishing workshops for teachers to give them a minimum background in one of these disciplines, as a first step in this new direction;
- extending the pilot program in comprehensive education to eleven additional schools;
- providing the opportunity for Vietnamese educators to participate in teacher training programs in the United States to prepare them for the new comprehensive high schools; and
- arranging observation tours in the United States for Vietnamese educators who were involved in the comprehensive secondary education program.

In 1965, 1966, and 1967 the first three pilot comprehensive high schools came into existence in Huế, Thủ Đức, and Cần Thơ respectively. These schools were under the supervision of the Faculties of Education of the respective universities. All new pilot schools were named demonstration high schools. Unfortunately, Huế School was forced to close due to political unrest. Cần Thơ school did not have facilities and staff to start. Therefore, Thủ Đức Demonstration High School turned out to be the only demonstration school that led the development of comprehensive high school for the RVN.

The principals of the first two pilot schools had received their training at U.S. universities. Most of the Vietnamese pilot teachers who were responsible for the new areas of study (including industrial arts, home economics, business education, and guidance counseling) were U.S. university graduates. The Student Guidance program in these new Vietnamese institutions was carried out by U.S.-trained Vietnamese specialists in guidance and counseling and considered a very necessary and important part of the school system. For the first time, at the Vietnamese secondary education level, a systematic guidance program was developed and implemented in the pilot comprehensive high schools.

In 1967, twelve more regular high schools received the green light from the MOE to start, step by step, the new comprehensive program as lead pilot schools. Several more high schools were permitted to start their comprehensive program a few years later. The burden of training new teachers for new subjects such as industrial arts, home economics, and business education was shouldered by the Saigon Faculty of Education.

The staff of the Thủ Đức Demonstration High School presented in 1968 a complete comprehensive secondary school curriculum to the dean of the Saigon Faculty of Education, who shared with the staff the responsibility of experimenting with this new curriculum. After several years of experimentation and after a seminar on revision of curriculum in 1971, the curriculum received approval from the MOE.

Also in 1971, all Thủ Đức staff in charge of new subjects who had received their BA, MA, or MS in the United States were transferred to the Saigon Faculty of Education as lecturers to provide training and in-service training for newly established pilot schools. The Vietnamese comprehensive high schools were still organized along the mono-track or four-track (mathematics, science, modern languages, and classical languages), which were to be found in regular Vietnamese general education high schools. The difference was that the newly established high schools had eight tracks, with four new tracks being industrial arts, agriculture, home economics, and business education; thus, students had a wider selection than the four-track regular high schools. Despite the wider selection of courses, a true flexible electives system for an ideal comprehensive high school had not yet been achieved in the Vietnamese secondary comprehensive high schools.

The emergence of comprehensive high schools in Vietnam was a cooperative endeavor between American and Vietnamese educators. Among the latter, some were U.S.-trained, others were trained in Vietnam, and some others received their education elsewhere.[3] Vietnamese educators, including those trained in the United States, possessed an educational background strongly influenced by the French classical tradition. Therefore, they brought to the Vietnamese comprehensive high schools some of their French orientations.

As of 1974, it was too early to know if the comprehensive schools were satisfactory in meeting the needs of Vietnamese secondary education. At that time, scientific and technical data development caused a proliferation of professions and careers, and the concept of comprehensive education appeared to meet the modern needs. Comprehensive secondary education was a worldwide movement at the time and needed a better understanding by the Vietnamese people for its development and implementation. Sadly, a few years after 1975 the Communist government abolished all comprehensive schools altogether.

Community Colleges

Prior to the concept of the community college in Vietnam, there were discussions about the concept of community education.[4] It was introduced to Vietnam in 1954 for elementary students. Four years later, some elementary schools became community elementary schools under the new formula that promulgated the idea of the interrelation between local and social life and the activities of the school. The idea was developed progressively, and by 1971, all the elementary schools in Vietnam were called elementary community schools. The development indicated a trend to eliminate the highly academic curriculum and to bring in a more practical approach to education. During the twenty years of its existence, community education in Vietnam became a familiar term especially to elementary teachers and administrators. However, many more discussions and studies as to content, functions, and the practices of community education were needed. The community school concept was not yet understood thoroughly.

The community college concept was introduced to Vietnam by Đỗ Bá Khê in 1970. He demonstrated in his doctoral dissertation the relevance of community colleges to postwar reconstruction in Vietnam.[5] He indicated that the establishment of community colleges in Vietnam was considered to be an answer to the need for practical education, an outlet to alleviate the overcrowded student enrollment at the University of Saigon, and most importantly, a training camp for middle-level technicians necessary for the economic development of the country.

We recognized the potential of community college. Presidential Decree no. 503 of August 15, 1971, established the system of community colleges. That same day, two further presidential decrees established the Duyên Hải Community College and the Tiền Giang Community College. These two new public community colleges were the results of the effort and cooperation between educators and educational authorities to improve higher education in response to the people's demands. Decree no. 503 stated two main functions for these institutions:

- To develop within a two-year program general and basic studies in higher education, with transferable programs of junior professional higher learning.
- To develop vocational higher education and specialized programs to meet the present needs of the community that sponsors the community college.

This decree also provided that each community college be directly associated with, and academically dependent upon, an existing national university. The president of the specific university would serve as the chair of the community college's local board of governance. The local board was to consist of laymen and government officials in the region of the community college. This board was to be responsible for determining policies and programs, and for budgeting, securing funds, administering, and disposing of financial matters, including all matters of college property.

This decree and other subsequent decrees represented the first innovation in Vietnam in the domain of governance and administration in which laymen acted in concert with government officials in the supervision of a higher institution of learning. In fact, however, these community colleges did not entirely reflect the meaning of "community" since they were totally supported by the national budget, which was very limited. Consequently, the admission of students was still based on rigid competitive entrance examinations. The programs offered had not been truly comprehensive. Teacher education programs were available at both of these colleges. Duyên Hải

Community College (which was located in central Vietnam) specialized in fishery and electronics courses, while Tiền Giang Community College (which was located in the upper Mekong Delta) specialized in agriculture. Neither of these institutions was able to offer transferable credits. This was mainly due to an acute shortage of qualified teachers in other fields, together with a serious lack of financing.

As new institutions in Vietnamese higher education, these first community colleges met many obstacles and struggled very hard to survive. The nonrecognition of university status, the cumbersome bureaucratic procedures, the lack of an adequate budget, the shortage of qualified personnel, and the difficulty in transferability to other higher institutions—all restricted greater development of public community colleges in Vietnam. However, these roadblocks did not discourage the community college movement in Vietnam: two private community colleges were also established. Educators proposed integrating existing normal colleges (elementary teacher training colleges) and other postsecondary institutions with community colleges. People were still demanding more community colleges to be established. In Đà Nẵng and Bình Định, for example, local communities expended great efforts in promoting the establishment of community colleges there.

Vietnamese educators and government authorities did recognize the potential of community colleges, and the philosophy of community college was generally accepted. Community colleges, as a means toward the democratization of higher education, would, in consequence, have blossomed in the RVN if not for the events of 1975.

The Polytechnic University

The MOE presented and introduced the concept of polytechnic higher education to the Culture and Education Council in 1970 as part of the educational policy.

The diffusion and development of cultural and scientific knowledge in every social class in order to raise national income is another objective many developing countries pursue. The training of technicians and servicemen must meet the real requirements of the country and at the same time conserve manpower and resources, so that these contributions in education may harvest results. This concept led to a polytechnic trend in higher education at the time.

The policy for the new concept presumed that a technical higher education system be considered as the continuation of the comprehensive secondary education program. Higher education Vietnam, influenced by the French tradition, considered technical higher education a separate system. Engineering was offered in different schools at the Vietnamese National Institute of Technology, that is, the Colleges of Civil Engineering, Public Works, Electricity, and Chemistry. Agricultural engineering was provided by the National Institute of Agriculture, which comprised the Colleges of Forestry, Husbandry, and Agronomy. The structure and organization of the Vietnamese universities were also based on the French system. Each university consisted of a number of faculties, or colleges, such as the Faculties of Letters, Sciences, Law, Medicine, and Pharmacy. Each operated independently. The same course might have been taught in different schools, even by the same professor (who has joint appointments), but credits could not be transferred from one school to another. In addition, there was no coordinating organization for graduate studies among the schools even within the same university. All public universities were administratively, financially, and technically under the supervision of the MOE.

All of these characteristics remained unchanged until the decade of the 1960s. Then, a movement toward integrating these professional higher institutions into the regular universities began to take place. The teachers of technical schools wanted to enjoy the same status as that of university professors. In addition, university professors recommended in the 1968 Higher Education Seminar that university learning should be vocationally oriented, which implied that the universities placed more emphasis on technical, professional, and agricultural education. Thus, during the last years of the 1960s, there was a tendency toward considering the university as a multidisciplinary institution, or a multifunction institution with a practical program to serve the new needs of Vietnamese society.

The idea of polytechnic higher education finally materialized through the establishment of Thủ Đức Polytechnic University by Presidential Decree no. 246 on March 29, 1973. The university's pamphlet stated that it offered a practical curriculum and an effective pattern of higher education.

The Thủ Đức Polytechnic University, by virtue of the official founding document, was not just another institution at the tertiary level in the Vietnamese educational system. It was founded to hopefully cure the ills of higher education in the country. The idea of a new university arose from a great enthusiasm for an institution to absorb, selectively, high school graduates, to demonstrate an effective pattern of higher education administration, and to offer curriculum of a practical nature, most essential to national development.

The decree of March 29, 1973, specified that Thủ Đức Polytechnic University was charged with the following tasks: to provide programs that would train leaders and specialists for economic and social development; to promote research and to expand useful scientific and technical knowledge; and to contribute to the design of projects and implementation of plans for economic development, with special emphasis on the areas of agriculture and industry.

The appointment of the president of Thủ Đức Polytechnic University followed the same tradition as in all regular national Vietnamese universities. However, Thủ Đức University had three new features that departed from the traditional university pattern: technical-professional schools and agricultural schools were brought onto the same campus and enjoyed the same status of other colleges; the Colleges of Letters, Arts, and Sciences were combined in one school, and there was also a graduate school; and the semester credit system was employed. This new university attempted to offer students a practical curriculum to help meet the nation's needs, which were felt but not yet filled by more established institutions. From observing the practically oriented curriculum at this university, an American educator stated that the polytechnic university "may become the Vietnamese version of a United States land-grant university."

As of March 1975, this polytechnic university had existed for only two years. It would be unfair to assess it, as it was still in its infancy. At that time there was the hope that it would be an important higher education institution responding to the present needs in Vietnam and a prototype of higher education for the changing and emerging patterns of the Vietnamese society of the RVN.

The Use of Objective Tests for the High School Diploma

Before 1967, four national examinations were regularly administered every year:

- the sixth grade entrance examination;
- the junior high diploma;
- the eleventh grade diploma; and
- the senior grade diploma or high school diploma.

These examinations consumed a tremendous amount of time, energy, and money. The number of candidates constantly increased, and in addition, essay-type questions, because of a subjective scoring process, were thought to be insufficient to measure a candidate's ability.

In 1963, the first proposal for changing the testing method emerged. A plan was developed by USOM specialists in educational testing and guidance and their Vietnamese counterparts for examination improvement. In 1964 the Testing and Guidance Center, which later became part of the Directorate of Examinations, was established. Its main purpose was to develop educational guidance services and to set up objective tests for use in national examinations. Six secondary teachers were sent to the Republic of China (Taiwan) for an intensive six-week course of study in testing and guidance. Upon their return to Vietnam, they constructed new objective-type tests for the sixth grade entrance examination.

Many conservative teachers opposed this innovative change, which required considerable provisions for the mechanics of testing. There was also an insufficiency of printed materials and a lack of facilities to keep these tests confidential, especially since the same tests were disseminated and used throughout the entire country. Therefore, until 1975, the old essay-type tests were still being used for the sixth grade entrance examination.

However, experiments with the new type of tests took place in the two pilot comprehensive schools. As early as 1965 the MOE ordered the Testing and Guidance Center to concentrate its effort on citizenship education and the preparation of objective tests for this subject. The first break with the traditional method of examination in this subject occurred in 1966 when the national examination used the objective tests. Some years later, objective tests were extended to the subjects of history and geography.

By the end of the 1960s, the number of candidates for high school diploma examinations increased so considerably that the examinations became a burden to the MOE. Officials realized the complicated traditional processes of administering the diploma would no longer be appropriate. The subjectivity of scoring continued to be criticized even though measures had been taken to assure fairness in the scoring process. Among the measures taken were an agreed scale of scoring and a guarantee of anonymity for candidates. Consequently, the MOE saw the need for urgently improving the process. In the academic year of 1972–73, the Committee on Examination Reform was established to study this problem and made the following recommendations:

- The objective-type test should be expanded to all subjects covered in the high school diploma examination. It was not only adaptable to the examination of large groups. It also would eliminate the subjectivity of the examiner, supply statistical data for other examinations, and prevent possible cheating.
- Computers should be used for registration, for examination scoring, and for the printing of certificates.

These recommendations were accepted by the MOE, which promulgated its ministerial decree on September 17, 1973. The summer of 1974 saw the beginning of the applications of the use of objective tests for all subjects in the high school diploma examination.

Objective tests were new neither to Vietnam's military schools nor to various schools of languages. The Thủ Đức Demonstration High School, under the supervision of the University of Saigon, had used objective tests in its sixth grade entrance examination since 1966. However, objective tests were not widely used before 1974 as part of the national examinations that affected so many students' lives. Applications of objective tests in the national examinations in 1974 evoked negative reactions. Vietnamese newspapers labeled this type of examination "the IBM high school diploma" because the IBM computer did the scoring. These examinations were referred to as the "A/B/C/D-circle examinations"—the implication being that students circled the correct answer by mere chance. The public criticized this new type of testing, probably because of their own confusion due to inadequate explanations of its purposes. Teaching professionals had doubts about the validity and the reliability of these tests with only multiple-choice questions.

Due to so many controversies among educators, the MOE decided to suspend the use of these national objective multiple-choice tests at the end of 1974 for further discussion and research. We will never know what would have been the decision of the MOE regarding high school diploma test since the RVN was wiped out by communist North Vietnam.

THE DEVELOPMENT OF TEACHER TRAINING

Normal colleges (NC) were the name of the institution in charge of training elementary teachers). From 1962 to 1971 the eleventh grade diploma was the prerequisite for the NC entrance exam. Since 1973 it was the high school diploma. The two-year general education program of professional training consisted of three parts: community education, professional education, and practice teaching. All the NC were established by ministerial decrees.

As of 1973 there was a total of sixteen normal colleges in the RVN that produced about three thousand teachers annually. All graduates from the NC were granted tenure after six months of satisfactory service as a teacher. According to the Directorate of Elementary Education (DEE), the number of graduates could supply only one half of the needed elementary teachers for the RVN. Therefore the DEE created different criteria for recruiting the needed elementary teachers. This led to a wide range in terms of status and salary scale among elementary teachers. Several short-term in-service training sessions (from one to three weeks) were organized by the National Elementary In-service Training Center in Saigon to provide on-the-job training for newly hired teachers who had had no formal training at normal colleges. With regard to the training of high school teachers, private and public universities contributed greatly through their Faculties of Pedagogy, the French equivalent terminology of American Colleges of Education.

Junior high school teachers were those who had a high school diploma, passed the competitive entrance exam, and completed two years of successful training at a public Faculty of Education. Also considered as junior high school teachers were those who had a high school diploma and a total of two years of experience in teaching at the junior high level. In addition, elementary teachers who held a high school diploma and who had received special training in teaching methods and had passed a practice teaching examination could become junior high school teachers.

Senior high school teachers were those who had the high school diploma and who had passed the competitive entrance examination and received four years of successful training at a Faculty of Education. Also considered high school teachers were those who had a four-year bachelor's degrees in arts or in sciences. Due to the urgent needs for senior high school teachers, the Faculty of Education at the University of Saigon offered a comprehensive three-year intensive training program during the academic school years of 1960–61, 1961–62, and 1962–63. It started the four-year training program in the 1964 school year.

Again, those who graduated from Faculties of Education were granted tenure-track teaching positions while those who graduated from private ones such as Vạn Hạnh and Đà Lạt Universities had to endure two years or longer in temporary positions until the budget for hiring them permanently could be approved. Therefore, there was a fierce competition to pass the yearly entrance examinations into Faculties of Education to fill budgeted positions. It was a chain reaction: the limited number of budgeted positions for high school teachers would lead to the limited number of public (free) high schools that could be opened. This situation led to the proliferation of private junior and senior high schools.

The development of junior high and senior high teacher training institutions was a great ongoing effort by all educators and all segments of society in the RVN even though it never caught up with the student population.

A Golden Age

From 1954 to 1975 Vietnamese education was subjected to many factors that influenced the educational system. Vietnamese educators urgently felt the need to improve an education system that was heavily under the influence of French colonialism so that it responded more readily to the demands of postcolonial Vietnam, which was still ravaged by an ongoing war and which was undergoing rapid social and political changes.

France, through its Mission Culturelle, made great efforts to continue its influences, with special attention directed toward the field of education. Various university educators and other education specialists worked with USAID, in planning, developing, and implementing programs for Vietnamese educational institutions.

The MOE first experimented with, then expanded several institutions, such as the comprehensive high schools, the community colleges, the polytechnic colleges, the testing/evaluation system, and the teacher training colleges. Unfortunately, a devastating war was going on from 1959 to 1975 between communist North Vietnam and republican South Vietnam. Nevertheless, the period appears in retrospect as a golden age for educators and for South Vietnamese people to experiment with and to enjoy a liberal education that was dynamic, future-oriented, and diverse in form. With the collapse of the RVN, the fate of its educational system also changed forever.

Notes

1 For a more extended analysis, see Nguyễn Hữu Phước, "Contemporary Educational Philosophies in Vietnam, 1954–1974: A Comparative Analysis" (PhD dissertation, School of Education, University of Southern California, 1974).
2 In other documents these terms were translated as "humanism" (*nhân bản*), "nationalism" (*dân tộc*), and "scientific methods" or "open mind for changes" (*khai phóng*). The 1964 National Conference reaffirmed these philosophies of education.
3 I was trained for a short time at the College of Education in Taipei University in testing, guidance, and counseling. I came back to serve for two school years as a teacher of history and geography for the Thủ Đức Demonstration High School when it opened its door for the first and second grades. Concurrently I also served in the Guidance Program as a trainee

led by a Vietnamese guidance expert (with a master's degree in guidance and counseling from a U.S. university) under the supervision of an American expert—who held a doctorate degree in counseling and guidance—from the Ohio University team. After this period, I was transferred back to the Faculty of Education, University of Saigon as a lecturer, and then an assistant professor in history, and guidance and counseling, and continued to train new staff to serve high schools including comprehensive schools.
4 See Vo Kim Son, "Selected Problems and Issues Related to the Development of Public Community Colleges in Vietnam" (PhD dissertation, School of Education, University of Southern California, 1974).
5 Đỗ Bá Khê, "The Community Junior College Concept: A Study of Its Relevance in Postwar Reconstruction in Vietnam" (PhD thesis, University of Southern California, 1970).

Chapter Nine

Personal Reflections on the Educational System

Võ Kim Sơn

Võ Kim Sơn earned her bachelor's degrees in biology and education at Saigon University, and a master's degree in botany at Washington University in St. Louis. Sơn taught at the National Wards High School and in 1967 became a lecturer at Saigon University's Faculty of Education. She received her PhD in education at the University of Southern California, and after April 1975, along with her Saigon University colleagues, attended a two-year brainwashing program required by the new communist government. Sơn escaped from Vietnam by boat in 1981 and was elected by the fourteen thousand refugees in the camp to be their first female leader. On her arrival in southern California, Sơn joined the Vietnamese Community of Orange County, a nonprofit organization, as executive director. Since 1984 she has served as special consultant on refugee affairs for the California State Department of Social Services. In 1987, Sơn added to her state job the position of director of the Intercultural Development Center of California State University at Fullerton where she was the founder and teacher of the Asian American studies program.

Despite an ongoing war and the lack of funds for spending on education (7 percent of the annual gross domestic product),[1] the Republic of Vietnam (RVN) government undertook a wide-ranging series of educational reforms. A major reform right at the beginning involved the transition from the French educational system into a Vietnamese one, which required new curricular programs and the training of new administrators, specialists, and teaching faculty.

The subsequent explosion of student enrollments at all levels demanded more and more schools to be constructed. The challenge was not simply financial but how to obtain parents' participation and community partnership in the development of new schools, from elementary and high schools in rural locations to colleges and universities in big cities.

The activities of the Ministry of Education (MOE) were constrained not only financially but also politically. Ministers were appointed by presidents. During the sixties, several military coups took place, and with a new government formed after each coup came a new minister of education. Fortunately, there were minimal disruptions.

In this chapter, I will first discuss the Vietnamization of the French educational system during the first decade of the republic. This process contributed to a sharp rise in the social demand for education at all levels, which in turn supported the growth of new kinds of schools such as private universities and community colleges. Through my personal experience working in the Faculty of Education, the National Wards High

School, and a private Catholic school, I hope to offer snapshots of the development of the diverse and dynamic educational system in the RVN. In the conclusion, I briefly recount my work as an expert on education from the United States to help the post-1975 Vietnamese government reform its educational system.

The Vietnamization of the Educational System

The year 1954 marked the end of colonialism and the beginning of the division of Vietnam into two regions under two different regimes. Nearly a million Northerners opted to move to South Vietnam following the division. After assuming office, one of the most important decisions President Ngô Đình Diệm declared was to implement immediately the Vietnamization of the old French system of education. The French language was replaced by Vietnamese as the instructional media in teaching all subjects from elementary to high schools. At the university level, due to a shortage of qualified faculty who could teach in Vietnamese, the French and English languages were still popular in such colleges as the Faculty of Education, the Faculty of Letters, and the Faculty of Sciences.

The programs of study, textbooks, and methods of examination modeled after the French system were changed to suit a now free society. The names and structure of the educational system were also changed. Different from North Vietnam with its ten-year educational system, South Vietnam adopted the twelve-year system from grades 1 to 12:

- The elementary level from grades 1 to 6. At the end of the sixth grade, students must take and pass the certificate of primary examinations in order to enter grade 7.
- The junior or intermediate level (or high school level 1) from grades 7 to 9. At the end of the ninth grade, students were expected to take examinations for the certificate of high school level 1. Even without this certificate, students could still attend grade 10.
- The high school level 2 included grades 10, 11, and 12. Right at grade 10, students could select their majors: "A" for sciences; "B" for mathematics; and "C" for French or English languages. At the end of grade 11, students take the Baccalaureate I (Tú Tài 1) examinations. Without Baccalaureate I, students could not proceed to grade 12. At the end of grade 12, students would take Baccalaureate II (Tú Tài 2) examinations that were equivalent to the high school diploma in American high schools. Only with Baccalaureate II could students hope to access the college level.

The Vietnamization of the education system allowed younger generations to make their education dream come true. Under the colonial period, those who wished to pursue higher education had to travel to Hanoi, where the sole university in the country (Hanoi University) was located. This university was initially focused on the training of medical doctors and later added some programs like pedagogy, law, and the arts. In the past, the French language used as the instructional media was a major obstacle in gaining access to schools for students in the countryside who did not have opportunities to meet French people and to learn French.

The replacement of French with Vietnamese created favorable conditions for parents to send their children to schools. The number of enrollments consequently increased considerably whereas the national budget for education did not change. It remained at about 7 percent of the annual gross domestic product, which was about US$2 billion at that time.

THE IMPLEMENTATION OF VIETNAMIZATION

Under the First Republic, the Ministry of Education had just enough time to plant the seeds of educational reform. The Second Republic was born after the coup that toppled President Ngô Đình Diệm. Throughout this period, military generals took turns leading the nation. Several coups d'état occurred in the sixties. After each change of the country's leader, a new minister of education was appointed.

From 1956 to 1971 alone, sixteen ministers of education took charge of the education portfolio. Specifically, in a short period from 1963 to 1967, nine ministers of education were appointed under the Second Republic. Fortunately, the education objectives deliberated upon by the previous ministers were implemented without interruptions by their successors. Both young and mature administrators were committed to better education to transform the developing Vietnam into a modern country. All the appointed education leaders, one after another, established the programs of study on the same philosophical basis: nationalist, scientific, and open minds. All the ministers of education favored centralization over decentralization in their administration of the educational system.

All the ministers of education were not education professionals, yet the best work all of them achieved was the recruitment of qualified staff. These education specialists knew how to develop good programs to be delivered to schools for implementation. All members of the Ministry of Education's administrative team were graduates from pedagogy training programs. They had been teachers who brought to the ministry their practical local experience. In the early 1970s many were sent for observation tours in developed countries. Upon their return to Vietnam, they developed new curricula, wrote new textbooks, and proposed to change the methods of student performance evaluation. Objective tests with multiple-choice questions replaced essay tests for the first time in 1972. The latter format was believed not to guarantee objectivity, consistency, and fairness.

In response to the sudden increase in enrollments beyond the ministry's control, the MOE encouraged the private sector to develop the system of private schools to accommodate students not being admitted to public schools. At the end of the sixth grade, students had to participate in a very competitive entrance examination to be admitted to public junior high schools. Depending on local schools, some admitted only 20 percent of applicants. It was natural that selected students proudly carried their school name attached to their uniform on their way to school.

The MOE also asked the Ministry of Defense to collaborate in providing education to fallen soldiers' children as a gesture of gratitude to those who sacrificed their lives for the nation. The system of National Wards, which will be discussed later, came into existence out of this call.

THE FACULTY OF EDUCATION

The Faculty of Education was officially established in 1957 along with two other colleges, the Faculty of Sciences and the Faculty of Letters, all of which belonged to Saigon University, the second university in Vietnam. (The first Vietnamese university,

Hanoi Medical University, was built in Hanoi in 1902 by the French. Its first headmaster was Alexandre Yersin.)

Sometimes translated into English as Saigon College of Education or as Faculty of Pedagogy, the Faculty of Education was responsible for training high school teachers, specifically for tenth, eleventh, and twelfth grades, to accommodate the expanding needs of teaching faculty. In the first few years, the dean of the faculty, Dr. Trương Công Cừu, invited professors of the Faculty of Letters over to the education school campus to train students of the Department of Humanities. For science and mathematics students, the school sent them to the Faculty of Sciences in the adjacent campus. To be admitted into the program, high school diploma graduates had to take very competitive examinations. Many candidates were interested in this new training program because of appealing annual scholarships awarded to each teaching student. Also, a guaranteed tenured high school teacher position was awaiting students who successfully completed a three-year training program. After 1964, the training program was extended into a four-year program.

Every year the Faculty of Education recruited forty teaching students of each subject category: French, English, Vietnamese literature, history and geography, mathematics, physics and chemistry, and natural sciences. Entrance examinations for the natural sciences class of 1958 (the year I took it) included translations of texts from French into Vietnamese, texts from Vietnamese into French, and an essay on the evolution of the horse.

As a member of the first cohort of admitted students, my French educational background was of great assistance not only to myself but also to my classmates when we began our programs of study. My classmates came in with a background of education obtained from the Vietnamese system of education. They earned Vietnamese high school diplomas; therefore, they had difficulty in taking notes from our French professors who delivered lectures without taking a breath. Among forty students with natural sciences majors, only two other students and I graduated from the French school system. We shared notes with our classmates. During my time at the Faculty of Education campus, from 1958 to 1961, I also enrolled in the Faculty of Sciences for a bachelor's degree in natural sciences. Most of my French or Vietnamese professors in both faculties used the French language as the instructional media; except in the Faculty of Education, few Vietnamese professors taught the foundational courses in Vietnamese. Upon my graduation, I was awarded a U.S. Agency for International Development (USAID) scholarship to continue my postgraduate education in an American university. Upon my return to Vietnam, I was assigned to teach at the National Wards High School from December 1963 to the summer of 1967; I was then transferred to the Faculty of Education in Saigon.

This time, my American educational background gave me unexpected barriers when I assumed the position as a professor of sciences. The new dean of the faculty, Dr. Trần Văn Tấn, received his education in France, whereas I graduated from an American university. Dr. Tấn may have preferred graduates from French schools rather than those from American universities. In addition, the dean might have wanted to demonstrate his independence from the Ministry of Education, and he liked to be free of all the foreign influences on appointment. Against my good will, I unexpectedly became a victim of conflicts between the traditional French influences and the new American approach. To demonstrate his power, the dean kept my American advisor and me waiting for two full hours for his audience. Finally, my advisor's great patience earned me the position.

My four years at the Faculty of Education did not give me much joy. I tried my best to make friends, but I received neither support nor friendship from my colleagues. My French high school diploma and my BS degree with double majors from the Faculty of Education and the Faculty of Sciences were not enough to testify that, like them, I too had received a French education. My teaching innovations could not attract my colleagues and motivate them toward the new trend of educational reforms. At the end of my first year, I organized a science exhibit on the school campus without a budget. I did not get any campus support to implement the exhibit while my students were excited and proud of their displayed experiments. My American advisor, Dr. Clark Hubler, and I collected empty food cans, milk cartons, used small batteries, trashed electrical cords, etc. from the trash bins in the Long Bình military base for my students of physics and chemistry to construct their experiments. My students of natural sciences subjects prepared the experiments with their collection of locally grown plants and animals. Sadly, Dean Trần Văn Tấn did not attend the exhibit's opening ceremony. Fortunately, however, Dr. Nguyễn Duy Xuân, Cần Thơ University president, and later minister of education, happened to visit our science exhibit. He later sent me an invitation to join his faculty. I became a "suitcase professor" for his new Cần Thơ University.[2] There, I taught the same science in education course to introduce some innovations in teaching sciences. My advisor, Dr. Hubler, highly valued my innovative teaching with simple science experiments to motivate my students toward the new teaching and learning methods. At the end of his contract, my advisor returned to Ohio University and wrote a textbook, *Science for Children*. In his book, he described the experiments prepared by my students with simple materials that could be collected from the backyard, supermarkets, and even trash bins.[3] These experiments could be replicated in any school without the luxury of being equipped with a science lab. Even today, I still have a dream to implement this innovative method of teaching sciences with demonstrations by simple experiments in any high school in Vietnam. My dream continues to remain just that.

NATIONAL WARDS SCHOOLS

The first school of the National Wards School system was located in Tân Bình District, Saigon. At their peak, the National Wards Schools or Trường Quốc Gia Nghĩa Tử (QGNT, Schools for Children of the Nation or Children of Martyrs) followed the same academic study program and student performance evaluation method of a regular public school. However, in terms of administration, the school was under the Ministry of Defense when it first opened its doors at the end of 1963. Later, National Wards High Schools were administered by the Ministry of Veterans' Affairs. The Ministry of Defense nominated the QGNT administrators, whereas the Ministry of Education provided the schools with the civilian teaching faculty in charge of core curriculum.

Along with the increase of war casualties, more and more fallen soldiers' children needed National Wards Schools throughout the nation. In response to students' critical needs, the Ministry of Defense established more schools in addition to the first QGNT in Saigon, including Huế (1967), Đà Nẵng (1968), and Cần Thơ (1971). Only one elementary QGNT school was available in Biên Hòa in 1969. All QGNT schools formed the so-called Quốc Gia Nghĩa Tử Cuộc, later changed into Viện Quốc Gia Nghĩa Tử (Institute of Schools for Martyrs' Children).

The National Wards High Schools system was conceptualized and built under the First Republic. The construction of the first Saigon National Wards High School was completed in August 1963. In the beginning, Lieutenant Colonel Trương Khuê Quan introduced the concept of this school system to the Republic of Vietnam after his observation tour in Holland. He adopted the model of the "Pupille de la Nation" in France and applied this concept in South Vietnam as a means to boost soldiers' morale and to express gratitude to those who sacrificed their lives for Vietnam's freedom. The founders of QGNT schools actively sought funds from the private sector to establish this kind of school, which was reserved solely for children of fallen soldiers. To be qualified for free QGNT admissions and benefits, students had to be granted a certificate as "quốc gia nghĩa tử." QGNT students studied the same programs and took the same examinations as their counterparts in a public school. Moreover, students who passed high school diploma examinations in the categories above average (bình thứ), excellent (bình), and outstanding (ưu) were recruited to the leadership program sponsored by the American government. These Vietnamese students enjoyed free education in American universities through a USAID program. Over 90 percent of them successfully completed their training program and returned to serve their country.

When the very first QGNT school opened its doors in December 1963, I was among the first seven civilian teachers assigned to the campus. For ranking and promotion, we were under the evaluation of the Ministry of Education, while a school principal who was a military officer reported our daily activities to the Ministry of Veterans' Affairs. In every examination season, like teachers of any public high school, we also had to participate in the national examinations center to grade students who took the high school diploma national examination. In addition, we had to spend our annual summer vacation with QGNT students at the Junior Military Academy (Trường Thiếu Sinh Quân) in Vũng Tàu. We were busier than any other public school teachers, subject to double control by the Ministry of Education and the Ministry of Veterans Affairs, working in a very special environment with unique students. Yet, my teaching time at QGNT was the best in my career. There, I shared my love to students in the absence of their loved ones.

However, I did not stay at the QGNT school for too long. An American advisor and education consultant at QGNT school, Dr. Clark Hubler from Ohio University, suggested and sponsored my transfer from this school to the Faculty of Education. Earlier Dr. Hubler had observed my teaching method in a biology class. For a class demonstration of photosynthesis, which is the influence of light on plant growth, I brought in green onions growing in milk cartons with a small hole on the side. I asked students to develop questions and hypotheses. At the end of his observation session, Dr. Hubler showed me his written report to the Ministry of Education and told me that I should move to the Faculty of Education where a teacher of science in education was needed.

Thánh Mẫu Gia Định Catholic School

The Second Republic witnessed the rapid expansion of private schools. Up to then private schools were only for children of the elites, with the most popular schools being the Taberd French Catholic satellite schools for boys in Saigon, Huế, Đà Lạt, and Sóc Trăng; and for girls, Saint Paul School in Saigon, the Providence in Sóc Trăng, and Couvent des Oiseaux in Đà Lạt. These elite schools continued to follow the French system and recruited students mostly from middle- and upper-class families that could afford high tuition fees for their children.

Following the change in instructional media from French into Vietnamese in the Vietnamese system of education, the student population expanded exponentially. Existing public schools could not satisfy the community demands. As a result, public schools administered entrance examinations at the end of sixth and ninth grades to select only the top students. To meet rising demand, the MOE encouraged the development of private schools with fewer regulations applied to the establishment of a private school.[4] Thánh Mẫu Gia Định School, which I helped found and at which I taught, took advantage of the circumstance and opened its doors in 1964. As its name indicated, Trường Thánh Mẫu Gia Định (TMGĐ), a Catholic private school located on the land belonging to the Gia Định Church of Gia Định Province, joined the new system of Catholic schools. This unusual Catholic school was totally different from any traditional parochial school that had only grades 1, 2, and 3 mostly to prepare students for their first communion.

In January 1964, upon my return from America as a member of his parish, I had a meeting with Pastor Anthony Phùng Sanh, the half-Chinese pastor of Gia Định parish, to propose the development of his parochial school into a K–12 school open to students from all walks of life. Father Phùng Sanh and his associate, Father Louis Phạm Tấn Nẫm who later became associate bishop of Saigon Diocese, welcomed my proposal with great enthusiasm. Both agreed with the transformation of this parochial elementary school, sheltered in a one-story building with 120 students, into three three-story buildings offering K–12 classes to students of diverse backgrounds. Using his ethnic Chinese connections, the pastor had no problems securing financial support from Chinese entrepreneurs to build our ideal school in time for the school year of 1964–65. Students were male and female, Catholic and non-Catholic, rich and poor. Wealthy parents volunteered to cover the tuition costs for their children's poor friends. To recruit students, Father Phùng Sanh got a big help from his brother, Reverend Phùng Thành who was the bishop of Bình Dương Diocese. The bishop sent students from Thủ Dầu Một and Lái Thiêu to TMGĐ School by van. At the same time, Chinese entrepreneurs donated vans to transport students from Chợ Lớn to Gia Định. The presence of Catholic nuns in the dormitory staff and several priests in school teaching faculty and administration gained parents' trust and confidence, whereas their children proudly wore school uniforms with an insignia to distinguish them from their counterparts in other schools.

I was responsible for all activities to ensure academic achievements by students. Recruiting excellent part-time teachers from public schools to teach the core curriculum was my most important assignment. In exchange for attractive hourly wages, teachers had to commit and dedicate themselves to serve students wholeheartedly. According to the military service law under the Second Republic, any male between eighteen and forty was subject to the draft for military service. Young men could be exempted from military service if they passed the high school diploma examinations and continued with their higher education. Understanding how important it was for male students to pass the examinations, TMGĐ teachers committed ourselves to maximizing the examination passing rate. We volunteered to provide review sessions for students in need. In response to our teachers' dedication, our students performed outstandingly. In the first year, twenty-three out of twenty-five TMGĐ male students in mathematics class passed the examinations.[5] What a relief it was for both students and their parents! From its opening in 1964, TMGĐ's enrollment rate increased every year. After four years, the school enrollments reached the maximum capacity with fourteen thousand students. This number of enrollments remained stable until 1975.

TMGĐ also developed a new project with a budget already allocated for the establishment of a private community college in the Gia Định Church surroundings. Unfortunately the collapse of Saigon on April 30, 1975, made the prospect of the community college project collapse along with it.

Growth of New Public and Private Universities

In the first decade there were only three public universities in Saigon (established in 1955), Huế (established in 1957), and Cần Thơ (established in 1966). The only private college was Đà Lạt University, which was established in 1957 based on the Catholic Pius X Institute. It offered teacher training programs of French language and philosophy. The public universities enjoyed their independence and autonomy from the MOE in most aspects. The public universities recruited teaching faculty and developed study programs on their own. In addition, there were three professional institutions that over time transformed into specialized universities. These included the National Institute of Technology (established in 1957), which was the predecessor of Phú Thọ Polytechnic University; the National Agricultural Center (established in 1959), which in 1973 would become Thủ Đức University dedicated to the sciences of forestry, agriculture, and husbandry; and the National School of Administration. The last one was established in Đà Lạt in 1952, then transferred to Saigon in 1955 and became the National Institute of Administration.

By the 1960s the existing universities and schools could not accommodate the overwhelming number of students and their aspiration to pursue higher education. The rising demand for higher education came to be met by new private universities and public community colleges—both of which grew rapidly in the early 1970s. Religious sects were the major player in private universities. Following in the footsteps of Đà Lạt was Vạn Hạnh Buddhist University, which was established in 1964 in Saigon and which was the first to offer a major in journalism among other arts and humanities majors. In response to demands from the Catholic community in Saigon, Minh Đức University, sponsored by the Dominicans and Jesuit priests, came into existence in 1970. This university's school of traditional medicine became especially popular. In the Mekong Delta region, Hòa Hảo University was established in An Giang in 1971 and earned the reputation of a weekend university because it offered classes on weekends only. The majority of students on campus were government employees in the surrounding areas. As its name indicated, the university was supported by followers of the Hòa Hảo religious sect. In Tây Ninh, another church-supported university was founded in 1971 by leaders of the Cao Đài religious sect.

By 1971, the Ministry of Education recognized the important functions of community colleges to train needed specialists for the economic development of the nation (see also chapter 8 on the development of community colleges). Dr. Đỗ Bá Khê, vice minister in charge of higher and technical education (1971–75), should be credited as the founder of community colleges in Vietnam. Under his leadership, the three principal functions of a two-year community college were to screen students for a four-year university that could not accommodate the explosion of enrollments; to provide adults, especially returning veterans, with basic skills to work in the development of new technology; and to offer recreational programs to senior citizens who nowadays enjoyed a longer life and would need a higher quality of life.

In the beginning, in response to local communities' aspirations for affordable higher institutions for their children, Đại Học Cộng Đồng Duyên Hải (Duyên Hải

Community College) was established in Khánh Hòa to serve five provinces along the coast. Đại Học Cộng Đồng Tiền Giang (Tiền Giang Community College) in Mỹ Tho, situated in the Mekong Delta, was reserved for seven provinces. Later, two more communities colleges, Đà Nẵng and Vĩnh Long Community Colleges, were added to make the total number of four.

The rapid expansion of university education in the early 1970s quickly ran into the shortage of college teaching professionals. To partially remedy the situation, many new public and private universities simply borrowed lecturers from the more established universities. The cost of travel and accommodation for visiting professors was high, yet private universities could not charge very high tuition fees; otherwise, many parents would not be able to afford to pay. Quality was therefore a real concern. Only church-supported universities, which largely depended on the contributions of their congregations, could maintain their establishment with quality education.

The Reorganization of the Ministry of Education

The Ministry of Education and Training was expanded into the Ministry of Culture, Education, and Youth in June 1971. Its new name defined additional functions of the ministry, which gathered the Departments of Culture and Youth into the Office of Education under one minister.

Under the First Republic, private schools had already enjoyed much more independence and less control by the MOE than their public counterparts. However, some investors took advantage of the circumstances under which the ministry encouraged the development of private schools in response to the constant increased growth of student population. These investors sought to maximize profits from their investment by establishing private schools without sufficient concerns for the quality of education. They hired nonqualified teaching faculty who were willing to accept low wages. Learning was students' responsibility, and the schools did not monitor their daily attendance. The schools even created fraudulent student profiles to sell to those who wished to evade the military draft. To prevent these fraudulent cases, the ministry was determined to reorganize the MOE office to expand staff and increase supervision over private schools. Dr. Nguyễn Thanh Liêm, formerly vice minister of education, culture, and youth in charge of elementary and secondary education, assumed the responsibility to develop the reorganizational plan.

The MOE reorganization in October 1972 addressed other issues as well. One such issue was the friction between some military officers and local education administrators. On some occasions, certain military officers interfered in the administration of national examinations while students were taking the tests. In some districts and provinces, education officials reported about the pressure from military officers who directly intervened in school administration and the recruitment of staff. Fortunately, such incidents did not occur often. At the same time, examples of assistance to schools provided by local military leaders were numerous. Education inspector Đào Hữu Ngạn happily shared with me the best time in his career when he was the principal of a high school in Chợ Lách District of Vĩnh Long Province. In this district, many parents still struggled to survive daily. Sending their children to a high school in Vĩnh Long or Cần Thơ province remained a dream for poor parents. In response to the growth of students' needs, the principal solicited support from local military leaders. With great enthusiasm, they provided enough construction materials to build a five-classroom high school. In subsequent years, the officers in Chợ Lách continued to transport students to selected sites for their excursion project whenever requested.

Traditionally, education officials were not well respected locally because of their position and status given by the MOE. Prior to the reorganization, the system of education, including elementary and high school in the province, was under the director of the so-called Ty Tiểu Học, meaning "Elementary School Office." According to this old-fashioned organization born out of the French administrative system, the director himself was not familiar with high school administration, yet he supervised programs and activities of high schools as well. Following bureaucratic hierarchy, the Elementary School Office director reported the school activities and program directly to the chief of the province who was typically a military officer. Vice Minister Nguyễn Thanh Liêm corrected this problem through a new strategy. The Ministry of Culture, Education, and Youth (MCEY) followed the administrative model used in the army.

According to the new reorganizational plan, the MCEY minister nominated his representatives in each military region (I, II, III, and IV) of South Vietnam. The representatives worked directly with the regional military commanders and reported to the vice minister of education. In each province, the Elementary School Office became the Educational Administrative Department (Sở Học Chánh) whose director also supervised the local Offices of Culture, Education, and Youth. Educational Administrative Departments adopted an administrative structure similar to a school district in America. At this level, the department head was free of local civilian and military supervision and control, reporting directly to MCEY. In this case the head would enjoy more freedom and privileges in the development of schools and educational programs. Unfortunately, for political or financial reasons, the implementation of the reorganization plan and all four MOE representative positions were eliminated one year later. Educational Administrative Departments were demoted to Educational Administrative Offices (Ty Học Chánh, and later Ty Văn Hóa Giáo Dục) to be placed under the authority of the provincial military chief. In 1974, fifty Ty Văn Hóa Giáo Dục in forty-eight provinces and in two cities functioned until the end of the regime.

Post-1975 Coda

After 1975, the educational system in South Vietnam was radically reorganized to follow the Northern model. Universities lost their autonomy. Private colleges and schools were nationalized. The Communist government suspected that any church-supported school existed for political and religious purposes. They confiscated all the denominational schools, regardless of whether they were sponsored by the Catholic, Buddhist, or other churches. All church-supported schools could no longer enjoy the independence granted under the RVN. Like the Catholic Nguyễn Bá Tòng High School and Buddhist Bồ Đề School, the Catholic Thánh Mẫu Gia Định School became a public school.[6] The National Wards Schools were similarly turned into normal public schools.

The new government did not favorably consider community colleges because of their two-year college status versus a traditional, well-established four-year university. The concept of a community college sounded strange to the new education administrators. Their main function was initially even suspected of serving to supply secret information to the American government because of the term "community." In a later effort to understand the true concept and the functions of a community college, the Ministry of Education and Training (MOET) in Hanoi had my thesis on the development of community colleges translated into Vietnamese for its staff. The MOET also invited a French educator to assist it in better understanding the functions of American community colleges. Unfortunately, the education ministry staff learned the concept of American community colleges from the lecture delivered in French through an interpreter who was not familiar with the education field.

As a faculty member at California State University in Fullerton (CSUF), I was invited by a congressional delegation under Senator Art Torres to visit Vietnam in 1990 for the first time since I left as a refugee. My responsibility was to conduct a survey about educational needs in Vietnam. In 1991, I came back with a team of volunteer teachers from California State Fullerton, California State San Francisco, and Santa Ana College to offer one session of ESL training to teachers in North Vietnam and one in South Vietnam. I was invited to do a presentation on American community colleges for the MOET staff. The audience realized that until then, they had a misconception of what community colleges really were.

From then the relationship between CSUF, the Vietnam Ministry of Education, and national universities in Hanoi, Huế, and Saigon has been building. The first group of Vietnamese students had been on the CSUF campus in 1971 under the auspice of USAID. Based on this record, President Milton Gordon of CSUF would like to renew the university's assistance to the educational reforms in Vietnam. Meetings after meetings at the national Vietnamese universities and at CSUF since 1992, and after several Vietnamese university staff have received their master's degrees from CSUF and returned to Vietnam, and still no program of education has been adopted.[7] CSUF made tremendous efforts to introduce such a general education program required in American universities to Vietnamese universities since 1996; however, no program of general education has yet been implemented in Vietnam's national universities today.

Despite such difficulties currently facing educational reforms in Vietnam, I hope that the model of National Wards Schools will be reconsidered and reestablished for the benefits of Vietnam's veterans' families and their descendants both before and after 1975. When the communists took over, children of deceased RVN soldiers were expelled from QGNT schools and banned from high schools because of their parents' previous services against the North. Today, children of these unfortunate QGNT students should be compensated with the benefits that their parents had missed. In addition, though war ended more than forty years ago, a large number of young Vietnamese men are mandated to enlist in the army to defend the country. There should be some benefits to compensate the descendants of those who sacrificed their lives because of their patriotic duties. If this model of Quốc Gia Nghĩa Tử schools were reestablished, school administrators could solicit financial aid from within and outside Vietnam. People might be willing to provide veterans' children with free education and scholarships to pursue their education overseas.

If the QGNT schools can serve a national purpose, the case of Thánh Mẫu Gia Định School clearly illustrated the potentials of church-supported schools. Religious leaders, by their exemplary lives, could successfully solicit the business community's financial support for education development. Laws against the establishment of church-supported schools in Vietnam today should be overturned, and instead the establishment of more church-supported schools should be encouraged. The denominational schools are built not for profits but for the noble educational purpose only, that is, to provide quality education to children.

Notes

1 Nguyễn Thanh Liêm, *Giáo dục ở miền Nam tự do* [Education in free South Vietnam] (Santa Ana, CA: Le Van Duyet Foundation, 2006), 380. The author was a former vice minister of education.
2 The humorous term "suitcase professor" referred to visiting professors who had to regularly pack their suitcases and travel from their main campus to other universities per annual contracts.
3 Clark Hubler, *Science for Children*, 1st ed. (New York: Random House, 1974), esp. chap. 9.
4 For example, founders of a private school were not required to be educators themselves. Due to the lack of government staff, private schools were not so closely supervised by government-appointed superintendents.
5 Based on students' preference, the school offered mathematics classes for boys, and sciences and languages and arts classes for girls.
6 Ironically, while the school is public today, parents in fact are required to pay tuition fees.
7 I came back to Vietnam every year from 1990 until 2008 and attended every meeting when the CSUF president traveled to Vietnam. Dr. Dennis Berg, CSUF associate vice president for academic affairs, had been with me since 1991. In 2006, he received a fellowship, which was renewed every year until 2012, to provide assistance to the MOET in educational reforms. I met Dr. Berg in the Southeast Asian Ministers of Education Organization in 2012. He concluded about his work: "In regard of performing education reforms in Vietnam, I cannot even move a brick."

CHAPTER TEN

LIFE AND WORK OF A JOURNALIST

Phạm Trần

Phạm Trần is a veteran journalist with over fifty years of experience in this field. During his fifteen years of working as a journalist in the RVN, he covered the war and politics for various news organizations, including the government's Vietnam Press News Agency (VP, Việt nam Thông tấn xã). During his tenure with the VP, he was assigned to cover both RVN's top leaders, Nguyễn Văn Thiệu and Nguyễn Cao Kỳ. He also worked for the Voice of America (VOA) from Saigon to Washington for forty-four years until his recent retirement. He left Saigon for the United States just twenty-four hours before the city fell to communist forces on April 30, 1975. Since then, he has continued to use his spare time to write about Vietnam. He contributes his free-of-charge weekly columns to various Vietnamese-language newspapers and news organizations. His articles have been carried by eight websites: SBTN (the largest Vietnamese television station in the United States), Thông Luận, Dân Làm Báo, Đối Thoại, Việt Catholics News, Basam News, Tin Mừng Cho Người Nghèo (Dòng Chúa Cứu thế Sài Gòn), and Dân Quyền Việt Nam, which is managed by prominent Vietnamese intellectuals living in Vietnam.

In this chapter I hope to recount the major events and developments in the press scene in the Republic of Vietnam (RVN), to which I had the honor to contribute throughout fifteen years in the First Republic (1960–63) and the Second Republic (1963–75). In the conclusion, I will briefly discuss the Press Law and other forms of press control in today's communist Vietnam for the purpose of comparison.

THE FIRST REPUBLIC

Under the First Republic the press was controlled in two ways to keep it from opposing the government. First, the government gave newspapers coupons to buy newsprint at subsidized prices.[1] Next, all the newspapers had to work with the exclusive distributor Thống Nhất, a commercial entity under government control. Publishers did not dare practice journalism the way they wanted either for fear of losing the coupons to buy newsprint at a subsidized price or for fear of their newspapers not being distributed and sold.

Though newspapers were not censored up until the beginning of 1956, they were constrained by the administrative decrees forbidding them to "violate national security" or "create panic in public opinion." These two provisions were quite vague and caused the newspapers to operate in constant fear of being shut down.

The Ngô Đình Diệm government's policy to control the press was also reflected in Article 16 of the 1956 constitution, according to which "every citizen enjoys the freedom of speech. This right cannot be exercised to slander, libel, violate the public morale, incite rebellion, or overthrow the Republic." With this vague language in the law, the press in the nine years under Ngô Đình Diệm's rule did not have total freedom by the standard of the European or American press. Political parties were not allowed to develop either.

One of the most prominent newspapers in the first years of the republic was *Tự Do* (Freedom) daily (first edition as opposed to its second edition to be discussed below). This daily debuted in 1954 following the migration of nearly one million Northerners to the South. It was considered the voice of Northerners in the South, with contributions from noted Northern writers and journalists such as Tam Lang (Vũ Đình Chí), Mặc Thu (Lưu Đức Sinh), Mặc Đỗ (Đỗ Quang Bình), Vũ Khắc Khoan, Như Phong (Lê Văn Tiến), Nguyễn Hoạt (Hiếu Chân), Đinh Hùng (Hoài Điệp Thứ Lang, Thần Đăng), and Phạm Tăng. At first *Tự Do* enjoyed financial support from the International Rescue Committee, but it was later able to sustain itself with income from sales, subscriptions, and commercial ads. *Tự Do* was clearly anticommunist, but it was completely independent from the Ngô Đình Diệm government. For this the paper did not earn any favors from the government or its supporters.

The situation changed around 1956. According to the late Như Phong (Lê Văn Tiến), who was the editor of *Tự Do*, the newspaper was brought to court for publishing an editorial by Nguyễn Hoạt criticizing the government and cartoons by Phạm Tăng that made fun of Madame Ngô Đình Nhu and of the regime. Phạm Tăng was exonerated, but Nguyễn Hoạt and Mặc Thu were sentenced to three months in jail. Soon after *Tự Do* closed down and was transferred to the government.

Together with *Tự Do* (second edition), now under the editorship of Phạm Việt Tuyền and Kiều Văn Lân, the government also issued a second daily, *Cách Mạng Quốc Gia* (National revolution), which was the mouthpiece of the National Revolution Movement spearheaded by Ngô Đình Nhu, brother and advisor of President Diệm. These two dailies were directed and funded at the highest level by the Office of Political and Social Research, that is, the intelligence agency directed by Dr. Trần Kim Tuyến, an energetic collaborator of Ngô Đình Nhu and advisor to President Ngô Đình Diệm.

Seeing what happened to *Tự Do* (first edition), other newspapers became more cautious and focused on entertainment and profit to avoid any trouble with the government. They avoided publishing news about the activities of communist forces that had just emerged in the Mekong Delta and the provinces of Quảng Ngãi, Quảng Nam, and Bình Định in central Vietnam. They were similarly careful with news about the activities of political parties and religious organizations, especially in the case of Catholicism as this was the religion of the Ngô family, for fear for being charged with malicious intent to foster disputes or antireligion sentiments.

However, the government did allow *Thời Luận*, an opposition weekly newspaper published by Nghiêm Xuân Thiện, a former military governor of North Vietnam in 1948, to operate for three years from 1956 until 1958. *Thời Luận* was the only newspaper that dared to criticize illegal and antidemocratic policies and practices by the authorities, such as the persecution of the opposition. Most antigovernment articles in *Thời Luận* were authored by Trần Văn Tuyên under the pen names of Chính Nghĩa or XYZ. Tuyên was a prominent lawyer and a leader of the Vietnamese Nationalist Party

(VNP). In 1958, the authorities ordered plainclothes security personnel to raid *Thời Luận*'s office and arrest Nghiêm Xuân Thiện. He was charged with the crime of "using newspaper to slander the government" and sentenced to ten months in jail. *Thời Luận* was permanently shut down.

That was the political environment when I began my journalist career in 1960. By this time, the government of President Ngô Đình Diệm was being condemned as a dictatorship. Opposition parties were placed under close surveillance. There were only ten newspapers, all based in Saigon. Except the tabloids, which were not interested in politics, other newspapers had no choice but to toe the government's line.

If the role of journalists had been limited since 1956, our activities were even more restricted after April 26, 1960, when the so-called Caravelle Group issued its manifesto calling on President Diệm to change his policy and reform the government. This group, called "Caravelle" because its meetings were held in the Caravelle Hotel in downtown Saigon, comprised eighteen leading personalities who came from all three regions (southern, central, and northern Vietnam) and who styled themselves as "the free and progressive patriots." Many members of the group were former government officials, including former economy and planning minister Trần Văn Văn, former Saigon mayor Trần Văn Hương, former defense and education minister Phan Huy Quát, former agricultural minister Phan Khắc Sửu, former foreign minister Trần Văn Đỗ, and former information and propaganda minister Trần Văn Tuyên.

The issuance of the manifesto was a brave act at the time given that all power was in the hands of President Ngô Đình Diệm. The South Vietnamese press did not dare to comment on or exploit this event. Some newspapers even tried to curry favors with the government by quoting Ngô Đình Nhu, who derogatively labeled the Caravelle Group "salon and night club politicians." President Diệm did not accept this peaceful recommendation. All the eighteen signatories and some others were brought to a military tribunal for causing "public disorder." Yet the government later yielded to international pressure, and a military tribunal on July 11 and 12, 1960, unexpectedly acquitted all the defendants. Though the Caravelle Group had not much of an impact on the general population, President Diệm took the opportunity to tighten his control over political parties and the press. Newspaper publishers at the time always cautioned journalists to be careful in their reporting.

A few months later, on November 11, 1960, Airborne Colonel Nguyễn Chánh Thi and Lieutenant Colonel Vương Văn Đông staged an unsuccessful coup against President Diệm. Many politicians who had supported the coup were jailed and tried in court for "treason" and "violation of national security."[2] An oppressive atmosphere enveloped Saigon, but no journalist dared to speak up. The press was warier than ever vis-à-vis the regime. At the time many newspaper editors thought that they were "fish on the chopping block" whose heads could be cut off by the regime anytime.

A few months afterward on December 10, 1960, came the announcement about the birth of the National Front for the Liberation of the South, known as the National Liberation Front, that vowed to oppose the Ngô Đình Diệm regime and his American supporters. The whole world knew that North Vietnam supported this front and helped it organize, but the Saigon press dared not report this important political development and had to wait for the official commentary from the government calling this front "the lackey and offspring of communist North Vietnam." Those of us who were journalists at the time dared not report on what we knew and heard from international media such as the BBC, VOA, and Radio France International. Most of the news stories at the time came from the Office of the President or sourced from Vietnam Press, the official news agency of the government.

The oppressive atmosphere we lived in at the time returned to more or less normal until February 27, 1962, when two South Vietnamese Air Force pilots, Nguyễn Văn Cử and Phạm Phú Quốc, bombed the Independence Palace. A bomb fell onto President Diệm's office but failed to detonate. The bombing was an attempt to assassinate President Diệm and his family, but all escaped harm. At the time the private press was cautious and only published news issued by the authorities, who dismissed the bombers as two traitorous pilots acting alone. Most of us knew that Nguyễn Văn Cử, one of the pilots, wanted to avenge the recent arrest of his father, Nguyễn Văn Lực, a VNP leader who opposed the Ngô government.

Ngô Đình Diệm was overthrown in the bloody coup of November 1, 1963, staged by a group of generals led by Lieutenant General Dương Văn Minh and supported by the Kennedy administration. The coup caused a serious rift between Buddhists and Catholics because the coup leaders killed President Diệm and his brother Nhu after they had surrendered. Reflecting this political cleavage, the press at the time was divided into three camps: pro-Catholic, pro-Buddhist, and "the middle." I had the privilege to work with all three camps from 1964 until 1975 on account of my specialization in political and military affairs.

The Second Republic

Though the press was unshackled to celebrate the coup, it did not take long before editors and journalists clashed with the military junta and the successive governments installed by the military. A number of new newspapers emerged after the coup, but they were controlled or would soon be bought by the various political factions. The victorious Buddhist faction had four newspapers—*Hành Động* (Action), *Chánh Đạo* (The right path), *Đất Tổ* (Holy land), and *Lập Trường* (Position)—but they were mired in internal dissent. Leaders of the Buddhist faction were split into three groups, and their newspapers also reflected that split. The group from the northern region was led by Abbot Thích Tâm Châu. The head of the group based in the southern region was Abbot Thích Thiện Hoa. And the group of the central region had Abbots Thích Trí Quang and Thích Thiện Minh as their leaders.

The Catholic Church, though with only about five million followers in 1963, was very influential due to the support from the Vatican and to its more cohesive organization. Three famous anticommunist priests who had fled the North to go South in 1954 were Bishop Phạm Ngọc Chi, Bishop Lê Hữu Từ (once an advisor to Hồ Chí Minh), and Reverend Hoàng Quỳnh, the legendary leader of the anticommunist Catholic resistance in North Vietnam before 1954. These three formed a significant political force in opposition to the military junta and the Buddhist faction.

After the 1963 coup, in order to counter the influence of the Buddhist faction and protect Catholic interests, Reverend Nguyễn Quang Lãm founded the daily *Xây Dựng* (Construction) and Reverend Trần Du launched the daily *Hòa Bình* (Peace). The political group behind the two newspapers was an organization named League for Great Unity (Lực Lượng Đại Đoàn Kết) founded by engineer Nguyễn Gia Hiến.

From 1964 until 1965 the press in South Vietnam was very much controlled by the various semicivilian, semimilitary governments and was heavily influenced by the armed forces. Just three months after President Diệm had been overthrown and killed, South Vietnam spiraled into a constant turmoil following what was dubbed as the Readjustment Coup (Chỉnh Lý) engineered by Major General Nguyễn Khánh that ousted General Dương Văn Minh on January 30, 1964. However, General Khánh was too weak to survive. Two civilian prime ministers, Trần Văn Hương and Phan Huy Quát, came and went. To stabilize the situation the group of young generals led by Lieutenant General Nguyễn Văn Thiệu and Major General Nguyễn Cao Kỳ took over and ruled the country, starting on June 19, 1965.

A Constituent Assembly was elected on September 11, 1966, to draft a new constitution, ushering in the Second Republic on March 18, 1967. General elections were then held in October 1967 to elect members of the House of Representatives, the Senate, and the first president of the Second Republic. In the new 1967 constitution, freedom of thought, freedom of speech, freedom of the press and publication were stipulated in Article 12. Censorship was rejected except for films and theater.

In accordance with the provisions of the new constitution, President Nguyễn Văn Thiệu promulgated the Press Law 019/69 on December 30, 1969. This law was, and still is, the most progressive piece of legislation ever in Vietnamese history because it guaranteed almost an absolute freedom of the press. This law also ended all concerns that the press was controlled as it had been in the First Republic.

Law 019/69 in its entirety had only eight chapters and sixty-nine articles. In chapter 1, the law affirmed that

> freedom of the press is a basic right in the Republic of Vietnam. This freedom cannot be used in violation of personal honor, national security, and cultural decency. The government cannot close newspapers without a judicial decision. Censorship of the press is not accepted.

Although "national security" was a vague phrase, the authorities could not use administrative means to close a newspaper but had to take the case to a judge.

On the freedom to publish newspapers, chapter 2 stated,

> Individuals or legal persons with Vietnamese nationality can publish newspapers without having to seek permission, and all they have to do is to register with the Ministry of Information of the Republic of Vietnam. Besides their identity documents, publishers need provide only evidence of the chief manager and editor's education and journalistic experience, as well as their legally certified résumés.
>
> When the above documents are submitted, the Ministry of Information is obliged to immediately issue a temporary registration certificate and an official certificate within a month. If not, the reasons must be provided. If the provided reasons are not legitimate, the temporary certificate will become official. Cases of disputes may be appealed to the Administrative Appeals Court.

Foreigners also could publish newspapers, but they were required to apply for a permit from the minister of information in consultation with the minister of interior.

On the rights and responsibilities of the press, chapter 3 stipulated that "newspapers cannot be temporarily suspended or permanently terminated without authorization by the court." If the government believed that a newspaper had violated national security, public order, or cultural decency, it could confiscate the newspaper and bring the case to the court within eight days. If the court issued a ruling against the government, it must compensate the newspaper for its wrong action.

Pros and Cons of the Press Law

The Press Law 019/69 had a number of notable changes. On the positive side, newspapers could be self-published or published and distributed through companies of their choosing instead of going through the government-sanctioned exclusive distributor as under Ngô Đình Diệm. The publishers were only required to pay a deposit of 500,000 Vietnamese Đồng (US$2,714 at the 1969 exchange rate) to insure against frauds.

According to the law, "newspapers cannot be prosecuted for reporting on the meetings, hearings, and speeches by members of Parliament. They have the right to cite all sources and to criticize the government as long as that is not for the sake of propaganda." (At the time "propaganda" was understood as publishing or reporting news that benefited the communist enemy or created panic in society.) Thanks to the new law, the press in South Vietnam began to thrive with the highest level of freedom since the November 1, 1963, coup.

However, on the negative side, the government required newspapers to provide their content at least two hours before publication in order for the Ministry of Information (later changed to the Ministry of Mass Mobilization and Open Arms) to archive them. Though the law stated that newspapers were not to be censored, the ministry used this requirement to censor them. In many cases, upon receiving the newspapers, the ministry ordered the publishers to delete those texts, news, or articles that the government deemed as violating the Press Law or creating public disorder.

The majority of newspapers went along in those cases, which meant that the newspapers were published with blank spaces and the acronym TYĐB (*tự ý Đục bỏ* or voluntary deletions). However, newspapers controlled by the opposition sometimes refused to comply or sought to circumvent the requirement. They tried to publish and distribute their newspapers before the authorities had had a chance to order deletions.

An example was when some newspapers (see chapter 12 in this volume) published on September 9, 1974, a document called the "Indictment No. 1" issued by Father Thanh, a Catholic priest who had led a vigilante group to fight corruption. The indictment was directed against President Nguyễn Văn Thiệu, charging his government with corruption. Before their publication, the Ministry of Mass Mobilization and Open Arms had phoned the newspapers and warned them not to print the document because its content was a total fabrication. Those papers that printed the document were later confiscated. After 1975, no documents emerged that substantiated the indictment from Father Thanh.

The main shortcoming of the Press Law under President Thiệu was that the law made it easy to publish newspapers, and as such, it was difficult for the government to control. There were procommunist elements and even communist agents who could easily take control of some newspapers and use them with the intent to generate public resentment leading to support for the violent overthrow of the government.

The two papers that opposed President Nguyễn Văn Thiệu and the United States and openly supported General Dương Văn Minh, who would become the last president of the RVN, were *Tin Sáng* (Morning news) owned by Representative Ngô Công Đức and *Điện Tín* (Telegraph) owned by Senator Hồng Sơn Đông. After April 30, 1975, when North Vietnam took over South Vietnam, many employees of those two papers turned out to be communist agents disguised as journalists.

Because it was quite easy to publish a newspaper, the number of dailies went from around twenty-five in 1970 to an astonishing fifty in 1972, not including hundreds of weekly reviews and magazines. In the gradually worsening war environment, in 1972 the National Assembly passed a law giving President Thiệu special rights to rule, thus freeing him up to cope with the situation. President Thiệu submitted and the National Assembly passed Press Law 007/72 limiting the number of newspapers in circulation.

However, the law created problems for President Thiệu because most newspaper publishers did not have 20 million Đồng (about $50,000) to deposit as required by the law and were forced to shut down their businesses. The opposition newspaper, *Điện Tín*, still survived (besides the two government newspapers *Dân Chủ* and *Tin Sống* and a few commercial newspapers). As a result, 70 percent of journalists were laid off, not counting many other employees of the newspapers. For that reason, four organizations, including the Newspaper Publishers Association, the Association of Journalists, the South Vietnam Union of Journalists, and the Vietnam Journalist Union, staged a protest to oppose Press Law 007/72.

This protest, which received the support of many representatives and senators, took place on October 10, 1972, with the participation of a few hundred journalists, many of whom were famous or senior. Calling the protest Reporters Go Begging Day (Ngày Ký Giả Đi Ăn Mày), protesters, including myself, were dressed like beggars with conical straw hats on our heads and bags on our shoulders. We walked from the building that housed the Association of Journalists right in front of the House of Representatives Building, to the Bến Thành Market, and back. The march was about one kilometer, and we were greeted by many people along the way. Many vendors and merchants in the area walked up and offered food and water to support us. The march generated tremendous domestic and international attention and was evidence of a free press and lively civil society in South Vietnam at the time.

Freedom of the Press in the RVN in Comparative Perspective

Press Law 007/72 did not help strengthen the government's authority. On the contrary, it had helped the opposition, communist agents who had infiltrated the press, the government in the North, and its protégés in the National Liberation Front in the South to get more ammunition to attack the young democracy of the Second Republic. However, without the U.S. decision to scuttle and run out of South Vietnam, Press Law 007/72 would not have caused the collapse of the Second Republic.

The reason for my claim is that among more than fifty dailies by 1972, there were only four papers that were leaning to the communists and whose owners and backers considered themselves as "the people's platform" against the war and were willing to enter into a political coalition with the communists. Even in the final stage of the war there were no newspapers or political organizations that openly advocated for ending the war and forming a coalition government with the communists.

I lived and worked for fifteen years as a journalist in South Vietnam, going from an apprentice journalist in 1960 to a reporter and an editor before I had to leave Saigon in April 1975. South Vietnam was not 100 percent free as in Western democracies, but like my other colleagues, I was never ordered to write by anybody. We were not controlled when voicing our opinions, nor did we encounter difficulties in doing our job under the Second Republic.

Though small, the South Vietnamese press had four organizations to assist us in our work. They were the Newspaper Publishers Association (Hội Chủ Báo), Union of Southern Journalists (Nghiệp Đoàn Ký Giả Nam Việt, which was established in 1953), the Association of Journalists (Hội Ái Hữu Ký Giả), and the Vietnam Journalist Union (Nghiệp Đoàn Ký Giả Việt Nam) that was created in the 1970s and that had assembled the majority of media professionals of Northern origin. Also supporting us was the PEN organization (Hội Văn Bút Quốc Tế) made up of writers, poets, and artists worldwide.

During the twenty years of the RVN, we worked hard and fought to defend freedom and democracy, in particular the freedom of thought, press, and other basic political freedoms according to the UN charter, whereas in the North and in all of Vietnam after 1975, the Communist Party has monopolized power. More than 90 percent of the members of their National Assembly and local assemblies today are party members. In South Vietnam before April 1975, we had more than a dozen political parties that participated in more or less free elections from 1956 until 1971, when the last presidential and National Assembly elections were held.

To appreciate the level of freedom and democracy under the RVN, it is useful to turn to the issue of press freedom in Vietnam today for a comparative purpose. The most recently revised Press Law of the Socialist Republic of Vietnam, which was promulgated on April 5, 2016, and registered as Law 103/2016/QH13, has a total of sixty-one articles. It is possible to read just a few articles to know what kind of press Vietnam now has.[3] Article 4 of this law states:

1. Newspapers in the Socialist Republic of Vietnam are essential information tools in the daily life of the people. They are the mouthpieces of the party, of the government, of the political, cultural, trade organizations. They are also the forum of the people.
2. Newspapers have the following duties and rights:
   a) to accurately inform about the situation of the country and of the world in accordance with the interests of the country and the people;
   b) to propagandize and to disseminate information; to contribute to the building and safeguard of the line of the party, the policy and regulations of the government, and the achievements of the country and the world; to contribute to political stability and socioeconomic development; to raise social knowledge; to meet the healthy cultural needs of the people; to protect and develop the nation's beautiful traditions; to develop socialist democracy; to strengthen national unity; and to develop and defend our socialist Fatherland.

These two provisions were not part of the various laws and regulations governing the press in the RVN before April 1975. Then, we only had a few progovernment newspapers and the rest were privately owned. On the contrary, in communist Vietnam today there has never been a privately owned newspaper because the ruling party forbids private citizens to own and publish newspapers, just as the regime has never accepted political pluralism and a multiparty system.

The Vietnamese Communist Party gave itself the exclusive right to rule the country as exemplified in Article 4 of the constitution, revised in 2013. This revision states that "the Vietnamese Communist Party, the vanguard of the Vietnamese workers and people, loyal representatives of the interests of the working-class working people, and the whole nation, with Marxism-Leninism and Ho Chi Minh thought as our ideology, is the leading force of the government and society."

In our South Vietnam throughout the twenty years of our existence, the press never had to serve the ruling party and government. On the other hand, in Vietnam today, journalists, as stipulated in Article 25 of their Press Law, have the obligation to "protect party line and platform, government policies and laws; to discover, disseminate, and protect the positive elements; to prevent and counter all erroneous thoughts and actions."

According to the statistics from the Vietnam Ministry of Information and Communications, in 2017 there were more than 861 press organs, "of which 199 were print, 662 were magazines, 2 national news service, and 66 radio and TV stations."[4] There were 18,380 newspaper people with press cards and "approximately 5,000 reporters though working for newspapers but do not yet meet the criteria to be issued press cards." When no private citizen can publish newspapers, to whom do the more than eight hundred newspapers and magazines in Vietnam today belong? Article 14 of the Press Law states very clearly:

> Organizations belonging to the party, the government, political and social organizations, the trade union, religious organizations from the provincial or similar level up to the central level, that operate according to the law, can establish news organizations.

Government control over the media is enforced not only through ownership but also through personnel. All the organizations that are allowed to publish newspapers are led by high-level cadres of the ruling party.

Due to the lack of press freedom, the state-owned media can only report corruption if the relevant authorities allow. An example is the corruption involving the Taiwanese company Formosa Hà Tĩnh Steel Corporation, which discharged toxic chemicals into the ocean causing massive fish deaths along the coast of four provinces in central Vietnam in mid-2016. Reporters have not dared to investigate the case. Things were quite different in South Vietnam prior to April 1975. Our press did investigate and uncover many cases of corruption and crime by government officials. Readers of our newspapers cooperated closely with the press in all areas. Even though we had to fight a savage war and lost, members of the press like myself are still proud that we lived in freedom for twenty years.

Many scholars in communist Vietnam have now admitted that the regime was wrong in trying to destroy the liberal democratic values nurtured in South Vietnam. This account hopes to contribute to a better understanding of the press under the RVN that embodied some of those values.

Notes

1 It was a common practice for many newspapers to exaggerate their circulation to obtain more newsprint from the government at discounted prices than they would need. They then would resell the unused paper in the market for profit.
2 Nhất Linh Nguyễn Tường Tam, the founder of the Self-Reliance Literary Group in the 1930s who cofounded the Front for Popular Unity to support the coup, was placed under house arrest for more than two years. After the Special Military Tribunal Court summoned him on July 6, 1963, to be tried for his role in the coup, he committed suicide on July 7 instead of appearing in court. He was fifty-eight.
3 See "Luật Báo Chí" [Press Law], issued by the National Assembly, April 5, 2016, available at https://thuvienphapluat.vn/van-ban/Van-hoa-Xa-hoi/Luat-Bao-chi-2016-280645.aspx.
4 Trương Minh Tuấn, "Quy hoạch, sắp xếp lại hệ thống báo chí, đáp ứng yêu cầu phát triển, bảo đảm thiết thực hiệu quả" [Reorganizing the media to meet demand for growth while guaranteeing effectiveness], Tạp chí Cộng sản [Communist review], September 13, 2017, http://www.tapchicongsan.org.vn/Home/PrintStory.aspx?distribution=46890&print=true.

Chapter Eleven

The Vietnam War in the Eyes of a Vietnamese War Correspondent

Vũ Thanh Thủy

Vũ Thanh Thủy, a Silver Star–awarded war correspondent in the RVN, became a fugitive living underground for two years after helping her fellow journalist husband escape from a reeducation camp. Fleeing Vietnam by boat and facing atrocities at sea, the couple made international headlines when they joined the multination efforts to rescue more than three thousand boat people in the South China Sea. During her subsequent thirteen-year stay at the San Diego Union-Tribune, *Thủy's personal and professional achievements earned her multiple awards, including "21st Century Woman Award" by the National Organization for Women in 1987; an honorary doctorate by Marist College in 1988; "Woman of the Year 1987" by the San Diego Press Club; and "2006 Lifetime Achievement Award" by the Asian American Journalist Association. Thủy and her husband founded Mass Media Inc. in 1999 and turned Radio Saigon Houston KREH 900AM, an operation of five employees, into a corporation that now employs thirty-five staff members and seventy contributing programmers. Radio Saigon Houston has expanded to include Saigon Directory, Saigon Weekly News, Radio Saigon Dallas—KTXV 890AM, and Saigon Network Television SGN-TV. Thủy currently serves on several boards, including the San Francisco–based New America Media, the New York–based Images and Voices of Hope, and Houston's American Red Cross.*

As a war correspondent in South Vietnam, my first frontline assignment was the battlefields of Cambodia in April 1970. Then I covered An Lộc in 1972 when it was under siege. And I walked on the Boulevard of Horror in Quảng Trị, witnessing thousands of South Vietnamese civilians killed instantly by North Vietnamese artillery covering up the two-kilometer stretch of National Highway One in the summer of 1972.

At twenty years old, I was awarded the Silver Star by the Republic of Vietnam's Armed Forces (ARVN) for bravery. But I really had no idea what true courage was. At the Cambodian frontlines, when sitting together on top of an M-113 tank amid enemy shellings, I met the famous war reporter Oriana Fallaci, who laughed at my youthful fearlessness and warned me, "Wait till you're older."

Five years later, at twenty-five, I found out how right she was when my country collapsed on April 30, 1975. I aged overnight. With millions of other South Vietnamese subjected to life under communism, brutality in "reeducation camps," or death in the open waters of the South China Sea, I came to know the pain of true courage. I faced persecution, imprisonment, and life as a fugitive in my own country for four years. When I finally escaped by boat, I thought I was free. Instead, I drifted at sea, ignored by every ship except pirate boats, which towed us to a deserted island in the Gulf of Thailand where we were victimized for twenty-one days.

In the face of such daily indignities, what did courage come to mean to me? When I finally reached freedom, courage meant that I dared to open up to share with the world the injustices my people endured as well as the goodness that persevered in the human heart despite great odds. To me, courage is the determination to tell the truth, to spare no details of the lowest depths of evil or the highest hopes of humanity. This is true journalism as I understand it.

In this chapter I will first share my personal experience as a war correspondent and a journalist employed in both government and private media in South Vietnam. Next, I will turn to the biases of the American media that affected the outcome of the war. Many foreign correspondents have spoken and written about the Vietnam War. But no matter how long they covered the war, nor how much they came to know the country, the war could never penetrate their soul in the same way as it did a son or daughter of Vietnam. I hope my perspective will offer a different view of the war than what was portrayed in the mainstream international media.

South Vietnam's War Correspondents

In the RVN, journalists who worked for government and private media were professionally untrained. Southern universities did not have journalism majors until the end of the 1960s (see chapter 9 in this volume). By the time the first generation of accredited journalists graduated, the war had almost ended.

Most South Vietnamese reporters were self taught on the job, attracted to the field by natural talent coupled with strong work ethics, not unlike famous American reporters such as Peter Jennings, Walter Cronkite, Oprah Winfrey, and Larry King, among others. I remember watching the movie *Teacher's Pet* in which Clark Gable played a managing editor of a New York paper who was very much against academic journalism. The only real training was on the field.

That being said, for every good reporter, there were also not so good ones. But thanks to the influence of Taoism, which instilled a sense of integrity and loyalty to family and country, the RVN media in the 1970s for the most part did not violate journalist ethics such as making things up or plagiarism to get published. There was an honor code among RVN's reporters.

Likewise, the operations were straightforward and equipment basic at best. My Western colleagues had sophisticated communication tools, transportation, and accessories. They seemed to have unlimited resources and financial support for expenses. We, South Vietnam's war reporters, had to make do with what little we had.

I used an old Uher recording machine like those in World War II movies. It was bulky and weighed over ten pounds. Because we worked with such limited resources, we were always on the move. We could not stay at the front line for very long because there was no equipment to send our reports back to the office. We had to physically deliver our reports every few days, traveling back and forth between the home base and the front line. There were times I had to hitchhike or talk my way back and forth. Instead of expensive gear, we relied on our social skills and blind luck to get our reports printed or broadcast on schedule. So you can forget about "breaking news" with us. We worked on a shoestring budget or out of our own pocket. Hotels and organized transportation were a luxury.

For that reason, many of my colleagues did subcontract work for the foreign media who covered the same fields to survive. They sold information or pictures and were paid a flat rate with no byline or credit. A foreign reporter would give a Vietnamese reporter a camera, usually a fancy Nikon with a dozen rolls of film. For every roll returned, they would receive 500 Đồng, which was about $1.50 for twenty-four prints. Sometimes my colleagues would exchange their labor for transportation or transmitting their reports home. The American news agencies rarely gave their Vietnamese subcontracted reporters or photojournalists official acknowledgment because they were unknown to the agencies. I always wondered who really took the iconic pictures of the war.

Looking back, I am amazed to have survived that period with nothing other than my youthful wits and the goodwill of those around me. Why did we do it? Why did I, a civilian female reporter, give up my city beat to risk my life at the front lines? The answer is simple: I believed the RVN needed its truth to be told. I needed to hear it, and there were not too many people around telling it. The Southern voice needed to be heard by locals from locals. And because the job was increasingly dangerous, those of us who persevered did so also to honor our fallen colleagues so their deaths would not be in vain.

I was deeply entrenched in the Southern media community but also an outsider in many ways because I was female and because I was more comfortable with foreigners. As a young journalist, I looked up to the seasoned foreign reporters. But looking back, I wondered whether they took me under their wing because they liked me personally, or was it because it was part of their job to get to know the Vietnamese perspective firsthand? Many of the foreign press did not have the opportunity to build a relationship that could better inform them of our point of view.

Battlefield Observations

Growing up in a war-torn country, I was devoted to understanding why my beloved Vietnam was at war. It was a personal duty to accurately report the experience I saw and heard throughout the country. When freedom is on the line, there is no time for fancy edits or second guessing. Everything happened very fast at the front, and the truth was the only way to keep up with constantly changing events.

The defining theme on the front lines was courage. The resilient strength of many leading generals of the ARVN was matched by the sheer patriotism of privates. In 1970, when communist forces used the Cambodian border as shelter to lead attacks into South Vietnam, I witnessed on many occasions the three-star general Đỗ Cao Trí, the commander of the Third Corps and Military Zone of Vietnam, keep the line time and time again by ordering his helicopter to land so he could jump on a tank to join a unit in combat.

Once, when a soldier next to him was wounded, General Trí rose to his feet on an M-113 tank to lead the convoy straight into the jungle from where the shot had come. His courageous, aggressive, and hands-on leadership style forged a bond with his soldiers and inspired them to keep their spirits up during the lowest of times.

I witnessed the emotional effect the death of General Nguyễn Viết Thanh, commander of the Fourth Corps and Military Zone, had on the soldiers when his helicopter went down over the front lines. I saw firsthand how South Vietnam mourned the death of General Đỗ Cao Trí, whose helicopter exploded on his way to battlefields in Cambodia. The general was killed along with his commanding staff and the *Newsweek* bureau chief Francois Sully, who had taken my seat on the helicopter when I had to cancel the trip at the last minute.

But most importantly are the unsung heroes I met at the front lines that reflected the strength of Vietnam's sons and daughters. From one soldier taking a shot for another and others risking their lives for their brothers in arms, I began to see a pattern of extraordinary acts of ordinary men. Fighting required not only courage to overcome the fear of death, but dignity to live with the fear. Serving on the front lines was beyond an abstract sense of patriotism. As soldiers developed reciprocal loyalty to each other in the face of death, the experience became very personal.

As a witness to such heroism, I get angry when foreign press dub the ARVN as "a puppet army." No puppet army could produce so many heroes that have cemented the legacy of the South. These heroes gave me the courage to face death in order to keep reporting. If I was killed on the front lines, I knew I would be among good company for a noble cause.

I do not understand why something that was so obvious to us Vietnamese could have been so hard for the American press to understand. One only needs to look at the pictures from the war to understand the relationship between an army and the people. In every picture, Southerners always ran *away* from the communists and toward the ARVN.

In the picture my frontline colleague Nick Ut took one can see a naked girl running away from the fighting toward the Southern troops. This iconic picture was awarded the Pulitzer Prize and came to represent the war to the American antiwar movement. But what exactly did it represent? It clearly shows some Vietnamese children terrified of the bombings and desperately running toward South Vietnamese troops for help.

Another picture of the mass killing on the Boulevard of Horror in Quảng Trị in 1972 shows the same thing: tens of thousands of people forming a human snake on Highway One to flee North Vietnamese troops. Unfortunately, the mass exodus made them sitting targets for their artillery. I was there to see the damage inflicted by the so-called People's Army under Võ Nguyên Giáp's leadership that massacred about five thousand civilians. These citizens of Quảng Trị risked instant death to flee from Northern forces. That does not paint a picture of people welcoming "liberators" but of people willing to die rather than live with the enemy.

Vietnamese people have a long-standing tradition of being attached to one's hometown, of staying on one's land, and of taking care of one's ancestral graves. Throughout Vietnam's history, there were no stories of mass exoduses from one's homeland until the communists took over the North. After 1975, when Hanoi took over the South, Southerners did not celebrate the "unification" of Vietnam. Instead, millions risked death to escape the country on foot, by sea, or by any means possible. The ignorance and antiwar bias of the foreign press and public haunt me and hurt me even today. As a journalist, it was my professional duty to report the facts. But as an older person, I owe it to myself to express my feelings. They affect me as much today as they did decades ago.

Last year in April, there was a Summit on the Vietnam War in Austin to commemorate the forty-fifth anniversary of the LBJ Presidential Library at the University of Texas at Austin. Who was present? John Kerry, Henry Kissinger, Ken Burns, Tom Hayden, Dan Rather, Peter Arnett, Peter Yarrow, and Phạm Quang Vinh, the ambassador of Vietnam. There was no representative of the large community of three million freedom-seeking Vietnamese refugees. There was no trace of the alliance between

South Vietnam and America. There was no mention of the Army of South Vietnam, as if it never existed.

Most of the talks were about the antiwar movement that caused the South to lose the war. I sat there, listening to the speakers, with a heart-wrenching pain that transported me back to the 1960s and 1970s. It was the same one-sided rhetoric all over again. The real winners were those in the antiwar movement, who emotionally and with pride recalled their efforts to end the war by abandoning South Vietnam to the communist North.

Even now, after forty-one years of hard evidence of communist war crimes and violations of human rights after the war, American media still do not acknowledge the RVN or its soldiers. There is a memorial wall in Washington D.C. to honor the fifty-eight thousand Americans who died in Vietnam. But the hundreds of thousands of South Vietnamese soldiers who died to protect democracy alongside Americans soldiers were ignored then and continue to be dismissed even now.

My observations on the physical battlefield then remain true about the historical battlefield of today: the truth presented to the public is a selective truth that favors one perspective while ignoring others. When voices are silenced, or remain silent, the loud voices become history itself.

South Vietnamese Media

The press in South Vietnam included government, private (Vietnamese), and foreign media. While being a war correspondent, for four years before the fall of Saigon in 1975, I also worked for the Voice of Freedom (VOF), a government-funded media that targeted Northerners. I believe our work was very effective, to the point that three other radio stations with a similar format were formed.

Based on feedback from deserted Việt Cộng and captured prisoners of war, the four stations reached many listeners in the North. Each station had a slightly different approach but shared the same goal of honoring the democratic ideals of the free state of the RVN. Each station featured the easygoing, comfortable lifestyle of Southerners who enjoyed private ownership in a free market in comparison with the restrictive nature of life under communism.

Although Northern officials denounced the stations as full of propagandist lies, the broadcasts succeeded in exposing the Việt Cộng, whose most powerful appeal to the poor population that made up the majority of their followers was the notion that the South was being liberated from foreign control and evil influences like capitalism and the unfair distribution of wealth.

At VOF, we also broadcast live reports of Việt Cộng killing civilians and destroying villages in Huế, An Lộc, and Quảng Trị. Reporters interviewed survivors who were driven from their homes, undermining the communist propaganda machine that claimed Southerners welcomed the Việt Cộng as saviors and heroes.

Further confirming the station's effectiveness were the testimonies of communist prisoners of war, who admitted that they and their families secretly listened to Southern radio stations. They wanted to learn about the world outside the communist iron curtain and the fate of their loved ones who were drafted by Hanoi to go to war in the South. Communist officials never informed their people of where their troops were or what happened to them. But our stations provided a daily list of the names of those Việt Cộng who were captured or killed in battles in the South and whose identities could be found.

For political and security reasons, the RVN government implemented a system of censorship over (Vietnamese) private newspapers. This system was under the control of the Ministry of Information led for some years by Mr. Hoàng Đức Nhã (see chapter 12 in this volume). Before going to print, all draft copies had to be submitted to the censorship bureau to be screened and approved. If any information was found to be harmful to national security or to benefit the communists, the article would be deleted, leaving a blank white space on the front page. By then, it would be too late to get another story approved, so the papers had to print as is.

By the end of the 1960s leading into the 1970s, it was common practice for Southern daily newspapers to have big white spaces in the middle of the front page labeled "voluntarily deleted." Sometimes, an entire circulation would be pulled and confiscated by the censorship bureau if there were too many unapproved articles. In wartime Vietnam, publishers accepted such financial loss and journalists swallowed their pride as part of the effort to protect the national security, but they occasionally sued the government or organized protests if the reasons for censorship had to do with politics.

The sad fact was the RVN government could control only the Vietnamese media, not the Western press. Contrary to censorship, the United States granted international news crews complete access to the battlefields in South Vietnam. ABC's former war correspondent Tim Bowden said, "The US strategy was to say, 'look, anybody can come in and see what great things we're doing for the Vietnamese people and attacking the communists.'"[1] This open approach turned out to be, in Bowden's words, "an utter disaster" that I will explain more below. I do not agree with a government-controlled media, but I do think the South would have benefited from stricter screening and monitoring of journalists. There were many communist spies disguised as reporters who took advantage of the free press in South Vietnam to misinform and influence the public. Their most devastating tactic was to befriend the foreign press and Central Intelligence Agency (CIA) officials to smear the RVN and to turn the Western world against the war.

Larry Berman wrote a book called *Perfect Spy* about Phạm Xuân Ẩn, a *Time* magazine and Reuters reporter who was actually a high-ranking communist agent working undercover for two decades. We all knew him in the South, and it is shocking that he was able to do so much damage in Saigon without being exposed, even by his "friends" at the CIA.

Ẩn befriended famous foreign correspondents, such as David Halberstam and Neil Sheehan, and high-ranking American advisors in South Vietnam, such as the CIA's William Colby and Colonel Edward Lansdale. American strategists who came to work in Saigon would look for Ẩn for information. In return, Ẩn gained access to high-security documents. His reports were so accurate that Hanoi's general Võ Nguyên Giáp would joke about "sitting in the U.S. war room."[2]

Spies like Phạm Xuân Ẩn were able to achieve power and influence over the American media because the South did not manage the media as it should have. It scares me to wonder how many other communist agents there were in our midst. The RVN's adoption of free speech rights for journalists caused much harm by opening the door to the enemy. But again, it would have been impossible for the RVN to have any control over the foreign press.

The American Media and the War

In general, the American media never understood the war the way we South Vietnamese did. In their eyes it was a war, first, between Saigon and Hanoi, then later between Hanoi and Washington. To us Vietnamese, it was beyond a civil war ignited by conflicting ways of life. It was much bigger than that: Hanoi was in fact an arm of the Cold War financed by the Soviet and Chinese governments pushing to expand communism.

At the time, the American press underplayed the Soviet and Chinese role in the war, and the world was under the impression it was a civil war between the North and the South. But we Vietnamese journalists often reported that it was Russian antiaircraft crews that shot down American and South Vietnamese pilots every day. We were not wrong. Reputable sources since the end of the war show that around 3,000 Soviet personnel served in North Vietnam in the 1960s and were responsible for shooting down many U.S. planes. Between 1965 and 1971, more than 320,000 Chinese troops were deployed to the North. At one point, there were 170,000 Chinese soldiers in North Vietnam.[3]

The American press overlooked the global nature of the war. Based on my honest and humble observations, at every battlefield I covered, the single clearest impression was the Southern soldiers' love of their country. Their love was unmatched, and their commitment was unwavering. The reason was simple: the South did not choose to fight. But when forced to, they fought with all their hearts to their deaths to defend their homes, loved ones, and national ideals.

In contrast, the Northern leadership waged a war against the South in part to spread global communism. Hồ Chí Minh emphasized this agenda in one of his speeches: "Our fight against the U.S. and victory over it is not only for our Fatherland's independence and freedom but also for the interests of our [socialist] camp, for all the oppressed people and progressive mankind."[4] Northern publications idolized Marx, Lenin, and Stalin. One of Hanoi's famous poets, Tố Hữu, wrote a poem entitled "Remember You Forever" on the occasion of Stalin's death on May 3, 1953. For many years the poem became part of the curriculum in grade schools throughout North Vietnam, and children were taught to revere Stalin. There was no such agenda in any Southern textbook or teaching, no praising of foreigners, not even our American allies.

The Vietnam War was the first televised war, so it comes as no surprise that the media's influence became a political force never before seen. By then, almost every American household had a television set around which families gathered. Imagine the impact of watching horrific images of real soldiers on the battlefields or tragic casualties of war night after night. Such raw footage had never before been shown to such a wide audience in such detail or frequency.

To watch a war unfold *live* was almost worst than being in it. When I was on the front lines, the realities of war were terrible, but it was tempered by the frantic pace to survive, the unwavering sense of solidarity, the energy of fighting for something noble, and the willingness to die for your loved ones and for your cause. When I was really there, I felt no fear, only a sense of being alive and having something worth believing in, something we could collectively stand behind. I never felt alone.

But when I saw the same images on TV in the comfort of my family's living room, with food and warm beds nearby or the sound of children playing outside, the fear of death and destruction was unbearable. To see live footage of hell while sitting in heaven, to watch the faces of young brothers desperately fighting for their lives or committing unspeakable acts in order to survive, one would be driven to take action. How could one not? How could anyone shut off the television and go about their lives in a normal manner? Unlike on the front line, where I would fall into an exhausted sleep, at home I would stay up all night, feeling tormented, alone, and guilty for not doing more.

The above-mentioned "utter disaster" Bowden spoke of was the U.S. government pandering to the public by opening the doors to the press, hoping for good publicity. That backfired horribly. The press not only made U.S. involvement in the war look bad but also turned the American public against its government and its soldiers. In the view of Ronald Boon who was a producer at CBS for twenty-two years, Walter Cronkite's reporting, after he became convinced the United States would lose in Vietnam, had the effect of a call to action for the antiwar movement in American government and society. I agree with Boon's opinion that the media influenced not only public opinion but also the outcome of the war. It is my professional belief that the United States triggered the fall of Saigon by first granting the press near-reckless access to the war, then submitting under the pressure of the media's biased and sensationalist stories' effect on the American public.

I do not attribute the fall of my country to American citizens involved in the antiwar movement. I might react in the same way under the same circumstances. But I do attribute the loss of the war to the media's recklessly and irresponsibly sensational reporting. There is a saying that "bad news makes good news." It is human nature for the public to pay more attention to sensational news. And it was sensational reporting that led to the RVN losing the war.

The alliance between the United States and South Vietnam made it a fair fight against the North, which was backed by Russia and China and their vast resources. Negative reporting by the press and the antiwar movement in the United States contributed to the "Vietnamization" policy to end U.S. involvement in the war. Although President Richard Nixon promised that the United States would continue to provide war supplies, that promise was eventually broken and the scales were tipped in the North's favor. The South standing alone against the North, the Russians, and the Chinese was a David-versus-Goliath scenario. The American media-triggered retreat effectively left David without a stone to throw.

American Media's Biases

As a South Vietnamese correspondent, what upset me the most was the ironic prejudice of the American media, who clearly favored the enemy. When the communists violated agreements or broke rules of war, they ignored it or glorified their senseless acts of destruction. On the other hand, they seemed to dig for every mistake made by American GIs or ARVN soldiers and blow it out of proportion.

One of the more notorious events that even a staunch supporter of the war could not stomach was when the Việt Cộng employed one of their favorite tactics: shooting at American troops, then running into a village. The troops would follow the shooter and, in a heat of rage, kill villagers that they thought were communists. Although military courts did their due diligence, such as convicting Lieutenant William Calley, the commander involved at Mỹ Lai, the antiwar movement presented such actions as common practice. Biased reporting made it seem like all American GIs were ruthlessly storming into villages to slaughter innocent people.

Likewise, the world saw the picture of General Nguyễn Ngọc Loan, the commander of the RVN Police, who executed a Việt Cộng prisoner in Chợ Lớn during the Tết Offensive in 1968. Again, the image planted the seed that the ARVN routinely killed POWs. What was left unsaid in the image was the fact that General Loan had just witnessed the Việt Cộng murder the wife and four small children of one of his men.

Although both events involved wrongdoing by both sides, only one side of the story stuck as the images were shown over and over on American television screens and reprinted in publications nationwide. Such biased reporting incited the antiwar movement and generated disdain for ARVN soldiers and American GIs. The media became judge and jury, condemning such cases as representative of the war and calling for the U.S. government to withdraw its troops.

This is not to imply that American journalists reported lies or intentionally ignored the truth. The stories and images presented to the American public did in fact happen, but they were accurate only to a point. They painted a one-sided picture, ignoring the other side of the story. But the problem was not journalists themselves but the media as a collective. I personally knew Western reporters who worked very hard to do proper research and to spend real time with Southern soldiers, reporters, and experts in order to share both sides of the story. Their reports included the ARVN perspective and highlighted their bravery and sacrifice. But once their reports left Vietnam, they never made it to the American papers or prime time. Editors sitting in their offices far away from the battles would toss such reports in favor of images or stories that fed into the antiwar movement. Such stories would run and images would play over and over like an endless loop. The result was not unlike the result of communist propaganda: to convince the public that that singular message alone was fact, isolated from its circumstances. When one piece of the puzzle is blown out of proportion, the big picture gets lost.

I make no excuses for incidents such as Mỹ Lai, which illustrates the worst of war for sure. However, I question why these events and images were invoked whenever the Vietnam War was mentioned. Why not the mass graves of civilians in Huế during the Tết Offensive of 1968 when the communists took over Huế for four weeks? Does the world know about the shelling of an elementary school in Cai Lậy, Tiền Giang, where communist artillery killed hundreds of children in 1974? I remember how horrified I was to hear about the shootings at Sandy Hook. The deaths of the innocents shocked the nation for weeks. But few foreigners inside Vietnam had ever heard of the students in Cai Lậy. The American media was certainly aware of such events but chose not to bombard the public with them. The stand the U.S. media took hurt us South Vietnamese very deeply.

Imagine that the media treated Nazis as patriotic underdogs willing to die for their nation, and ignored the gas chambers killing millions of innocent people and millions of others who were condemned in concentration camps? Or treated the terrorists of 9/11 as heroes, willing to sacrifice themselves for their cause, and ignored the innocent victims? These analogies may seem extreme, but to Vietnamese people who fought against communism, it cuts us *that* deeply.

The tendency of the American media to glorify enemy soldiers can be observed in their seeming obsession with communist fanaticism, focusing extensively on communist soldiers who chained themselves to tanks or cannons. They romanticized such acts as heroic and patriotic. I could not understand why they were enamored with the communists who threw their lives away so easily and yet ignored the Southern soldiers who fought hard every day to follow the rules of engagement and to defend their country honorably.

We Vietnamese reporters who spent time with Southern soldiers or directly interviewed Việt Cộng POWs knew the truth. Our interviews with the POWs suggested how Hồ Chí Minh and his party used misinformation and propaganda to control their soldiers, giving them no choice but to blindly follow orders. They became dispensable tools, horses with blinders on moving along to the whip of their masters—the communist officials. There was nothing heroic about people willing to manipulate men into death. The truth was a sad one: poor and uninformed people were manipulated and exploited to further the communist agenda.

During my years covering the front lines, I had seen other foreign correspondents, European, Asian, and Australian, following the South Vietnamese soldiers at the front lines, but I rarely saw American press covering the ARVN troops long enough to understand their devotion or to witness their fighting spirit. Instead, I did witness the U.S. press paying more attention to what should have been our common enemy: the communist soldiers.

Because it was Vietnamese fighting Vietnamese, it was difficult at times to distinguish who was who and who was fighting for what. Perhaps it required too much of an investment to penetrate the surface similarities between the North and the South. Perhaps it was easier to appeal to readers and viewers with sensationalism. To research history and interview experts may have been less saleable than adopting sound bites.

Also, another reason for the bad press was that foreign reporters had daily deadlines to meet. Under pressure to provide stories, they sometimes did not have time to fact check. Furthermore, once the stories were published, retractions were unheard of. Corrections put reputations on the line and required a great deal of integrity, courage, and humility. Most mistakes were left as is and sometimes repeated or picked up in other reports. There was no going back; it was hard enough to keep up with the breakneck pace of the war. Remember CBS's Dan Rather who neglected to double-check the fake document about President George W. Bush and was too proud to admit his mistake? Or NBC's Brian Williams, who exaggerated his war story and lost his job because the little lie quickly grew too big to contain?

As a young correspondent in the 1970s, I had great respect and admiration for the Western media and tried to learn from them as much as I could. Never once did I suspect the American press of corruption. As I got older, I continued to be bothered by the negative stories that cost us the war. My subsequent research revealed that journalists were not above accepting bribes. According to an investigative report by *USA Today* in 2005, the Bush administration used the national budget to pay hundreds of thousands of dollars to famous editorial writers, such as Armstrong Williams, Maggie Gallagher, and Michael McManus, to publish articles supporting Bush's No Child Left Behind and marriage initiatives. If high-ranking journalists could be bribed to write for money under modern notions of transparency and threat of exposure by citizen journalists on the Internet or by social media, then could the same have been true of journalists during the Vietnam War? Did politicians or antiwar leaders bribe editors and editorial writers to push their agenda?

What Journalism Is All About

U.S. senator Hiram Johnson said in 1917 that "the first casualty when war comes is truth." This implies people whose duty it is to present facts may have a conflict of interest between that duty and their personal opinions. As a Southern Vietnamese war correspondent, I did not find that to be true. I never felt conflicted. My editors never told me to report in a certain way. My job description never included a duty to support the war or government policy. I needed no agenda, no directive to keep up morale for the troops, society, or anyone else.

I, along with my Vietnamese colleagues in South Vietnam, only needed to tell the truth. We had no need of propaganda. There was no conflict of interest between my professional duty to report the truth and my personal duty to serve my country. Unfortunately, when it came to the foreign press, our truth became the casualty of war as had been warned by Senator Johnson.

Courage, to me, now means I must dare to tell the world about the injustice my people endured, as well as the good that prevailed in their hearts. So I will continue to be brave and to do my job as a journalist by speaking up for those whose voices were and are still silenced. Isn't that what journalism is all about?

Notes

1 See "Long Tan: The Vietnam War through the Eyes of War Correspondents," Australian Broadcasting Corporation, August 18, 2016, http://www.abc.net.au/news/2016-08-18/long-tan-vietnam-war-through-the-eyes-of-correspondents/7748916.
2 Larry Berman, *Perfect Spy: The Incredible Double Life of Pham Xuan An, Time Magazine Reporter and Vietnamese Communist Agent* (New York: HarperCollins Publishers, 2007), 14.
3 See a summary in Jennifer Llewellyn, Jim Southey, and Steve Thompson, "Chinese and Soviet Involvement in Vietnam," Alpha History, http://alphahistory.com/vietnamwar/chinese-and-soviet-involvement.
4 "Lời kêu gọi của Hồ Chủ Tịch" [President Ho's address], *Văn Nghệ*, no. 265 (July 25, 1968): 3.

Chapter Twelve

Sóng Thần's Campaign for Press Freedom

Trùng Dương

Trùng Dương, whose real name is Nguyễn Thị Thái, was born in Sơn Tây in 1944 and migrated to South Vietnam in 1954. Among the best-known young female writers in the late 1960s in South Vietnam, she is the author of several collections of short stories about love and urban life published between 1964 and 1975, including such works as Vừa Đi Vừa Ngước Nhìn (Stargazing while strolling) (1966) and Mưa Không Ướt Đất (Dry rain) (1967). She cofounded the daily Sóng Thần (Tsunami) published in Saigon during 1971–75, known for its uncompromising criticisms of the government. In this capacity, she partook in the newspaper's campaign to raise money and collect thousands of corpses of civilians killed by communist artillery in Quảng Trị during the Easter Offensive in 1972. After 1975, Trùng Dương settled in Sacramento, CA, obtained a BA degree in government-journalism and an MA in international affairs from the California State University, Sacramento, and worked for more than a decade as a journalist, copy editor, news librarian, and researcher for several local newspapers before retiring in 2006.

On October 31, 1974, the daily newspaper *Sóng Thần* (Tsunami), of which I was the publisher, was put on trial. This trial followed the confiscation of the paper's issue of September 21, 1974 for having published Father Trần Hữu Thanh's corruption indictment against President Nguyễn Văn Thiệu. There were two other dailies sharing the same fate as *Sóng Thần*, the *Đại Dân Tộc* (Great nation) and *Điện Tín* (Telegraph), but their court appearance was for a later date.

The trial drew pledges from 205 lawyers, including several prominent figures, to join the paper's defense team. It also drew mass demonstrations demanding the government, first, to deal with the corruption issue perceived as damaging to the republic's war effort against the communists and, second, to abolish a new press law that bankrupted newspapers while restricting freedom of expression and the public's right to information. Various groups demonstrated, including writers, journalists, and publishing industry workers whose lives had been hurt by the law issued two years earlier, known as Press Law 007/72, part of the National Assembly–issued Martial Law (Luật Ủy Quyền no. 005/72), June 28, 1972. The law, which "delegates the president of the republic the power to decide and issue decrees as he sees fit to deal with national situations," came after the North Vietnamese military crossed the demilitarized zone to invade South Vietnam that spring.

This chapter will examine the events leading to the protests of the press community, culminating in the trial of *Sóng Thần*. Its purpose is, first, to provide a primary source for future studies of the Republic of Vietnam, with a focus on the press, and, second, to show that despite governmental efforts in controlling the media, South Vietnamese journalists did not just submit but fought back, without communist influences as many people believed, to defend freedom of expression recognized by the 1967 constitution, and to do their job as journalists to inform the public of state affairs and the progress of the war against communism. This is a personal account of the trial of *Sóng Thần*. The main source of materials for this paper is from our paper's internal dossier compiled by journalists Uyên Thao and Lê Thiệp in 1974.[1]

THE 1967 CONSTITUTION AND PRESS LAW 019/69

Following four years of political turmoil and social unrest after the overthrow of President Ngô Đình Diệm, the Second Republic was born with the promulgation of the constitution in 1967.[2] Section 12 of the constitution recognized "freedom of thought, speech, press, and publishing as long as it does not harm personal honor, national security or good morals." In the same section, censorship was "abolished except for motion pictures and plays."

Two years later, within that constitutional framework, President Nguyễn Văn Thiệu signed Press Law 019/69 on December 30, 1969.[3] The new law began with chapter 1 reaffirming the constitution's Article 12, "Freedom of the press is the essential right of the Republic of Vietnam. The limits to this right are not to harm individual honor, national security, and good morals. Newspapers cannot be shut down unless by a court ruling. Censorship is not accepted."

As for publishing, chapter 2 recognized the right of citizens or legal entities to publish. They needed only to inform the Ministry of Information via application procedures. A foreigner could also get a publishing license from the Ministry of Information at the Ministry of Interior's recommendation.

Chapter 3 set down the rights and responsibilities of the press. "The press cannot be shut down either temporarily or permanently without a judicial decision," it stated. However, if the government believed a publication had violated national security, public order, and/or good morals, it could confiscate that issue and sue the publisher within eight days. If the government was wrong, it had to compensate the defendant. The press was forbidden to slander high-ranking officials, private persons, and the deceased.

The law also stated, "The press cannot be prosecuted when reporting or publishing accounts of meetings, presentations, political opinions by elected officials, and when quoting various sources. The press may criticize the government as long as it does not aim at propaganda." Newspapers could use their own distribution system or hire a private enterprise, unlike under the Ngô regime, which monopolized such activity.

Although censorship was forbidden, newspapers were required to submit one or more copies of each issue, known as "nạp bản," to the Ministry of Information.[4] By this provision of "nạp bản" at least two hours before newspapers hit the streets, the ministry could advise that certain news items or sections of them be removed ("tự ý Đục bỏ") if deemed as violating certain rules. I will return to further examine this "nạp bản" issue when discussing the 007/72 decree, amending the 019/69 press statute, which became effective following the communist 1972 Easter Offensive.

No doubt the still infantile democracy of South Vietnam needed a press law. It not only ensured that the rule of law would reign but also helped stabilize the then rather chaotic journalistic and publishing activities. The publishing community now had a press law of its own, unlike before when the press was regulated by an assortment of decrees that were "extremely complicated and inconsistent," as observed by Judge Trần Thúc Linh.[5]

The Birth of *Sóng Thần*

In 1970, South Vietnamese concern about corruption peaked with the death of Hà Thúc Nhơn, a medical doctor at the military hospital in Nha Trang killed while leading a campaign against corruption. According to Vân Nguyễn-Marshall, "the events surrounding the death of Ha Thuc Nhon were highly controversial and the details remain, even to this day, murky." As she describes,

> According to his supporters, Ha Thuc Nhon was a highly principled physician who exposed corrupted hospital administrators of the Nguyen Hue military hospital in Nha Trang city. As tension escalated between Ha Thuc Nhon and hospital administrators, he was accused of murdering one of the administrators. This eventually led Ha Thuc Nhon, along with a number of wounded soldiers who were currently patients, to take over the hospital by force. The stand-off lasted several days, ending with the death of Ha Thuc Nhon along with a number of bystanders. The government claimed that Dr. Nhon had committed suicide, but others believed he was shot by the police or someone connected to the corrupted officials. While Nhon's supporters did not condone his radical action, they believed that the severe and endemic level of corruption had driven the doctor over the edge. . . . His death moved many people in the city of Nha Trang and also throughout the country. It was reported that 5,000 people came to his funeral. Newspapers carried reports and discussion about various theories about his death.[6]

The weekly *Đời* (Life) of the famed writer Chu Tử published an extensive report of the Hà Thúc Nhơn case, written by journalist Uyên Thao, who was the weekly's managing editor and a close friend of mine. With the support and encouragement of many *Đời* readers, the two, along with like-minded intellectuals, professionals, and elected officials, established the Hà Thúc Nhơn anticorruption group in November 1970, using *Đời* as the organization's mouthpiece. However, they felt they needed a daily, but none of the group's few members, who had been blacklisted by the government for their adversarial activities, could get a publishing license. One day as I wandered into the office, Uyên Thao casually asked, "How about you apply for a publishing permit?" I remembered staring at him and saying, "Me? You must be kidding. I'm a fiction writer, not a journalist. Besides, you need to have lots of money to publish a newspaper." Uyên Thao said the Hà Thúc Nhơn group already had a plan.

And a plan it had. The daily *Sóng Thần* was born in September 1971 as the first ever cooperative newspaper in the history of the Vietnamese press, funded in part by sales of shares to concerned citizens from all walks of life. And that was how I became involved in journalism, out of idealism—fighting corruption for a better and just society, like the hundreds of people around the country who bought shares. According to Vân Nguyễn-Marshall:

People were encouraged to contribute by buying shares and thereby become collective owners of the paper. The Hà Thúc Nhơn group estimated that it would need 10 million Đồng ($25,000) to begin publishing and wanted to raise half this amount through selling shares and the other half through loans. In order to allow people of all economic circumstances to participate, shares were available at a low rate. People could contribute as little as 500 Đồng (approximately $1.30) and as much as 500,000 Đồng. As explained in a Đời article, every six months dividends would be assessed and sixty percent of the profit would go back to the shareholders, while the other forty percent would go to pay for employees of the daily (20%), reinvesting in the paper (10%), and help support the work of the group (10%). The management committee for the cooperative would be elected at an annual general meeting to which all shareholders would be invited.

Again, according to Nguyễn-Marshall,

This list of shareholders and the amount of their contributions demonstrate the geographic and economic diversity of Sóng Thần's supporters. While many contributed on average between 20,000 to 50,000 Đồng, there were some who contributed only 500 or 1,000 Đồng and a few who could afford to buy 50,000 Đồng worth of shares. Some contributors wrote letters of support, which were published in various issues of Đời. Huỳnh Trung, a supporter from the rural district of Xuyên Mộc, explained that he bought shares not for financial gains, but in order to be among the ranks of those fighting corruption. Vĩnh Linh of Qui Nhơn city explained that he would skip breakfast and reduce his smoking in order to buy more shares in the near future. Lê Kim Hiền, a low-ranking military officer's wife with six children, had debated whether or not their modest income could be stretched in order for her to buy shares. Fortunately, her pig gave birth to ten piglets and the sale of these enabled her to pay for her children's school tuition and clothing, and to buy two shares of Sóng Thần.

By August 20, 1971 the paper received a little over 3.5 million Đồng from 209 people (averaging 17,000 Đồng or $43 per person). While this was less than what the newspaper organizers had hoped, it was still a substantial and impressive amount of money to raise.[7]

We were able to borrow money to pay for the rest, thanks in part to journalist Chu Tử's past reputation as a successful fiction writer and publisher/editor. Chu Tử, a Northerner who was born in the same city of Sơn Tây as I, had previously published the daily Sống (Live) in the mid-1960s. The paper, widely circulated, was later shut down by one of the short-lived governments during the turbulent years between the First and Second Republics. In mid-1966, he was also a target of communist assassination along with Từ Chung, the managing editor of the daily Chính Luận. Từ Chung was shot dead in front of his house as he returned home for lunch, just a few months before a failed attempt on Chu Tử's life that left him seriously wounded and handicapped.[8]

Thanks to its characteristics as a cooperative, Sóng Thần was also the first daily that maintained several regional offices in Huế, Quảng Ngãi, Đà Nẵng, Qui Nhơn, Đà Lạt, Nha Trang, Pleiku, Phan Rang, and Cần Thơ. Such provincial presence helped not only to reflect local issues and perspectives, but also to keep a check on local governments through investigations of residents' grievances.

The publication of *Sóng Thần* came amid the controversial one-ticket presidential election (after other candidates withdrew to protest perceived governmental manipulations) in September 1971, which reelected President Nguyễn Văn Thiệu for a second term. The paper was widely received, reaching at one point one hundred thousand copies in circulation, thanks again to the reputation of Chu Tử and to the fact that it was a collaborative enterprise, making it a so-called people's paper. Thanks to the paper's presence through regional offices, *Sóng Thần* could run several unique news stories that most other Saigon-based newspapers could not as most of them relied on press agencies such as the state-run Việt Tấn Xã (Vietnamese News Agency) and foreign news organizations.

The Martial Law 005/72 and Press Law 007/72

This provincial presence of *Sóng Thần*, while serving as a check on local authorities besides news gathering and advertisement sales, proved to be a big asset when the Easter Offensive occurred in early 1972 as Hanoi sent tanks rolling south across the demilitarized zone to attack Quảng Trị, and the paper's local correspondents could provide breaking news and detailed, vivid reports from the battlegrounds. The paper's two daring young reporters Ngy Thanh and Đoàn Kế Tường of the provincial offices, themselves active servicemen, were the first to enter and report about the so-called Đại lộ Kinh Hoàng (Highway of Horror), a stretch of road of a few miles between the cities of Quảng Trị and Huế, where some two thousand people, mostly civilians with many women and children, perished by communist mortars from the eastern range of Trường Sơn while they tried to flee to Huế. *Sóng Thần* later started a campaign to raise funds and help collect 1,841 remains of these victims for burial. Nguyễn Kinh Châu of *Sóng Thần*'s Huế office undertook the humanitarian work with help from several volunteers. The so-called *Hốt xác* (Collecting corpses) campaign lasted several months while battles were still raging and civilians were forbidden to enter the area to look for missing loved ones.[9]

The war intensified, and as a result, the government saw the need to tighten control of the press again. The National Assembly passed Martial Law on June 28, 1972, empowering President Thiệu to issue laws as he saw fit. This law was to last for six months, meaning it would end on December 28 of the same year.[10] The decree 007/72 became the new Press Law beginning August 4, tightening the government's grip on the press. While still recognizing freedom of expression and publishing according to the constitution, the new law laid down new restrictions, of which two stood out: each daily must deposit a sum of 20 million Đồng (about $50,000), 10 million Đồng for each periodical, and so on; and each newspaper was required to "nạp bản" a few copies for review of each issue four hours (instead of two as in the 1969 law) prior to distribution, therefore further delaying its distribution in an intense competition among dailies. During those agonizing hours for a newspaper, ministerial personnel would scrutinize the paper's content to ensure no violations of any of the restrictions listed in the new Press Law. If any violation was detected, the paper was to remove it or the issue would be confiscated. Where the content removal occurred, the paper had to write in that slot this ridiculous phrase, "tự ý Đục bỏ" (voluntarily deleted). Confiscations of issues perceived as violating certain restrictions still occurred at an alarming rate as the war intensified, the public was hungrier for news, government personnel were stressed out searching for perceived violations, and the newspaper ran out of time to run the press then package its product in time for distribution.

Confiscation was damaging to the newspaper's finances as it caused the loss of readers and advertisements—the only two sources of revenue for most publications.

If the "nạp bản" and "tự ý đục bỏ" practices killed a newspaper slowly, the required deposit of 20 million Đồng gave newspapers an instant death, if publishers could not come up with the cash. The 007/72 decree said the deposit was to ensure that a newspaper had funds available to pay for possible fines. For publishers and journalists, the decree raised the question of how they could have such a huge amount of deposit to continue publishing, not to mention how to feed their families should they become unemployed. The 20 million Đồng deposit was twice that of the fund required to publish Sóng Thần when we started a year before. Several newspapers closed, due to an inability to come up with the deposit. Veteran journalist Trần Tấn Quốc shut down his four-year-old, respectable daily Đuốc Nhà Nam (Southern torch) in protest although he was financially able to pay the deposit. There were about sixteen dailies and fifteen periodicals that had to cease publishing. The Sóng Thần staff debated in anguish on whether to continue. We decided to raise funds again and borrow the rest.

According to the state-run Việt Tấn Xã issue of September 16, 1972, a total of twenty-nine dailies met the deposit deadline to continue publishing, including seventeen Vietnamese, eleven Chinese, one English, and five periodicals. Among the dailies, two were state funded and at least two known among the press community as communist sympathizing.

The 007/72 decree was believed to "prevent disorders on the home front and infiltrations of communist operatives in the mass media," according to the author of Lược Sử Báo Chí Việt Nam, compiled as a high school textbook for twelfth graders, with a progovernment view. What happened in the next two years, however, proved to be the opposite of preventing "disorders on the home front."

Tumult before the Trial

On August 31, 1974, two years after the implementation of the 007/72 press decree and twenty months since the supposed expiration of the Martial Law, the daily Hoà Bình (Peace) declared it had to cease publishing after many a confiscation that had bankrupted the publication. In an open, rather emotional letter dated the same day to the president and the prime minister, the publisher/Catholic priest Trần Du accused the government of violating the constitution and freedom of the press.

Built upon the tragic Hoà Bình demise, the editorial board of Sóng Thần, which had suffered several confiscations itself, launched a campaign for freedom of press with an editorial titled "The National Assembly and the Government must bear the responsibility for the crises harmful to the Fourth Estate of Vietnam," published on August 31, 1974. In this article, the editors pointed to two main causes for the crisis of the publishing industry and the press in particular: the Press Law 007/72, and the narrow-mindedness of those in charge of its implementation at the Ministry of Information.

The next day, on September 1, Trung Tâm Văn Bút Việt Nam (PEN Vietnam, a member of International PEN), then headed by the respectable scholar Thanh Lãng, a Catholic priest and author of several books on Vietnamese literature, called an emergency meeting to discuss the Hoà Bình issue and government publishing policy. The 160-plus-member PEN Vietnam had to be concerned. Several writers made a living by writing serial fictions, known as *feuilleton*, for dailies, and for many writers, that was their main source of income. Thus, with the closures of several dailies and periodicals due to the harsh "ký quỹ" (deposit) requirement imposed by the 007/72 press decree, several writers, journalists, and other publishing workers had become unemployed. Some estimated the unemployment rate was about 70 percent for the press, but no such estimates were available for other publishing activities. PEN Vietnam later issued a proclamation to denounce current press policy and support the campaign for press freedom.

The next day, September 2, Minister of Information Hoàng Đức Nhã explained that the confiscation of *Hoà Bình* was not a work of negligence of his agency. Dismissing any speculations or conspiracy theories regarding the *Hoà Bình* shutdown, including religious oppression (the daily was owned by a Catholic priest), the minister said he was seeking a dialogue, having sent a letter to the president of the Association of Newspaper Publishers (Hội Chủ Báo) to request a meeting date be selected so he could clear up any misunderstanding.

The minister's letter of invitation addressing the president of the association, Senator Tôn Thất Đính, was published in newspapers on September 4. The date of September 10 was selected for the meeting. Before then, however, the press community was swept into yet another unnerving incident, involving one of the most respectable dailies, *Chính Luận*, and even more disturbances that would follow.

In its September 3, 1974, issue, *Chính Luận*, known for its solid reporting with few confiscations and thus enjoying a steady revenue from subscribers, paper sales, and advertisement, raised an alarm after its managing editor Thái Lân and journalist Ngô Đình Vận were detained because of a news item about the smuggling of fifteen thousand tons of copper worth 7 billion Đồng by a high-ranking official at the prime minister's (PM) office, Huỳnh Huy Dương, who had forged the PM's signature. *Chính Luận* reporter Ngô Đình Vận picked up the news item at a daily briefing at the Ministry of Information along with other reporters. The report in the daily's July 4 issue when submitted at the ministry prior to press run was not recommended for "tự ý Đục bỏ" ("not even a comma," meaning harmless, *Chính Luận* reported). However, the daily said the very next day it received a phone call from the PM office requesting a correction of a few details that might create misunderstanding, with which the paper dutifully complied. Then a week later, on July 11, the paper's managing editor Thái Lân was summoned to the National Police Headquarters and questioned from morning until 6 pm. In the following days, the reporter of the copper-smuggling news, Ngô Đình Vận, was also summoned several times to the National Police, then wound up being detained for the last three to four weeks. Thái Lân had also been ordered back for further questioning, and on August 31 he was detained until the afternoon, had to surrender all personal information along with fingerprints, then was told to return Monday, September 2. When he returned as told, he found himself sent to court.

Meanwhile, also on September 4 when *Chính Luận* raised the alarm, eleven elected officials of an opposition group called Quốc Gia in the National Assembly declared their support for the press's campaign for freedom of expression and removal of decree 007/72. In response, government spokesman Nguyễn Quốc Cường said during a daily briefing that these elected officials were too quick to jump to such conclusion. He also criticized PEN Vietnam's September 1 letter of protest as the work of some "erroneous and ambitious individual," who had "smeared mud on his own shirt and then asked foreigners to help clean it" by sending it to international organizations, while refusing the invitation of the minister to come and discuss writers' grievances. The spokesman's remarks had helped open a can of worms.

PEN Vietnam immediately responded with a long letter dated September 4, 1974, stating it had never received any such invitation while it had actually requested twice, in vain, in early 1973 to meet with the minister to discuss its members' grievances, followed by a total of twenty-eight letters specifically listed in the PEN Vietnam letter, asking for help from the president, the vice president, the prime minister, various ministers, and various culture-related committees in both houses of the Congress. With no responses to their plight, therefore, PEN Vietnam had no choice but to ask for help from International PEN for the first time on December 9, 1973, after a meeting attended by over two hundred writers, artists, journalists, and heads of publishing houses, who all signed a declaration on the crisis of current publishing situations. The government spokesman's criticism was, therefore, groundless, if not "malicious," the PEN Vietnam letter concluded.

Following the September 4 letter presenting its case to the public, PEN Vietnam decided to hold a conference at its headquarters on Đoàn Thị Điểm Street, but the area was cordoned off by several police and ministerial personnel, who told those arriving for the meeting that it had been cancelled. The meeting took place nevertheless among a few members already present inside the club. And again PEN Vietnam issued a letter of protest. *Sóng Thần* reported the whole incident in its issue of September 6, 1974.

Also on September 4, two incidents occurred: *Sóng Thần* was sued by Vice President Trần Văn Hương for having "slandered and defamed" him; and another twenty-five elected officials known as the Dân tộc Xã hội (National-Social) bloc of the lower house headed by the famed lawyer Trần Văn Tuyên announced their support for the campaign for freedom of press. Together with the eleven-member Quốc Gia group mentioned above, they issued a declaration promising to work with other progressive groups at the National Assembly to achieve democratic goals that included freedom of press.

The next day, September 5, a Committee for Freedom of Press and Publishing was established with members from various organizations including the Association of Publishers, the unions of journalists and distributors, PEN Vietnam, elected officials, intellectuals, professionals, and the Society for Human and Civil Rights Protection. The next day the committee issued a declaration dated September 6 to demand the government to withdraw all decrees and to cease its campaign aiming at suppressing freedom of expression that adversely affected the livelihood of reporters and writers, among others. On September 7 the Union of Reporters released the content of an urgent telegraph to the International Unions of Reporters in Brussels to inform and request support for the struggle of Vietnamese journalists.

As the campaign for press freedom gathered momentum in Saigon, on September 9, breaking news came from the city of Huế. Father Trần Hữu Thanh's group of 301 Catholic priests, the People's Front against Corruption, for National Salvation and for Building Peace, announced it would join the press campaign. The group released its six-point accusation of corruption against President Thiệu.[11] Wasting no time, on September 10 the Ministry of Information issued an order forbidding newspapers to publish the document. However, *Sóng Thần* went ahead and published a summary of the indictment in its next day's issue. At 2:30 pm the same day, upon receiving the "nạp bản" copies of the paper, the ministry again repeated its order, demanding the paper to "tự ý đục bỏ" the summary, and *Sóng Thần* adamantly declared it "cannot publish at government order." At 3 pm, police surrounded the paper's printing plant, insisting "if the paper refuses to 'tự ý Đục bỏ' the item, then the edition will be confiscated." *Sóng Thần* assistant publisher Hà Thế Ruyệt, also a Saigon city councilman, supposed to be among the publishers meeting with Minister Hoàng Đức Nhã as previously scheduled, declared he would not "go and meet with the minister if the issue is confiscated." However, the police still surrounded the printing plant to prevent the paper distribution. At 4:30 pm, the ministry confirmed the paper would not be confiscated, and a *Sóng Thần* representative agreed to meet with the minister.

However, what happened afterward revealed the opposite from what *Sóng Thần* had been guaranteed. Thus, we learned of another set of tactics used by the Ministry of Information: Scores of ministerial personnel descended on newsstands and bought all available copies, as newspaper sellers later informed us. Meanwhile, at other newsstands, confiscations occurred, and sellers even got actual receipts for the confiscated copies stating that the issue had been printed in two different editions, which was against the 007/72 decree forbidding newspapers to publish different editions of one issue. However, it was difficult to abide by such a rule because of the "tự ý đục bỏ" system: from the time a newspaper submitted its copies for review at the ministry until it could hit newsstands was a good four hours, during which several "tự ý đục bỏ" recommendations reached the printing plant, where distribution staffers were impatient to roll the press while newspaper sellers waited outside, equally impatient, to grasp whatever bundles were just off the press for delivery, especially when an issue carried a hot news item. Therefore, it was inevitable for the press to run, then stop for certain "tự ý đục bỏ," then restart, and so on. More than one edition per newspaper issue, therefore, had become unavoidable, an unwritten norm. *Sóng Thần* felt it had been betrayed as its representative had been promised that the issue would not be confiscated as a condition to meet the minister.

The entire incident was reported in the paper's issue no. 973 dated September 13 in the form of a letter of protest to the Council of the Press (Hội Đồng Báo chí, a civilian body established by the Press Law but consisting of at least two members from each publication, the publisher and a reporter). "We determine that the life or death of a newspaper is not important. However," the letter concluded, "the life or death of a free press goes hand in hand with the very existence of the regime. In the current situation, the absence of any [free] newspapers due to oppressive measures above poses a serious threat to the regime's democracy."

Meanwhile, a flurry of declarations from various organizations, including PEN Vietnam and the Cooperative of Periodicals, demanded the press decree to be dismantled. The latter claimed the decree had killed 150 periodicals, leaving a mere four, due to the required deposit of 10 million Đồng per publication. On September 12, the Association of Newspaper Publishers issued a five-demand list to the government: (1) remove both Press Laws 019/69 and 007/72 and replace them with one that is based on the constitution's Article 12; (2) cancel all press violation cases, including those that have been tried and those that still await their day in court; (3) end all government harassment of publishers and reporters, which goes against the principle of freedom to perform one's profession and freedom of press, and release currently detained reporters; (4) abolish the deposit requirement and terminate confiscations while awaiting a new press law; and (5) allow all publications that had been shut down due to the Press Laws 019/69 and 007/72 to reopen. At 7:30 pm the same day, a symbolic gesture took place at the National Assembly's conference hall when Hà Thế Ruyệt publicly set a copy of decree 007/72 afire. About two hundred participants including assembly officials, publishers, editors, reporters, religious members, and lawyers, placed themselves under the protection of the constitution's Article 12.

On September 16, Nguyễn Liệu, a member of the Hà Thúc Nhơn anticorruption group, wrote an opinion piece suggesting President Thiệu should resign in order to preserve his leadership's integrity and avoid disorder for South Vietnam. The next day, in the September 20 issue, *Sóng Thần* columnist Lý Đại Nguyên reviewed the past seven years under President Thiệu, who had campaigned in 1967 promising "to end the war, promote democracy and reform society," but none of these promises had been fulfilled. Also in the same issue, the paper announced it would publish the entire four-thousand-word corruption accusation by Father Thanh's group against the president in the next day's issue. The issue was ordered confiscated by the Ministry of Information. Instead of letting the police take the freshly printed copies away, *Sóng Thần* decided to set them on fire as their staff, printing shop workers, and newspaper sellers stood by watching mournfully. Among those witnessing the newspaper's "self-immolation" were representatives of the international press corps.

The daily *Chính Luận*, in its next day's issue, reported the entire incident in a detailed narrative of the press campaign for freedom of expression since the demise of *Hoà Bình* twenty days before, under the headline "*Sóng Thần* sets self afire against press oppression." The daily *Trắng Đen* ran a special banner across its eight-column front page of the issue no. 2226 dated September 21: "We protest the government's confiscation of *Sóng Thần*." The Civil Rights Group (Nhóm Dân Quyền), a group of sixteen elected officials in the National Assembly who in 1972 had opposed the Martial Law, also issued a declaration in support of the press campaign.

In a show of solidarity, and with the support of the Committee for Freedom of Press and Publishing, which had met till 10 pm following the paper-burning incident, five other dailies announced they would also publish the entire anticorruption exposé. In the end, however, only two papers, *Đại Dân Tộc* and *Điện Tín*, remained committed to share the journey with *Sóng Thần* and published the entire four-thousand-word document in their issue dated September 21. Anticipating confiscations, the committee mobilized supporters to come and protect the printing plants of these dailies, which were already surrounded densely by the police since the early afternoon of September 20, awaiting orders from the Ministry of Information. When such orders arrived in the late afternoon, the three dailies with the help of supporters chose to toss freshly printed copies to the public crowding the streets in front of their printing shops, and setting remaining copies on fire. The daily *Công Luận* dated September 24, 1974, had a detailed report describing the day's turbulence by the hours.

The last week of September saw the press community in a so-called confiscation and burning fever. To add fuel to the crisis, Minister of Interior Lê Công Chất, whose agency would initiate lawsuits against the three dailies, said during a hearing at the National Assembly that those who had burned the papers would be prosecuted for having "destroyed the evidence." Despite the government threat, on September 28, the Association of Newspaper Publishers of nineteen dailies, including those in English, French, and Chinese, met to examine the dire press situation after the release of its five-demand letter of protest two weeks prior to no effect. Toward the end of the meeting, the association issued its Declaration No. 1 reaffirming its stand by placing the press under the protection of the constitution's Article 12, demanding that the government cease all measures against the press and be accountable for all consequences, and calling on all newspapers and periodicals to cease publishing until its demands were met.

On September 30, thirty-seven assemblymen of the opposition signed a letter of protest to Prime Minister Trần Thiện Khiêm, warning of increasing communist risks as "the entire regime is on the road to self-destruction for having wiped out the basic freedom and becoming an enemy of the people." On October 1, just one day before President Thiệu was to speak on the state-run television, the archbishop of Saigon released an announcement signed by Archbishop Nguyễn Văn Bình affirming the church's stand for what was right and fair and encouraging its members to engage in the struggle for a better society. Meanwhile, calling themselves Legion of Activist Lawyers (Lực lượng Luật sư Tranh Đấu), eighty-five members from the Association of Attorneys issued a proclamation affirming that South Vietnam must exist beyond the communist realm as defined in the constitution, and the rule of law must be respected, and pledging to stand by the people in their struggle for freedom and a corruption-free society.

On October 2, all South Vietnam was glued to television screens to watch the much-anticipated address by President Thiệu. According to a declassified U.S. State Department cable dated October 3–9, compiled from various sources across South Vietnam on reactions to the presidential speech, "the speech was too long (2 hours) and that its rambling, extemporaneous format weakened its impact." According to the cable, Trần Quốc Bửu, leader of the Vietnamese Confederation of Labor, was disappointed that Mr. Thiệu failed to address recent criticisms and that he suggested no solutions to the problems of South Vietnam or mentioned the problem of his government's performance but blamed current difficulties on outside factors (e.g., foreign aid reduction and the communists). Summing up these reactions to the speech, the cable stated,

> Most other newspapers paralleled the views of the independent, though somewhat strident Saigon Daily, Song Tanh [sic], which reported that "Contrary to the expectations of the people, president Thieu . . . did not directly answer (Father Tran Huu Thanh's) Indictment No. 1 in which the anticorruption movement charged (Thieu) with corruption practices." What he did say was, "I assert that these slanderous and defamatory allegations are in fact exaggerations and pure fabrications."

The positive reports about the speech came from a few progovernment publications, the cable noted.[12]

Meanwhile, the living conditions of unemployed reporters and publishing workers had reached a point that the three organizations of Vietnamese Union of Reporters (Nghiệp Đoàn Ký giả Việt Nam), Union of Southern Journalists (Nghiệp Đoàn Ký Giả Nam Việt), and Association of Journalists (Hội Ái Hữu Ký Giả) felt they could no longer afford not to do something, even only symbolically. Having seen their funds depleted from helping members' families, in order to show their support for one another and at the same time to draw attention to their plight, these groups on October 4 announced that October 10 would be Reporters Go Begging Day (Ngày Ký Giả Đi Ăn Mày). The groups also issued their statement regarding the president's October 2 speech, demanding that he withdraw his negative remarks about reporters as extortionists ("ký giả đi làm tiền") and the press as serving as loudspeakers for communists ("báo chí là ống loa của cộng sản"), and that the government abolish decree 007/72 that was destroying the free press and their livelihood.

On October 10, the symbolic Reporters Go Begging Day took place in downtown Saigon, attended by hundreds of journalists, elected officials, veterans, and prominent figures, such as Fathers Thanh Lãng and Nguyễn Quang Lãm marching side by side with scholar Hồ Hữu Tường, each wearing an old conical hat and holding a walking stick, a sack over their shoulder—typical accessories of a beggar. Members of the public including many elderly men, women, and children held one another's hands to create a human barrier between demonstrators and the police. It was billed as the largest spontaneous demonstration ever in Saigon in recent years. Many people actually offered cash and rice to these one-day beggars. There was some confrontation between the police and a few participants trailing the parade, apparently hopeful to stir up violent clashes to make their case, but the police had seemed rather self-restrained from using any force other than their bare hands and batons. Many among those trailing the parade called themselves "Lực lượng thứ ba" (Third Force) but were suspected communist sympathizers, such as Huỳnh Liên, a Buddhist nun, and Nguyễn Ngọc Lan, a Catholic priest, among others. Despite some push and shove, the demonstration went without any serious incidents, generating domestic and worldwide reports, many of which were sympathetic toward the press community's plight. *Sóng Thần* ran a lengthy feature of the Reporters Go Begging Day, illustrated by several moving photos, in its issue dated October 11, 1974.

Then, as expected, on October 11, as publisher of *Sóng Thần*, I received a subpoena from the Ministry of Interior for a court appearance on October 31, 1974. The charge was the publication of the Indictment No. 1, defaming and slandering the president. The court order listed as evidence of the accusation the entire Indictment No. 1 of Father Thanh's anticorruption group, for which the issue, along with those of *Đại Dân Tộc* and *Điện Tín*, were confiscated by Ministry of Information order. A trial date of November 7 was scheduled for these two dailies.

Assemblyman Lý Quí Chung wrote an article published in the *Sóng Thần* issue dated October 16 questioning what kind of verdict the paper, which only did its job as a messenger, could expect. Chung wondered why Father Thanh, the author of the Indictment No. 1, and those who had read the accusations out loud in public had not been sued. Chung continued to question why the president, if he felt that he had been defamed and slandered, did not do the normal thing, which was to demand a correction by the paper, before resorting to a stronger measure, which was to sue the paper. He could not see how the court would be ruling when the paper had been confiscated before anybody got to read the document. Whatever verdict the court had for *Sóng Thần*, Mr. Chung concluded, "the public would also have a verdict for the court."

On October 13, the Legion of Activist Lawyers informed the Committee for Freedom of Press and Publishing that there were a total of 175 lawyers who had signed up to defend the press. The number eventually reached a total of 205 just before the trial date, including prominent lawyers such as Bùi Tường Chiểu, Hồ Tri Châu, Lê Ngọc Chẩn, Vũ Văn Mẫu, Trần Văn Tuyên, Bùi Chánh Thời, and the famed lawyer Mrs. Nguyễn Phước Đại, among several of the younger generation. Two of the legal team coordinators hard at work from beginning to end were young lawyers Đinh Thạch Bích and Đặng Thị Tám, in cooperation with *Sóng Thần*'s counselor Đàm Quang Lâm.

Meanwhile, paper confiscations did not let up. As of October 19, the Association of Newspaper Publishers informed that there had been a total of eleven incidents between October 13 and 19. Furthermore, the government had also shut down the printing shop of *Đại Dân Tộc*, it said. It was even more troubling for *Sóng Thần* when its regional representatives were ordered to remove the paper's signs from the front of their offices by local governments, at the order of the Ministry of Interior. As a consequence, the association declared, beginning October 21, all newspapers would not report any government-related news and would not send their correspondents to attend any government-organized press conferences, including the daily briefing at the Ministry of Information.

On October 23, to appease the press, the prime minister agreed to dismiss four ministers of the Ministries of Information, Commerce and Industries, Finance, and Agriculture. These ministers were, however, still on the job functioning as interim. And the press continued its suffering.

On October 24, for the first time Father Thanh of the anticorruption campaign met with the Legion of Activist Lawyers and the Committee for Freedom of Press and Publishing to coordinate strategies for the day of the *Sóng Thần* trial. The three groups selected October 31 as the day to demonstrate their will of cooperation. Also during this meeting, Father Thanh said he was willing to go to jail in lieu of *Sóng Thần*'s publisher should that be the case. And should the court impose a fine, he would call on his congregation to contribute ten Đồng each until the goal of 5 or 10 million Đồng was met.

On October 25, the 1,900-member International Press Institute sent a telegraph to President Thiệu to protest the oppression of the Vietnamese press, according to the Voice of America. It also requested press freedom be restored. Also on the same day, the Council of Coordinators consisting of presidents of ten press and publishing organizations met to plan actions for the trial day, which became Justice and Press Persecution Day (Ngày Công Lý và Báo Chí Thọ Nạn). Before that day, a planned vigil was to take place at the Press Club at 15 Lê Lợi Boulevard; all newspapers were to cease publishing on October 31; and on November 1 the council was to send its ultimate letters to the government's three branches to demand solutions according to democratic principles. Father Thanh's anticorruption campaign together with the local congregations were also planning vigils on October 30 and 31 with mass to pray for the nation and to enlighten the national leadership. Campaign organizers also promised to march to downtown Saigon in support of the press while appealing to the judiciary's conscience.

Meanwhile, on October 30 *Sóng Thần* gave a farewell party, filled with apprehension, at the PEN Vietnam club in late afternoon. This was the same place where four years ago we had held a reception to introduce the first cooperative newspaper of South Vietnam to friends and the public. After the party, I went with representatives from the Legion of Activist Lawyers, who took me into hiding for the historic next day since the entire downtown area, within which was situated the courthouse, would be cordoned off by barbed wire and riot police. My hiding place was lawyer Đặng Thị Tám's law office only a couple of blocks from the courthouse. With me were young reporter Triêu Giang and photographer Nguyễn Tân Dân of *Sóng Thần*.

"The Longest Day," as declared a banner across the front page of *Sóng Thần*'s issue dated October 31, 1974, came with several demonstrations by hundreds of supporters of the free press heading to the city center. However, they were barricaded from entering the cordoned area, where deserted streets looked like a ghost town. There were clashes between protesters and the police, but nothing lethal. The stage for a dramatic press trial was all set as the nation held its breath, watching nervously.

The trial never took place. It had been cancelled by the Ministry of Interior, no reason offered. Three months later, on a February day just after a Tết celebration amid apprehensions as the war intensified, an order from the Ministry of Interior arrived at the *Sóng Thần* office. It announced that the paper's publishing license was from then onward revoked. It gave no reason.

Past, Present, Future

As I was writing this chapter the American press is experiencing a crisis with the Republican president who called the media "an enemy of the American people" via a tweet on Friday night, February 17, 2017. Criticizing President Donald Trump for calling media "the enemy," Republican senator John McCain said: "That's how dictators get started." There have been plenty of reports and analyses of the matter; however, the incident brought back the famous quote by one of the founding fathers, Thomas Jefferson. In a letter from Paris to Edward Carrington, a soldier and statesman from Virginia whom Jefferson sent to the Continental Congress from 1786 to 1788, on the importance of a free press to keep government in check, Jefferson wrote: "Were it left to me to decide whether we should have a government without newspapers or newspapers without a government, I should not hesitate a moment to prefer the latter."[13]

Such a choice would definitely not work with an infantile democracy that was also undergoing a ravaging war while trying to build a nation, a young and fragile one, such as the Republic of Vietnam. The press in South Vietnam understood the need for certain government restrictions, especially when there were undercover communist operatives among them. Journalists were fully aware of communist agents and sympathizers in their midst, but out of respect for democracy and the rule of law, they had pretty much left these agents alone or sometimes, out of a humanitarian sense, even petitioned, as needed, for the release of someone arrested by the government, as with the case of communist sympathizer and writer Vũ Hạnh.

However, I believe, then and now, that had there been an honest dialogue between the government and the press, it would have been helpful and turmoil may have been much less and/or controllable. The government could have listened with genuine concern to the press's grievances and asked what could be done to ease them, and in turn asked for the community's assistance in making the South a better place while helping to fight against communism. It may sound idealistic, if not naïve, but that was how I and many of my friends felt during the last few months of the republic's existence when we had also wished the president would have convened a Diên Hồng–like conference as King Trần Thánh Tông of the Trần Dynasty had in 1284 to ask for advice from the elder populace on whether to fight or surrender to the Chinese that were threatening to invade the country.

Unfortunately, neither an honest dialogue with the press in late 1974 nor that with the people in early 1975 took place. For years I have hesitated to write about this experience as a participant in the South Vietnamese quest for freedom of the press, mainly out of humility. I have finally overcome it, inspired in part by what has been going on here in the United States as the media has taken on the task to check on an apparently runaway government.

I want to demonstrate what the South Vietnamese press had striven to do just over forty years ago despite all odds. I would also like to use this opportunity to honor those journalists and writers, many of whom no longer with us, for their courage and a strong sense of journalistic responsibility. I would like also to offer my late appreciations to all those who had stood up with the press then, and who apparently had shown a clear understanding of the importance of the press while the government did not. I wish the American press to prevail, firmly believing it will, thanks to its long-standing democracy and a solid check-and-balance political system. And finally, I hope once democracy is restored in Vietnam, the press and whoever will be charged with governing and rebuilding my native land would learn from the experience of republican Vietnam and, especially, America.

Notes

1 Uyên Thao and Lê Thiệp, comps., *Sóng Thần: Vụ Án Lịch Sử 31–10–1974, Ngày Báo Chí và Công Lý Thọ Nạn* [Song Than: A historic trial, October 31, 1974—a day of tribulation for the press and for justice] Saigon: *Sóng Thần*, 1974), author's private collection.
2 "Hiến pháp Việt Nam Cộng hoà 1967" [The Republic of Vietnam's 1967 constitution], Wikisource, https://vi.wikisource.org/wiki.
3 "Luật số 019/69 ngày 30 tháng 12 năm 1969 ấn Định QUY CHẾ BÁO CHÍ—Sửa Đổi bởi Sắc Luật số 007-TT/SLu Ngày 4–8–1972 của Tổng thống Việt Nam Cộng Hoà" [Revision to Press Law 1969 based on Decree no. 007-TT/SLu by the president of the Republic of Vietnam] (Saigon: Bộ Thông Tin, 1972).
4 This ministry's name was later changed to Ministry of Mass Mobilization and Open Arms (Bộ Dân Vận Chiêu Hồi); however, for this paper, I will use the former name for simplicity.
5 Trần Thúc Linh, "Góp ý kiến về Luật báo chí Việt Nam" [Comments on the Press Law], *Báo Chí Tập San* 1, no. 2 (Đà Lạt University, Summer 1968), author's private collection. This *Báo Chí Tập San* issue was edited by Nguyễn Ngọc Linh and had a section that listed forty-one press laws and decrees issued from 1881 to 1968, in both French and Vietnamese. In another source, Nguyễn Việt Chước listed twenty-three press-related decrees between 1949 and 1969, when the Press Law 016/69 came into existence. Nguyễn Việt Chước (Hồng Hà), *Lược sử Báo chí Việt Nam* [A brief history of Vietnamese press] (Saigon: Nam Son, 1974); a PDF copy is available for download at http://tusachtiengviet.com/author/post/19/1/hong-ha-nguyen-viet-chuoc?r=L3AxMDdhNDkyL25odW5nLXRyYW5nLXN1LXZlLXZhbmctcXV5ZW4tMg.
6 Vân Nguyễn-Marshall, "Working for Social Justice in Wartime South Vietnam," paper presented at the "New York Conference on Asian Studies," Poughkeepsie, NY, October 2015.
7 Ibid.
8 For more on this case, see Trùng Dương, "Báo Chí Miền Nam: Nhân kỷ niệm 38 năm ngày giỗ Chu Tử, Nhìn lại vụ Chu Tử bị ám sát hụt, ngày 16-4-1966" [South Vietnamese press: On the 38th anniversary of Chu Tu's death, reexamining his failed assassination on April 16, 1966], Diễn đàn Thế kỷ, http://www.diendantheky.net/2013/05/trung-duong-bao-chi-mien-nam-nhan-ky.html.
9 Vân Nguyễn-Marshall, "Appeasing the Spirits along the 'Highway of Horror': Civic Life in Wartime South Vietnam," paper presented at "Nation-Building in War: The Experience of Republican Vietnam, 1954–1975," University of California, Berkeley, October 17–18, 2016. See also Giao Chỉ, Ngy Thanh, Trùng Dương, and Nguyễn Kinh Châu, "Quảng Trị Mùa Hè Đỏ Lửa 1972: Hốt xác Đồng bào tử nạn trên 'Đại lộ Kinh hoàng'" [Fiery Summer in Quang Tri: collecting the remains of the dead on the Highway of Horror], *Thời Báo*, November 20, 2009, 54–59, 104–9.
10 Luật Ủy Quyền 005/72, *Công-Báo Việt-Nam Cộng-Hoà* [Official Gazette of the RVN], No. unknown, dated June 29, 1972.
11 Rev. Father Trần Hữu Thanh, "Letter from Vietnam, Hue, September 8, 1974. Indictment No. 1." Father Thanh's actual indictment is available at Texas Tech University's Vietnam Archive, file no. 14510325042. The indictment lists six charges of corruption: (1) real estate holdings of President Nguyễn Văn Thiệu, (2) land holdings in Đà Lạt, (3) fertilizer speculation, (4) hospital Vì Dân (For the People) established by Mrs. Thiệu, (5) heroin trafficking involving President Nguyễn Văn Thiệu, Prime Minister Trần Thiện Khiêm, and General Đặng Văn Quang, and (6) the rice affair in central Vietnam. Some charges, such as the fifth charge about heroin trafficking, are said to be unfounded as all those involved were finally allowed to resettle in the United States. See Trần Gia Phụng, *Chiến Tranh Việt Nam, 1960–1975 (Việt Sử Đại Cương Tập)* [The Vietnam War, 1960–1975, brief history of Vietnam] (Toronto: Non Nước, 2013), 7:378.

12 State Department Cable, Embassy Saigon Mission Weekly for October 3–9, 1974. Declassified/Released US Department of State EO Systematic Review, June 30, 2005, https://aad.archives.gov/aad/createpdf?rid=219521&dt=2474&dl=1345.
13 Letter from Thomas Jefferson to Edward Carrington, January 16, 1787, National Archives, Founders Online, https://founders.archives.gov/documents/Jefferson/01-11-02-0047.

Chapter Thirteen

WRITERS OF THE REPUBLIC OF VIETNAM

Nhã Ca (translated by Trùng Dương)

Nhã Ca, whose real name is Trần Thị Thu Vân, is a writer with forty works published in Saigon under the Republic of Vietnam. She was awarded the National Prize in Poetry in 1966 with her collection of poems titled Nhã Ca Mới *(New Nhã Ca). Her* Giải Khăn Sô Cho Huế *(Mourning Headband for Huế) won the National Fiction Prize in 1970. Many of her novels have been translated into French and English and made into movies. After April 1975, together with other Saigon artists and writers, she and her husband Trần Dạ Từ were imprisoned under the communist regime. Thanks to international intervention, the couple were released in 1988 and allowed to leave Vietnam for Sweden. In 1992 she moved to southern California and founded* Việt Báo Daily News, *which is one of the largest dailies in the Vietnamese language in the United States. Among more than four thousand pages that Nhã Ca has written since 1975 are her memoir* Hồi Ký Một Người Mất Ngày Tháng *(Memoir of a person who lost the sense of time); novels such as* Hoa Phượng Đừng Đỏ Nữa *(Blooming flamboyant flowers, please stop!),* Đường Tự Do Sài Gòn *(Freedom street in Saigon),* Chớp Mắt Một Thời *(An old time that seemed so recent),* Sài Gòn Cười Một Mình *(Smiling to oneself in Saigon); and a collection of poems titled* Thơ Nhã Ca *(Poems by Nhã Ca). In 2015, her* Giải Khăn Sô Cho Huế *was translated into English by Olga Dror and published by Indiana University Press as* Mourning Headband for Huế. *The book won the 2016 INDIEFAB Book of the Year Bronze Award in the category of War and Military/Adult Nonfiction.*

As a survivor of wartime massacres and postwar imprisonment, I have often reminded myself to reflect on the past—as I have done when confronting death or while imprisoned, and as I do when I want to maintain hope, keep my eyes open, and take a step forward.

This chapter is about literary and artistic achievements under the Republic of Vietnam from 1955 to 1975. I believe that these achievements belonged not just to South Vietnam but to the entire Vietnamese people as they emerged from colonial rule.

The Beginning

In September 1945, scholar Phạm Quỳnh was murdered in a forest near Hue, and Confucian scholar and poet Nguyễn Bá Trác was executed at a public market in Qui Nhơn. Those are the incidents that occurred right after the Việt Minh seized power. In

1946, while calling on the people to participate in the resistance against the French, the communists assassinated Phan Văn Hùm, a scholar from the South. In 1947, as they urged people to unite to fight for national independence, the communists murdered Khái Hưng, the talented novelist and journalist of the Tự Lực Văn Đoàn (Self-Reliance Literary Movement) of the 1930s. In November 1949, the communists assassinated Nhượng Tống, a scholar, poet, and translator in Hanoi. The remains of these scholars and writers were scattered around the country, but their spirits still live on.

In 1954, the first international agreement for Vietnam was signed in Geneva, ending the First Indochina War. The result of the nine-year resistance was a divided Vietnam. In South Vietnam, the nationalist government quickly regained independence. A rich cultural heritage from France as well as China still continued to exist there. But the eighty-years-long colonial rule had been overthrown, and the Republic of Vietnam was born in 1955. With assistance from the United States, South Vietnam became an independent nation, recognized by all the nations of the free world.

Meanwhile, the North was unable to free itself from communist China. Based on the communist ideology and one-party system, Hanoi became a dictatorship that took orders from Beijing. The country and the people were devastated by a bloody Chinese-style land reform. Writers and artists were brutally oppressed. The *Nhân Văn-Giai Phẩm* Affair alone saw hundreds of them being "hạ phóng," meaning demoted or stripped of their right to write, including composer Văn Cao, author of the North's national anthem. Three hundred people were publicly denounced and sent to be reeducated, meaning imprisonment. Phan Khôi, the publisher of *Nhân Văn* and a scholar, journalist, and poet since the turn of the twentieth century, was publicly insulted, fired from his job, and evicted from his house. A few well-known literary figures were allowed to continue but forced to "self-criticize" and publicly condemn their own works, to display their full submission to the Communist Party's power ("biết sợ" in the words of famed writer Nguyễn Tuân). There were no longer true artists in the North. Everyone was assigned to his or her proper place. Their only job was to embellish the regime with their pens and brushes per orders from above. The fields of culture and education were severed from tradition and history. All traditional performing arts such as *chèo cổ, ca trù, hò Huế, vọng cổ,* and *cải lương* were forbidden for as long as a decade before the ban was lifted.

Meanwhile the South welcomed nearly a million Northerners who were evacuated and resettled following the partition of the country. Among the Northern refugees were many writers and artists who contributed to the presence of both regions in all cultural activities. By the side of Lê Văn Đệ, a Southerner and director of the College of Fine Arts, was Nguyễn Gia Trí from the North who continued to produce lacquer paintings. Exhibition halls exuded the lights from the youthful lines, shapes, and colors in the works of artists such as Trương Thị Thịnh, Nguyễn Trí Minh, Duy Thanh, Ngọc Dũng, and Nguyễn Trung.

Saigon nights became more lively. Over here was a troupe performing the traditional *hát bội* (a form of theater with origins in Peking opera); over there was another show of *cải lương* (a Southern form of popular opera) play. At this street corner displayed the usual banner of the Thanh Minh-Thanh Nga company, which was beloved across Nam Kỳ Lục Tỉnh (the old name referring to southern Vietnam when it had only six administrative provinces). At another street corner rose the new sign of the emigrated Kim Chung company, the "golden bell" of Hanoi.[1] In the meantime, the seventh art of motion picture, after a fifteen-year dormancy during the war, sprang back alive as never before.

The year 1955 marked the start of a journey shared by many generations representing the literati of a unified Vietnam. Among the first generation of writers who produced the *quốc ngữ* (romanized Vietnamese) literature were Hồ Biểu Chánh, one of the first and best known novelists of the South, and Á Nam Trần Tuấn Khải, the classical poet from the North. Among those who were between fifty and sixty years old, who belonged to the pre–World War II generation of writers, were Nhất Linh Nguyễn Tường Tam, leader of the Tự Lực Văn Đoàn of the 1930s who continued to write novels and publish magazines, and Đông Hồ, the famed poet from Hà Tiên who began his career in the *Nam Phong* magazine era (1917–34) but who kept on writing poems, contributing to newspapers, and publishing books. Others of this generation were writer Đỗ Đức Thu, playwright Vi Huyền Đắc, and scholar Vương Hồng Sển. In their forties were mature writers such as Bình Nguyên Lộc for fiction, Vũ Hoàng Chương for poetry, Vũ Khắc Khoan for plays, Nguyễn Mạnh Côn for novels and essays, and poet Đinh Hùng who led the well-received radio program *Tao Đàn*, a poetry-reciting forum. Full of creative energy were writers in their thirties, such as Sơn Nam and Võ Phiến, among others. On the pages of literary journals there emerged scores of writers in their twenties who were eager to explore new literary trends such as Mai Thảo, Nguyên Sa, and Thanh Tâm Tuyền. Free-form poetry and new-style novels appeared with numerous authors who helped shape Vietnam's postcolonial literature.

As for the press, during the first years after Geneva, one could see the then well-established Saigon-based newspapers such as *Thần Chung*, *Tiếng Dội*, *Sàigòn Mới*, and *Tiếng Chuông*, with the works of prominent journalists Nam Đình, Trần Tấn Quốc, and Bút Trà, side by side on newsstands with Northern-style dailies such as *Tự Do* published by emigrated journalists from the North, such as Như Phong, Mặc Thu, and Hiếu Chân, and *Ngôn Luận* by Hồ Anh and Từ Chung. Among magazines, the best-selling was *Đời Mới* whose publisher was the Southern-born, respectable Trần Văn Ân and whose editor was Northern scholar Nguyễn Đức Quỳnh, who, together with Đặng Thái Mai and Nguyễn Đổng Chi, had earlier established the scholarly Hàn Thuyên Group and *Văn Mới* magazine well-known in prewar Hanoi.

During Tết (lunar new year) of 1955, *Đời Mới*'s special edition promoted for the first time "Tình Ca" (Love song) by composer Phạm Duy, sung by the legendary singer Thái Thanh. "For four thousand years my mother's tongue has cried and laughed with the country's changing destiny" ("Tiếng nước tôi bốn ngàn năm ròng rã buồn vui, khóc cười theo vận nước nổi trôi"). As the lyrics implied, preservation of our historical traditions and promotion of the people's unified sentiments were shared goals of the South's literature and arts.

On stage as well as over the air, we heard *vọng cổ* songs by artists from both the South and the North, such as Út Trà Ôn and Huỳnh Thái. The chorus Thăng Long celebrated Southern life with "Ly Rượu Mừng" (A happy toast to you) by Phạm Đình Chương; Minh Trang expressed the sadness of "Đêm Tàn Bến Ngự" (Night fades over Bến Ngự) by Dương Thiệu Tước; Trần Văn Trạch promoted "Xổ số kiến thiết quốc gia" (Lottery for national reconstruction), alongside the chorus of "Hòn Vọng Phu" (The warrior's wife rock) by composer Lê Thương. Meanwhile, prewar songs by composers such as Văn Cao, Lưu Hữu Phước, Tô Vũ, and Tô Hải, who remained in the North, were still being performed in the South regardless.

In history books, school curricula, and language-study textbooks from elementary through high school and college, authors representing prewar literature, including those who stayed in the North and who now had to write and speak according to the communist regime's orders, were still present. At bookstores that sprang up all over the South, readers still could easily buy earlier literary works, from prewar novels by Thế Lữ, Nguyễn Công Hoan, Nam Cao, and Nguyễn Tuân, to collections of poems by Xuân Diệu, Huy Cận, Chế Lan Viên, and Tế Hanh, among others.

Government monopoly of writing, publishing, and distributing did not exist. Associations and unions of all professions enjoyed the same freedom. Their autonomy enabled social groups that were active in culture, media, and literature to easily connect and mingle with their peers around the world.

The Association of Asian Cultures established by Nguyễn Đăng Thục and Lê Xuân Khoa joined the International Association of Asian Studies. The Union of Journalists and the Association of Newspaper Publishers founded by journalist Hồ Văn Đồng were official members of the International Union of Journalists.

PEN Vietnam, with a membership of two hundred of various ages and different viewpoints, was recognized by International PEN. Writer Nhất Linh was elected as the first president of PEN Vietnam. The organization's charter emphasized the right of free speech and opposed any forms of censorship.

From 1955 to 1960, during the first five years of the First Republic when the whole South still enjoyed peace and stability, Southern writers embarked on an auspicious journey. However, their spectacular achievements actually appeared only during the troubled time of war under the Second Republic.

At War

Before making a living as a full-time writer, I was just a student who liked writing, and I sent my stories from Huế to literary magazines in Saigon. Among young writers in Huế at the time I remember Lê Hữu Bôi, Nguyễn Xuân Hoàng, and Trịnh Công Sơn. I remember the latter once got into a near-fatal accident and had to be hospitalized for a whole year. It was during this episode that he wrote his first songs such as "Sương Đêm" (Night dew) and "Ướt Mi" (Teary eyes).

The year 1960 was when I adopted the pen name Nhã Ca and when my first poem was published in *Hiện Đại* magazine's first issue. This publication was established by poet Nguyên Sa. When leaving Huế for Saigon to live as a writer, I met my husband Trần Dạ Từ, a poet and journalist who had emigrated from the North in 1954. Từ headed the editorial section of the daily *Dân Việt*, one of eight newspapers in Saigon at the time. In addition, we and a group of friends published the weekly *Ngàn Khơi*.

In 1963, when the Huế government forbid the display of Buddhist flags and oppressed church members as they celebrated the birthday of the Buddha, protests erupted and quickly spread across the land. Saigon was placed under martial law. Buddhist temples were attacked. Then a coup d'état took place, ending the First Republic. Following this were years of political upheaval. Taking advantage of the situation, the North launched its military offensives, prompting the United States and other allies' militaries to join the fight in 1965. And the Second Republic came into being in 1967.

In the late 1960s, along with increased involvement of the United States and allies, South Vietnam was inundated with American goods, technologies, and culture—from television to movies and from music to fashion. As in other areas of civilian life, music, art, motion pictures, books, and other literary and artistic activities in South Vietnam quickly adapted, developed, and evolved, achieving remarkable accomplishments.

The press also experienced tremendous changes. The three newspapers *Tự Do*, *Ngôn Luận*, and *Dân Việt* no longer existed. In their places were, to name a few, the daily *Chính Luận* with Từ Chung as managing editor, and the daily *Sống* with Chu Tử as publisher and with the combined editorial staffs of *Dân Việt* and *Ngàn Khơi*. The latter soon became a best-selling newspaper of the era. Most papers increased their number of pages. Not just newspapers saw their circulation increase but other publications—literary magazines, books, etc.—did as well. Bookstores and newsstands sprang up everywhere. Any writer, who so wished, could publish his or her own books if there were readers wanting to buy them. As a result, several authors became their own publishers and distributors.

News from the battlefields became dominant. War ravages still occurred in remote areas, in the jungles or the countryside. Yet Saigon and the large cities in the South were still secure and vibrant. New universities, including those privately operated, came into existence in Saigon and the western region, and the student population increased (see chapter 9 in this volume on the growth of higher education in the early 1970s).

Ten years following the country's division, more than a generation of the South had become adults who began to take part in shaping the destiny of the country. It was their youthful energy that contributed to and changed every aspect of the republic, including literature and arts.

Since 1966, the open space behind the Faculty of Letters (Đại Học Văn Khoa) that bordered four avenues in the heart of Saigon became a center of activity for the young generation. It was there that poetry recitals took place on many evenings. The audience consisted of hundreds of students, sitting on the ground and listening to free-form poems. From there these poetry recitals eventually entered academic curriculums. They became literary shows on television and radio hosted by Trần Dạ Từ, a new venue for poetry writing, reciting, and listening.

It was at a corner of this open square where the Society of Young Fine-Arts Painters was born, with its own large wooden headquarters opening onto Lê Thánh Tôn Avenue where the works of its members were displayed. The place offered a safe sanctuary for the young composer Trịnh Công Sơn who chose to write music over military service. It was there that Trịnh Công Sơn and Khánh Ly rehearsed his new songs during the day to share with a student audience at night at the open space behind the society's building. Sơn's songs, performed together with or by Khánh Ly alone, were recorded on cassette tapes already available then and soon spread over the air, touching many a heart.

Like Sơn and me, our small group of school friends from Huế had all grown up. Nguyễn Xuân Hoàng had now become a teacher and writer. Lê Hữu Bôi now presided over the Union of Student Associations, then went on to become a civil servant.

During the Tết of 1968, also known as Tết Mậu Thân, the three childhood friends, Lê Hữu Bôi, Trịnh Công Sơn, and myself, converged in Huế for the holidays. On Tết's Eve, the cease-fire was broken. The North's infiltrated forces opened attacks on major cities of the South (see chapter 6 in this volume). Huế during Tết Mậu Thân turned into hell.

Lê Hữu Bôi forever remained in Huế, his body buried somewhere. Trịnh Công Sơn and I survived. Returning to Saigon, we met and remembered "young Bôi" as I sat listening to Sơn sing his newly composed "Hát Bên Những Xác Người" (Singing by cadavers). Sơn wrote the song as he walked by the Bãi Dâu area (in Huế) littered with corpses of war victims, he told me. Done with singing, he turned to me and said, please write about what happened, dear Vân. I told him, you should write too. Though different in viewpoints, we quietly knew together we had to do something for Huế.

Sometime later, I got to listen to the songs in his collection titled *Ca Khúc Da Vàng* (Songs for the yellow-skinned), which opened with the song "Gia tài của Mẹ" (A mother's heritage): "Một ngàn năm nô lệ giặc Tầu. Một trăm năm nô lệ giặc Tây. Hai mươi năm nội chiến từng ngày" (One thousand years ruled by the Chinese / One hundred years enslaved by the French / Twenty years of civil war). Sơn also composed a few songs for chorus by students during their gatherings. The leader of the student chorus was Ngô Vương Toại. He was later shot in the stomach by a communist operative when he went on the mike to introduce his ensemble during a gathering.

As for me, just after a few pages of *Giải Khăn Sô Cho Huế* (Mourning Headband for Huế) were published as a serial in the daily *Hoà Bình* of Saigon, a typewritten death-threat letter signed by a member of the "Đặc Công Thành" (Inner City Commando Assassination Squad) was sent to the newspaper, telling me to stop writing or else. That communist operatives could kill a writer or journalist had been a reality. Journalist Từ Chung, the managing editor of the daily *Chính Luận*, was assassinated on his way home from work. Writer-journalist Chu Tử, publisher of the daily *Sống*, was shot in the face on his way to work, but survived.

The death-threat letter to Nhã Ca was published in *Hoà Bình*. *Giải Khăn Sô Cho Huế* continued, then was published in book form.[2] The entire proceeds from the book went to Huế and helped restore the libraries of the Đồng Khánh High School and the College of Medicine.

The 1970s began with all hidden or open communist networks destroyed following their defeat in the Tết Offensive. The Second Republic became more solidified. With national security under control, several important reforms were carried out. It was the time in which the South's literary and artistic activities reached a higher level, not just within but also without. The voice of Khánh Ly went on to Paris and Washington D.C., and was recorded and broadcast in Japan by the Japanese national broadcasting company (NHK). Songs by Phạm Duy and Trịnh Công Sơn were performed in various languages at many Asian capitals. Saigon-styled rock music and songs by Nguyễn Trung Cang and Lê Hựu Hà were appreciated by the youth in Singapore and Seoul.

Journalist Hồ Văn Đồng became a vice president of the Union of International Press Associations, representing Asian nations. Cartoonist Nguyễn Hải Chí, whose works appeared in several Western newspapers, entered the list of World's Top 10 editorial cartoonists. Paintings by Nguyễn Trung were among top art works sought by Western collectors. PEN Vietnam held a contract-signing ceremony in which translator Barry Hilton received the right to translate Nhã Ca's works. Saigon also became a gathering place for international silver-screen artists when the Republic of Vietnam hosted the Asian Film Festival (see chapter 14 in this volume).

Scores of novels were made into movies during this period, including works by Phan Trần Chúc, Khái Hưng, Nguyễn Mạnh Côn, Chu Tử, Ngọc Linh, Văn Quang, Duyên Anh, and Nguyễn Thụy Long. I myself had a total of four film contracts based on my novels. By 1972, two films had been made. One was titled *Hoa Mới Nở* (Blossoming flower), based on the novel *Cô Híp Py Lạc Loài* (The lost hippy girl).

My memoir *Giải Khăn Sô Cho Huế* was later combined with another novel of mine, *Đêm Nghe Tiếng Đại Bác* (Listening to thundering cannons at night), to become the film *Đất Khổ* (Land of sorrows). This film was directed by Hà Thúc Cần, with me writing the dialogue and Trịnh Công Sơn playing the main character.[3]

In *Đất Khổ*, besides Trịnh Công Sơn, several other artists also appeared, such as writers Sơn Nam and Hà Huy Hà; composers Lê Thương, Lê Trọng Nguyễn, and Vũ

Thành An; and performers such as Bích Hợp, the famous actress who had emigrated from Hanoi, and the beloved, Southern-born Kim Cương. They were representative of different regions, ages, or political views. Although each would follow his or her own path, during the filming all were dedicated and respectful toward one another. The diversity among those who appeared in *Đất Khổ* was similar with that in other areas of politics, literature, arts, and media—a diversity characteristic of the Second Republic.

The Republic of Vietnam from 1955 to 1975 experienced great political discontinuity. The First Republic enjoyed several years of peace, but it was a total war during the Second Republic between 1967 and 1975. Even in the latter period, however, no writers were ever actually imprisoned.

Postwar Tribulations

It is true that the Republic of Vietnam has long fallen.

It is true that the whole community of Southern writers and artists went to prison.

It is true that the entire corpus of books, newspapers, poetry, music, and films of the South were condemned and destroyed.

It has been more than forty years, and the regime has carried out countless campaigns to completely eradicate the so-called "cultural poisons of America and its South Vietnamese puppets" (*Mỹ Ngụy*).

Yet the republic's achievements still live on.

The Republic of Vietnam's cultural, educational, literary, and artistic accomplishments still live on.

Dương Thu Hương, a woman writer from the North, has confessed that she burst into tears on entering Saigon and seeing how much freedom Southerners enjoyed compared to Northerners. Hương realized that she had been deceived, that several generations of the North had been fooled by their leaders.

I believe what she said.

As with human beings, roads, rice fields, and fruit gardens, the South's literature and arts have revealed their accomplishments in their very destruction. That has become clearer and clearer as time goes by. One cannot erase them no matter what.

In fact, a Southern writer confidently expressed this very idea forty years ago.

This happened on a spring afternoon at an intersection by the residential complex named Chu Mạnh Trinh in the Phú Nhuận suburbs of Saigon, where a local police unit was busy leading a youth team to burn books. The scene took place right across from the house of writer Nguyễn Mạnh Côn. Standing with us on a balcony on the first floor of the building, watching piles of books being burned, Côn said while smiling, "Just wait and see. Those words of Southern writers and those songs and voices of Southern artists would forever exist no matter what is being done to them."

A week afterward, the public security force orchestrated an unprecedented, all-out campaign of terror. In the night of April 3, 1976, hundreds of writers and artists in Saigon were rounded up. Côn, myself, and my husband were among those arrested and sent to prison. While held at the prison no. T20 in Gia Định, once we were shepherded onto trucks and taken along with others artists to the "Exhibition Hall of Mỹ Ngụy Crimes." The exhibition area was in a former university lecture hall, and the "crimes" on display were many books by Southern writers. Among them were Nhã Ca's works—my works—with *Giải Khăn Sô Cho Huế* prominently displayed. All of us writers stood at attention. Face forward. In silence. Respectfully saluted our own works.

The campaign to burn books and imprison the writers of the South made the whole civilized world protest. Thanks to the assistance and intervention of several individuals and organizations such as International PEN, Amnesty International, and the Swedish government, my husband Trần Dạ Từ was released after nearly thirteen years in prison and our family were allowed to leave Vietnam and resettle in Sweden afterward.

In April 1976, I was the only woman writer in the communist prison in Saigon. The following was my first exchange with a police interrogator in prison:

The interrogator spoke first:
"Do you know the crime for which you were arrested?"
"I do. For surviving."
"Millions are surviving, why would we arrest only you?"
"Because you are afraid of me, I guess."
Ha, ha . . . He laughed loudly, surprised by my answer.
"Afraid of you? Ha ha . . . If the revolution wants to kill you, it doesn't even have to expend a bullet. We arrested you only because we wanted to apply to you the lenient and humanitarian policy of the Party. Had we wanted to kill you, we would have done so. How can you say we are afraid of you?"
"Why arrest if you are not afraid. Why don't you let me go?"
He shook his head, probably exasperated at the funny logic of a woman.
The logic may sound funny but it is no less real for that.[4]

A renowned Northern writer visited Saigon after all the years of living in the communist North. Asked why a full-scale internationally recognized state would have to resort to a trick to put nearly a million people in reeducation camps, the Northern writer had to look all around him before he could whisper the answer: "Please, don't ever put such a dangerous question to me again! You mean you people don't really understand? It's rather simple. Fear. In one word, fear. They are the most apprehensive people that you know. For what is their real strength? They don't have a thing. Anything they found in the South goes well beyond their wildest dreams, from a home, a school, cultural facilities, to the streets, cars, a suit, and educated people. How can they understand that?"

It is fear that transformed a whole country into a vast Gulag; it is fear that led them to burn books and put many Southern writers in jail and to believe that they could imprison a nation's mind by putting its most creative minds behind bars.

Among those who had perished while imprisoned included three former leaders of PEN Vietnam: Vũ Hoàng Chương, poet who was president twice; Hồ Hữu Tường, politician and writer who was vice president three times; and Hiếu Chân Nguyễn Hoạt, writer and one-time secretary general. Nguyễn Mạnh Côn never returned. He died in a prison somewhere amid the jungles of Xuyên Mộc. However, his belief in the staying power of Southern literature and arts has become a reality.

Forty years later, Hanoi residents enthusiastically went to the theater to listen to Southern singers Chế Linh and then Khánh Ly sing *nhạc vàng* (literally "yellow music," a communist epithet referring to the South's romantic music) that they previously were only able to listen to clandestinely. Sampling through Vietnam-based websites today, one finds out that millions have visited the sites where they can read books by the Republic of Vietnam's authors. Looking closer, one would notice that among the most sought after and read today are many Southern authors who were in their late teens in 1975.

Literary works created by South Vietnamese authors during the 1955–75 period are not just treasures of the South. They reflected a mutual journey, shared accomplishments of the entire people. The people in Vietnam from South to North have confirmed this fact.

I am a writer of the South during the division of the nation.

I am a writer of the Republic of Vietnam.

Yes, and I am a Vietnamese writer.

Notes

1 "Kim Chung" means "golden bell."
2 Nhã Ca, *Giải Khăn Sô Cho Huế* (Saigon: Thương Yêu, 1970). The English translation is Nhã Ca, *Mourning Headband for Hue: An Account of the Battle for Hue, Vietnam 1968*, trans. Olga Dror (Bloomington: Indiana University Press, 2014).
3 Director Hà Thúc Cần was a cameraman for CBS during the Vietnam War. In 1965, he accompanied journalist Morley Safer to cover the battlefields of Cẩm Nê. When receiving the Pulitzer Prize for his reportage of this campaign, Safer praised Hà Thúc Cần as an "extraordinary man."
4 Nha Ca, "The SRV Campaign Against Writers and Artists," trans. Nguyễn Ngọc Bích, in Trần Dạ Từ, *Writers and Artists in Vietnamese Gulag* (Elkhart, IN: Century Publishing House, 1990), 10.

Chapter Fourteen

The Cinema Industry

Kiều Chinh

Kiều Chinh is an actress and movie producer who was involved in the development of the cinema arts in the Republic of Vietnam from the beginning. She first appeared briefly in the movie The Quiet American, the very first American movie shot in Vietnam in 1956, and played her first leading role in the Vietnamese movie Hồi Chuông Thiên Mụ *(The bell of Thiên Mụ pagoda). By 1975, Kiều Chinh had been the leading actress in twenty-two other movies made in South Vietnam, Thailand, India, the Philippines, Singapore, and Taiwan, including several American movies that were filmed in Asia, such as* A Yank in Vietnam, The Devil Within, Operation CIA, *and* Destination Vietnam. *She relocated to California after April 1975 and has appeared in more than one hundred TV shows and movies such as* M*A*S*H, The Letter, Vietnam-Texas, The Joy Luck Club, *and* Journey from the Fall. *She has won numerous awards and prizes, such as Best Actress (Saigon, 1969), Best Leading Actress (Taipei, 1973), and three Lifetime Achievement Awards at Viet Film Festival (2003), San Diego Film Festival (2003), the Cinema Della Donne Film Festival in Italy (2003), and Global Film Festival in San Francisco (2015). Together with the late veteran Lewis P. Puller and journalist Terry Anderson, Kiều Chinh cofounded and cochaired the Vietnam Children's Funds, a nonprofit organization that has built fifty-one schools for more than thirty thousand children in Vietnam since 1993.*

Being a movie actress and not a government official or a researcher, my contribution to this volume is simply an artist telling a story about her personal life experiences in a unique time period in the Republic of Vietnam.

I was blessed to be part of South Vietnam's cinema industry from the beginning and to interact with the international motion pictures industry as early as in 1956. The very first "Action" sound—the acting command—that I received in my career was from director Joseph L. Mankiewicz, when I had a brief appearance in the movie *The Quiet American*—the very first American movie shot in Vietnam. Later, in 1957, I actually entered into the motion pictures industry with the leading role in the movie *Hồi Chuông Thiên Mụ* (The bell of Thiên Mụ pagoda) produced by Tân Việt Studio, with Bùi Diễm at the helm.

From then, I played the female lead role in twenty-two other movies that were made not only in Vietnam but also in Thailand, India, Taiwan, Singapore, and the Philippines, including a number of American movies that were filmed in Asia, such as *A Yank in Vietnam, Operation CIA, Devil Within,* and *Destination Vietnam*. The last movie in my twenty-year career in Vietnam was *Full House*, which was filmed in Singapore. The shooting was completed on April 15, 1975, and I returned to Saigon just when South Vietnam was collapsing.

After many days wandering as a refugee without a country, I finally reached America and was introduced to Hollywood with help from actress Tippi Hedren and actor William Holden. And it was here that I decided to stay for the "seventh art"—knowing that I would have to restart from the beginning. And since October 1975, I have appeared in more than one hundred TV shows and movies such as *M*A*S*H*, costarring with Alan Alda, *The Letter*, costarring with Lee Remick, and *Welcome Home* with Kris Kristofferson. I also had a lead role in several movies, such as *Vietnam-Texas, The Joy Luck Club, Face, Tempted*, and *Journey from the Fall*. Most recently, I was a coproducer for the movie *Ride the Thunder*. I received a Lifetime Achievement Award at the Global Film Festival 2015 in San Francisco.

In the last forty years in the United States, I have played many "roles." I make movies. I also work with the Greater Talent Network, Inc., in New York, as a professional speaker for cultural and university events throughout the United States. And, more significantly, the late veteran Lewis P. Puller, journalist Terry Anderson, and I cofounded and cochaired the Vietnam Children's Funds (VCF), a nonprofit organization comprising many American veterans. VCF seeks to build a network of elementary schools in Vietnam in areas that were most damaged in the war—as a dedication to over two million lives lost in that war. VCF aims to seat fifty-eight thousand students in a school year—the same number of the names on the wall of the Vietnam Veterans Memorial. We have already built fifty-one schools for more than thirty thousand children.

Significant Milestones in the History of Cinema

The year 2016 marked 120 years since the world's motion pictures industry was born. It also marked 120 years since the day that Vietnamese first knew about cameras. This shows that cinema came to Vietnam very early, before many neighboring countries. However, more than a century later, Vietnam's cinema industry remains underdeveloped relative to other Asian countries.

The reason for this underdevelopment is this: cinema, just like any other profession or enterprise, always shares the same destiny as its country. Therefore, before recalling the development of the film industry during the Republic of Vietnam period, I would like to briefly mention the significant milestones of world cinema.

Cinema officially began in France, when the Lumière brothers invented a set of film camera, film printer, and film projector, which was generally called *cinématographe* (from which the term *cinema* derived). Three days before the New Year of 1896, Salon Indien (an Indian-style guest room), located in the basement of the Grand Café in Paris, was turned into the place to host the first public movie screening at which admission was charged. Since then, the seventh art was introduced to whole world.

Also in 1896, Pathé Studio made a movie introducing France and its colonies, which included a few scenes of An Nam (the old name of Vietnam), from Huế the capital to popular festivals across the country. People were shown how movies were made and got to watch them for free. At that time, the king of electrical equipment in the United States was Thomas Edison, who had just unveiled the Kinetograph, a camera that could only record motion pictures rudimentarily, and the spectators needed to shine a light and watch through a magnifying glass.

Nevertheless, French hegemony in cinema was unsustainable. The *cinematographe*, the amazing invention of the Lumière brothers, did not have the time to develop. Eighteen years later, World War I started in 1914. Though this war lasted for only four years, France and Europe were greatly devastated. Meanwhile, the United States quickly developed into a scientific and cultural center of the world. Hollywood subsequently became the premier player with many illustrious artists in silent films such as Charlie Chaplin and Buster Keaton.

The silent film era, which was initiated by the French, also ended in 1927, when a number of studios such as Warner Bros and Fox Pictures successfully produced the very first sound films, *The Jazz Singer* and *The Lights of New York*. Shortly after World War I, France did attempt to reclaim its dominance of cinema, but it turned out to be too late.

In August 1920, near Hoàn Kiếm Lake (the Returned Sword Lake) in downtown Hanoi, the first movie theater—the Pathé—was inaugurated. Pathé Studio and Indochina Film Studio were also established. From 1923, a series of new movies was made, including the first feature film *Kim Vân Kiều*, which was premiered at the Cinema Palace movie theater, on Tràng Tiền Street in March 1924. Though *Kim Vân Kiều* was made based on the work of poet Nguyễn Du, actors were classical opera singers from Quảng Lạc Troupe. All scenes were shot in Hanoi, but the technical crew and director were from France.

However, at the end of silent movie era, Vietnamese cinematic talent in Hanoi was showcased when Nguyễn Lan Hương made and screened several documentaries such as *Đám Tang Vua Khải Định* (King Khải Định's funeral) and *Tấn Tôn Đức Bảo Đại* (King Bảo Đại's inauguration).

Moving to the speaking film era, now it was the turn of Saigon to show the technical ability of the Vietnamese. In 1938, a film company in Hong Kong, the South China Motion Pictures Co., made a movie named *Cánh Đồng Ma* (The haunted field) with collaboration from the Annam Artist Union for the story and cast. Among the actors from Hanoi going to Hong Kong was writer Nguyễn Tuân. Stories about film making were later recalled in his memoir *Một Chuyến Đi* (A trip). Consequently, people long mistook *Cánh Đồng Ma* as the first speaking film in Vietnam.

The truth is, it was neither Hanoi nor Hong Kong, but Saigon where the first 35mm "speaking movie" was made in Vietnam. That film was *Trọn với Tình* (A love commitment), which was ninety minutes long, produced by Nguyễn Văn Đinh of Asia Film in 1938. Everything from scripts and direction to machinery, visual, and sound techniques was created by Vietnamese. In Saigon then, besides Asia Film, there was also Vietnam Film. In 1939 alone, these two studios produced seven feature films.

Yet, 1939 was when World War II began. The allies' aircraft repeatedly bombed both Hanoi and Saigon after Japanese troops moved into Indochina in 1942. (A bomb that fell on the maternity ward in the Phủ Doãn Hospital in Hanoi killed my mother who was there to give birth to my newborn brother.) After this war ended, there came the national resistance movement against French colonialism, and then the Vietnam War. Having the same fate as the country, Vietnam's cinema industry, despite its attempt to rise, continued to be immersed in the darkness of wars and dependence. During this gloomy period, movie theaters in all cities controlled by the French only showed French films or French dubbed films. I witnessed that during my adolescent years in Hanoi when my father took me to the Philamonique Theater or Cầu Gỗ Theater. I still remember watching *Limelight* by Charlie Chaplin, *The Best Years of Our Life* (in French, *Les Plus Belles Anne de Notre Vie*) by American director William Wyler, which won seven Oscars in 1947, and *All about Eve* (in French, *Ève*) by American director Joseph Leo Mankiewicz in 1950, which received fourteen Oscar nominations.

Reading *Ciné Revue* with my father's explanation, I understood that most movies then were produced by the Americans and that the French were only the exclusive distributors in their colonies. Real French films were indeed rare, let alone Vietnamese films.

From 1954 to the First Republic

After fifteen years of complete paralysis due to wars, in early 1954 Hanoi finally produced *Kiếp Hoa* (The fate of flowers), with the script and cast from Kim Chung Troupe, but the director and movie set were from Hong Kong. Just like *Cánh Đồng Ma* before, only one film was made.

At the same time, in Saigon, Việt Thanh Film made *Quan Âm Thị Kính*, while the director Tống Ngọc Hạp made *Lục Vân Tiên* with actress Thu Trang playing the heroine in the story. Notably, Alpha Film produced *Bến Cũ* (The old station), which was the first color movie made in Vietnam, even though it was only recorded by a 16mm film camera. The lead male actor was Hoàng Vĩnh Lộc, and the director was Thái Thúc Nha who also owned Alpha Film. These two people would continue to contribute greatly to the development of the Vietnamese cinema industry.

Three weeks after the French defeat in Điện Biên Phủ, in June 1954, an American military mission led by General Edward Lansdale started establishing operations in Vietnam. Two months later, an armistice between Việt Minh and France was signed in Geneva. Vietnam was thereby divided into two parts: the (communist) Democratic Republic of Vietnam in the North, and the Republic of Vietnam (RVN) in the South. American aircraft and ships brought nearly a million people from the North to the South in a campaign called "Passage to Freedom." I was among this group and became a refugee within my own country.

As the coordinator of this exodus, right after arriving in Vietnam, General Lansdale, together with a few Philippine cinema professionals, quickly finished a film called *Ánh Sáng Miền Nam* (The shining light in the south) as propaganda. Following that, still with the topic of migration, came the film *Chúng Tôi Muốn Sống* (We want to live) with Bùi Diễm as the producer and Vĩnh Noãn the director. More than a year after the exodus, in October 1955, the RVN officially became an independent state. Simultaneously with the last French soldier going home, Vietnam's cinema ended sixty years of French dependence.

At that time, the story of Americans helping dislodge the British and French colonial influences in South Vietnam was truly an enticing topic that inspired a novel called *The Quiet American* by Graham Greene, published in 1955. The female character named Phuong was a Saigonese girl who was pulled between a British writer and an American CIA agent. It was Edward Lansdale who arranged for *The Quiet American* to be filmed in Saigon by Director Joseph Mankiewicz in 1956, with leading actors Michael Redgrave and Audie Murphy.

I was offered the script and casting invitation for the lead female role by Director Mankiewicz, but due to objections from my family, I could only make a brief appearance in the movie. The consultant for Mankiewicz at that time was Bùi Diễm, who later left the film studio to enter politics. (His last position was ambassador of the Republic of Vietnam in the United States.) Understanding this situation, later on in 1957, Bùi Diễm personally arranged for me to officially undertake a cinema career, with the lead female role as a nun in the movie *Hồi Chuông Thiên Mụ* (The bell of Thiên Mụ pagoda) of which he was the executive producer.

Both movies, before the premiere day, had a formal reception at the Continental Hotel on Tự Do Street (meaning Freedom), the new name for Rue Catinat under the French. These two American–Vietnamese movies indeed marked a special progress in the film industry of Vietnam, from a French colony to an independent republic.

Due to historical circumstances, Vietnam was deeply influenced by French culture. After the French left, the Republic of Vietnam was assisted by the United States, and American films and English-language films imported by Cosunam began to come into the country. In the South, with nearly a million recent migrants from the North, ethnic cultural heritage still remained its unified identity. Talents came from all regions of the country—for example, in *Hồi Chuông Thiên Mụ*, the producer Bùi Diễm, lead male actor Lê Quỳnh, and lead female actress Kiều Chinh came from the North while director Lê Dân was a Southerner, and the movie was shot in Huế, with crews from both south and central Vietnam!

With these proper first steps, South Vietnam in the First Republic period properly inked the very first page in the history of the national film industry. Whereas cinema and media in the North were under the control of the state, in the South the government only provided support to help the private cinema industry to recover. International studios were invited into Vietnam to cooperate and help develop the private cinema industry.

In 1957 alone, together with *Hồi Chuông Thiên Mụ* by Tân Việt Studio, the South had thirty-seven other movies produced by private studios. Among them were *Người Đẹp Bình Dương* (The beauty from Bình Dương) of Mỹ Vân Studio with Thẩm Thúy Hằng, and *Lòng Nhân Đạo, Ngọc Bồ Đề* (The good heart and the Bodhi Jade) with Kim Cương. In addition to actors such as Thu Trang, Trang Thiên Kim, Khánh Ngọc, Mai Trâm, Lê Quỳnh, Nguyễn Long, Long Cương, along with Thẩm Thúy Hằng, Kim Cương, Kiều Chinh, and Thanh Nga, there came a new generation of talented actors such as Đoàn Châu Mậu, Trần Quang, Minh Trường Son, Xuân Phát, La Thoại Tân, Huy Cường, Ngọc Phu, Hùng Cường, Vân Hùng, Thành Được, Tuý Phượng, Nguyễn Chánh Tín, Túy Hồng, Kim Vui, Thanh Lan, and many more.

Also during this First Republic period, the foundation for the national cinema industry's technical facilities, from governmental to private sector, gradually formed. In 1959, the National Film Center was established. This was a state agency that assembled directors and technicians to produce movies. From a destitute cinema room in 1955 with neither personnel nor machines, only a few years later, with new technical equipment and a number of professional staff trained in the United States, the National Film Center, under director Đỗ Việt, was then able to produce many kinds of documentaries and feature films. Right after its establishment, its movie *Đứa Con Của Biển Cả* (Son of the sea) won the special prize at the Berlin International Film Festival.

Along with the 1960s came another achievement: the film *Chờ Sáng* (Waiting for daybreak), directed by Thân Trọng Kỳ, received another award for feature film at the Berlin International Film Festival. The leading actors, Lê Quỳnh and Kiều Chinh, were there in person, marking the first time Vietnamese actors representing the government-sponsored film sector attended an international film festival.

And the private movie sector also took a big step forward. In 1954, Thái Thúc Nha's Alpha Film Studio was able to produce *Bến Cũ* in which the picture and sound quality were still bad, but the spirit was high. Only a few short years later, Alpha Film became the first mainstream private film production in Vietnam. A typical success of

Alpha Film is *Mưa Rừng* (Forest rain), an adaptation of Hà Triều Hoa Phượng's opera of the same name. It was in color, with widescreen and starring Kiều Chinh, Kim Cương, Lê Quỳnh, Hoàng Vĩnh Lộc, Xuân Phát, Ngọc Phu, and still directed by Thái Thúc Nha.

Saigon had more than thirty private film studios, which made hundreds of new films (which cannot be listed here due to space constraint). This achievement was due to the steady technical and professional support both from the government (the National Film Center) and from the private sector (Alpha Film). These two entities and other private film studios had exchanged personnel and technology support, regardless of origin. Besides nationally acclaimed directors such as Hoàng Vĩnh Lộc and Bùi Sơn Duân, there were several French-trained directors like Lê Dân, Lê Mộng Hoàng, Hoàng Anh Tuấn, Võ Doãn Châu, and Đặng Trần Thức. And they all worked comfortably with directors Lê Hoàng Hoa, Thân Trọng Kỳ, and other film professionals trained in the United States. It was from this foundation that the Vietnamese cinematic talents were able to grow, as I will show below.

The Vietnam Cinema Industry Took Off

With two studios fully equipped and staffed, the owner of Alpha Film, Thái Thúc Nha, became chair of the Vietnam Movie Producers Association. As a producer and director, fluent in both English and French, Thái Thúc Nha established a stellar international reputation. Alpha Film Studio would be the first studio that foreign studios looked for, and Thái Thúc Nha would be the first person to help integrate Vietnam cinema into the international arena.

In 1963, when a Hollywood filmmaker came to Saigon to make *A Yank in Vietnam*, Thái Thúc Nha became the coproducer and I the lead actress. And also at this time, Vietnam started to attend Asian film festivals. In 1965, Thái Thúc Nha and I took part in to the Tokyo Film Festival and, in the following years, Taipei and Hong Kong. Joining us were Mỹ Vân Film and actresses Thẩm Thuý Hằng, Kim Vui, and Thanh Lan.

In the mid-1960s, when the war escalated, U.S. troops officially entered the war, and television techniques also came to Vietnam. Initially, the U.S. military TV stations broadcast from aircraft, with tucked antenna, hovering over the city. Later, the Vietnam television system was formally established, and technical facilities were built, one by one, gradually covering all of South Vietnam. With five local TV stations and more than 350,000 TV sets, 80 percent of the population was able to watch television at home.

The war continued to escalate. U.S. military personnel increased. The television network of the U.S. military (the Armed Forces Vietnam Network/AFVN) was established, showing a number of then popular series, such as *Combat!* starring Vic Morrow and *Rawhide* starring Clint Eastwood. During this period, I was also invited to a few shows on AFVN to welcome U.S. celebrities and dignitaries who came to Vietnam to visit the troops. Thus, I had the opportunity to meet many Hollywood stars such as Tippi Hedren, Diane McBain, Glenn Ford, Danny Kaye, and Johnny Grant. I also recall receiving President Nguyễn Văn Thiệu and Minister Hoàng Đức Nhã, when they visited AFVN to send New Year's wishes to the allied soldiers.

At that time, the presence of a large number of American and allied troops in Vietnam led to many profound changes, attracting the attention of international media. Saigon became an international exchange center. Many new techniques from the United States, such as electronic music and the latest movies, were always updated.

Influenced by the small TV screen and the widescreen at newly built theaters such as Đại Nam and Rex, the audience of the seventh art in Vietnam increased rapidly. Hence, although it recovered in the mid-1950s, only in the 1960s, in the Second Republic period, did Vietnam cinema really become matured and was officially recognized as an important art form.

In 1969, an annual award dedicated to cinema was approved. I was honored to receive a national film prize in the first year, awarded by President Nguyễn Văn Thiệu. The year 1969 also saw the launch of an annual film festival called "Vietnam Cinema Day." With effective support from the government, on September 22, 1969, all movie theaters showed Vietnamese films free of charge. The Movie Producers Association (chaired by Thái Thúc Nha) successfully organized this special activity.

After that, the film industry became a foreground industry to be boosted. Thanks to supporting policies to promote investment, the businesses in the film industry could join force in making better movies. It was then that Liên Ảnh Company was formed. With the participation of many studios and coordination by Quốc Phong (publisher of *Phim Ảnh* magazine), Liên Ảnh quickly gathered sufficient funds needed to make the films that met audiences' demands. Larger capital meant bigger movies and stronger support. From the success of *Chân Trời Tím* (The purple horizon), story by Văn Quang and directed by Lê Hoàng Hoa, starring Kim Vui, Hùng Cường, Quốc Phong, and Lưu Trạch Hưng, Liên Ảnh made many more successful movies and enjoyed a large number of spectators. In addition, with specific aid measures for private filmmakers, the artists were encouraged to produce movies themselves. Kim Cương, Thẩm Thúy Hằng, Tuý Hồng, and other artists eventually established their own studios.

For me, it was time for Giao Chỉ Studio to be established. With special help from the Ministry of Information and Mass Mobilization (under Ngô Khắc Tỉnh and Hoàng Đức Nhã), the National Film Center, and many branches of the Armed Forces of the Republic of Vietnam, Giao Chỉ Film and Hoàng Vĩnh Lộc successfully produced *Người Tình Không Chân Dung* (The faceless lover). In this movie, besides working as the executive producer, I costarred with Vũ Xuân Thông, Minh Trường Sơn, Trần Quang, Tam Phan, and Hùng Cường. This was the first Vietnamese film to receive the best movie and the best actress awards at the Asian Film Festival in 1972.

Also on this occasion, the Third Film Festival was set out to increase cooperation between Vietnam and foreign countries. The chair of the Movie Producers Association suggested that only one association specializing in production would be inadequate, and hence all artists and professionals would need to participate. Therefore, the conference decided to establish a Vietnam Cinema Association, and I was nominated to be the first chair.

After the establishment of Vietnam Cinema Association, due to the contacts made at the many film festivals and from starring in U.S. movies shot in Asia, I was able to help improve international relations. In 1973, the Republic of Vietnam became the host country of that year's Asian Film Festival. Saigon turned into the meeting venue of the international film industry, including filmmakers, directors, and actors from Bangkok, Tokyo, Taipei, Hong Kong, Singapore, Seoul, and other Asian capitals. Thanks to support from the government's National Film Center, as well as generous assistance from many officials, businessmen, studio owners, movie theaters, and especially the dedication of all artists and professionals in the Vietnam Cinema Association, the Asian Film Festival Week 1973 in Saigon was a great success. From these activities, many contracts were made, and many joint projects between Vietnam and Thailand, Singapore, Taiwan, and Japan were discussed.

The Paris Accords of 1973 on the cessation of hostilities in Vietnam were announced early in the year; therefore, even though skirmishes still happened, most Southern cities were relatively unharmed. During Christmas in 1973, New Year's Eve in 1974, and then the Lunar New Year of the Tiger in 1974, Saigon was more crowded than ever, and all major theaters were showing Vietnamese movies.

On the Sixth Vietnam Cinema Day, in September 1974, the chair of the Movie Producers Association excitedly declared that the Vietnam cinema industry had truly taken off. Lưu Trạch Hưng, the owner of Mỹ Vân Studio, announced the promotion for the construction of a large film set on Biên Hòa Highway. Tôn Thất Cảnh and Đỗ Tiến Đức, directors of the National Film Center, were really confident that the Vietnamese People Watch Vietnamese Films movement would be stronger and stronger.

Everyone was excited about the future. The Vietnam Cinema Association and I were requested to quickly invite a few international actors to participate in the VII Vietnam Cinema Day in September 1975. And then the Vietnam Cinema Day of 1975, or any since, never came!

A Beautiful Dawn in Memory

From 1920, when the first movie theater was inaugurated near Hoàn Kiếm Lake in Hanoi until the country was divided in 1954, Vietnamese citizens mostly watched foreign films. Vietnam's cinema industry at that time was just scattered fragments buried in the shadows of wars and dependence.

Yet, in just twenty years, even during the most intense times of the war, the cinema industry in South Vietnam was able to produce all movie genres. In the Lunar New Year of 1975, all major theaters in Saigon were still full of audiences who came, not for Western, Chinese, or Indian movies, but for Vietnamese movies.

That was the twenty-year history of the cinema industry during the Republic of Vietnam period as I personally experienced and based on my recollections. It was a beautiful dawn, an exciting beginning.

CHAPTER FIFTEEN

THE NEGLECT OF THE REPUBLIC OF VIETNAM IN THE AMERICAN HISTORICAL MEMORY

Nu-Anh Tran

Nu-Anh Tran is an assistant professor at the University of Connecticut, where she holds a joint appointment in history and Asian and Asian American studies. She studies Southeast Asian history, with a specialization in Vietnam. Her current project examines the conflicts between anti-communist nationalists in the Republic of Vietnam during Ngô Đình Diệm's tenure (1954–63). Nu-Anh holds a PhD at the University of California, Berkeley, and a BA from Seattle University.

One of the most common grievances I heard growing up in the Vietnamese-American community was that American movies and television did not accurately portray the Vietnam War. I came to the United States as a refugee in the early 1980s, and my family's first decade in this country coincided with the release of iconic films such as the Rambo series, *Full Metal Jacket* (1987), *Platoon* (1986), and *Born on the Fourth of July* (1989). The war also served as a backdrop or back story for a number of contemporary television shows, including *The A-Team* (1983–87), *Tour of Duty* (1987–90), and *China Beach* (1988–91). My parents and their friends decried the absence of Vietnamese people in popular depictions and were outraged by the portrayal of the Republic of Vietnam (RVN, better known as South Vietnam), the defunct anticommunist government that many refugees still championed. Gathered at the dining table over holiday meals or lecturing me and other children during weekly language classes, my elders would say indignantly, "American movies only show American soldiers, as if they did all the fighting, and we did none." Someone would invariably add, "And if they show the Vietnamese at all, it's only the communists. The movies don't show anyone on our side except for prostitutes, corrupt generals, and cowardly soldiers." At issue was the very legitimacy of the war. Although my elders acknowledged the shortcomings of the Saigon government, my parents and their friends valorized the war as a nationalist struggle against communism. They especially resented the implicit suggestion the regime was not worth saving, a suggestion that they believed cheapened our plight as refugees and the sacrifices of loved ones who fought for the anticommunist cause. Ultimately, I think the refugees feared that their experiences of the RVN would never become part of the collective historical memory.

I have repeatedly mulled over those many conversations I heard as a child. The grievances of my parents and their friends appear to beg two distinct questions: Why has the anticommunist regime been ignored in the dominant American discourse, and what can Vietnamese-American refugees do to remedy the situation? I want to consider this problem as both a trained historian and a member of the community. This article is a personal reflection and an appeal to other Vietnamese-Americans rather than a work of academic analysis. My elders sometimes suspected that there was a deliberate attempt to silence anticommunist voices, but I believe that the reasons were far more mundane.

Let me begin by briefly discussing the representation of the Vietnamese in American popular culture in the late 1980s and early 1990s. At the time, mainstream film and television focused almost exclusively on the American experience, just as my elders alleged.[1] According to several studies, the media typically relegated Vietnamese people—if they are included at all—to minor characters or shadowy figures. Those affiliated with the RVN were depicted as corrupt, inept allies, while Vietnamese communists were either perfidious enemies or idealized heroes.[2] I have no expertise in American popular culture, but I would wager that the majority of filmmakers were white Americans who were interested in their own stories, and the result was a vision of the war dominated by characters made in the filmmakers' own image. (I hasten to point out that American movies about other historical events have been and continue to be equally riddled with problems of representation and accuracy.) Perhaps part of the solution is that there needs to be more Vietnamese-American filmmakers. Many members of the community hailed Ham Tran's *Journey from the Fall* (*Vượt Sóng*, 2006) as an accurate portrayal of their experiences, especially the film's depiction of reeducation camps and the boat people experience. Indeed, Tran's film was revolutionary as the first full-length narrative film made in the United States to privilege an anticommunist Vietnamese perspective.

The problem of representation extends to the English-language academic research. The Vietnam War has generated a tremendous volume of scholarship, but the bulk of the research has focused on the United States. While a significant portion examines the communist Democratic Republic of Vietnam (DRV, or North Vietnam) and the communist-led National Liberation Front (NLF, colloquially known as the "Vietcong"), there is very little scholarship on Vietnamese anticommunists and the RVN. Below, I identify four main reasons for the past scholarly neglect and explain how Vietnamese-Americans can help rectify the problem.

The first reason is that the Vietnam War is a research topic that straddles two starkly different fields: American diplomatic history and Vietnam studies. The former is large and robust and has disproportionately shaped academic understanding of the war. Diplomatic historians are Americanists by training, and they study the conflict as an event in the history of U.S. foreign relations. In the past, these scholars have discussed the RVN only as an extension of American foreign policy rather than a distinct unit of analysis, and they argued that the Saigon regime was a foreign creation devoid of indigenous origins.[3] Vietnam studies was a potential corrective to the American-centered research. Students of Vietnam conceptualized the war as an event in Vietnamese history and pointed to the conflict's inextricable ties to French colonialism, the Vietnamese nationalist movement, and the rise of communism. But Vietnam studies, itself a subfield of Southeast Asian studies, remains underdeveloped and cannot match the influence of American diplomatic history.

Second, scholarly trends within Vietnam studies have mitigated against research on the RVN until recently. American academic research on Vietnam did not begin in earnest until the latter half of the 1960s. This first generation of Vietnam specialists was eager to examine the Vietnamese dimension of the war, but they were selective as to which group of Vietnamese to study. Influenced by growing antiwar sentiments and seeking to explain the strength of the NLF and the DRV, researchers devoted their attention to the communists instead of the Saigon regime. The communist-centric trend continued into the 1980s and produced what has become the dominant historical interpretation.[4] In brief, scholars argued that Vietnamese communism was the direct outgrowth of the colonial-era nationalist movement and that the communists won the war because they were more convincingly nationalist. The narrative cast the communist movement as the main trend in modern Vietnamese history while dismissing the RVN as a deviation. Researchers discussed the anticommunist regime not as a topic in its own right but merely as a foil to the other Vietnamese belligerents.[5] Although the vagaries of academic trends affect virtually all disciplines, the communist-centric scholarship exercised unusual dominance because of the small size of Vietnam studies.

The limited availability of sources was another reason for scholarly neglect of the RVN. For decades after the war, the absence of diplomatic relations between Vietnam and the United States meant that American researchers could not consult the Vietnamese archives. Instead, scholars could only draw on American and French archives, published materials available in Western research libraries, and publications and oral history produced by the Vietnamese diaspora. These sources, although valuable, could not substitute for the RVN's own documents, arguably the best material for understanding the regime's identity and aspirations. Finally, the language barrier constituted a serious obstacle. Vietnamese-language skills are essential for conducting serious research on Vietnam, but few American scholars had the opportunity to learn Vietnamese because most universities did not offer any courses in it. Even at institutions that did, the pedagogical quality lagged behind more frequently taught Asian languages such as Mandarin Chinese and Japanese.

Yet the tide of academic scholarship is turning, and prospects for research on the RVN are now brighter than ever. In the latter half of the 1990s and the early 2000s, a young generation of American diplomatic historians began studying Vietnamese just as the reestablishment of diplomatic relations made the Vietnamese archives more accessible. Several of these scholars seized upon the opportunity to examine government documents produced by the RVN as well as rare books and periodicals housed at the regime's former national library. Other historians explored the DRV's archives to better understand the inner workings of the wartime government in Hanoi. The new sources facilitated the emergence of a scholarly trend known as the "new Vietnam War scholarship," which was distinguished by a major conceptual shift. Instead of the American-centered framework, several historians devoted equal attention to both sides of the Washington–Saigon alliance. Whereas earlier research had cast Ngô Đình Diệm as a reactionary mandarin that obstructed American reforms, historians such as Philip Catton and Edward Miller argued that the RVN's first president possessed distinct ideas for transforming South Vietnam. Catton's and Miller's studies found that Diệm and his American advisers disagreed sharply on how to modernize Vietnam, and their differences ultimately led to a breakdown in relations.[6] Jessica Chapman demonstrated that earlier research had failed to appreciate the significance of the southern sects and their impact on international relations,[7] and Geoffrey Stewart examined

Diệm's largely forgotten civic action program.[8] Quickly following on the heels of these Americanists is an emerging cohort of Vietnam specialists who have made the RVN the main focus of their current research projects. I include in this cohort scholars such as Van Nguyen-Marshall, Jason Picard, Phi Vân Evelyne Nguyen, and myself.[9]

The Vietnamese-American community can contribute to the new Vietnam War scholarship by creating primary sources. I urge everyone who lived under the RVN to write memoirs, to grant interviews, and to share their memories. Although there are many published autobiographies and interviews, most of them feature political and military leaders, almost all of whom are educated men.[10] Valuable as these perspectives are, historians also need to understand the experiences of women, youth, ethnic minorities, artists, journalists, teachers, religious leaders, artisans, laborers, market vendors, cyclo drivers, bargirls, enlisted soldiers, and peasants. Such diverse sources will give scholars a richer understanding of the RVN as a dynamic and complex society, and historians will be better able to examine topics such as popular political attitudes, sexual mores, youth culture, class stratification, urban-rural divisions, and the effect of the war on ordinary people. Personal accounts are also useful in teaching. I regularly assign Vietnamese-American memoirs in my courses on the Vietnam War. Most of what my students know about the war comes from American movies, and the memoirs help my students understand how different Vietnamese groups experienced the conflict.

The prospects for future research on the RVN are partially dependent on the strength of Vietnam studies as a field. I believe the Vietnamese-American community can support the field by teaching our children our mother tongue, by sharing with them our family history, and by fostering their interest in Vietnamese culture. We can also encourage our children to seek out universities that teach about Vietnam and enroll in Vietnam-related courses. The objective is to pique young people's interest in Vietnam studies and to build a constituency for the field. I myself would not have chosen to study the RVN had it not been for my parents' captivating stories and their decision to raise me bilingual. In fact, roughly half of the Vietnam specialists in my acquaintance share my background: diasporic Vietnamese who learned the language and culture from their parents. I fully acknowledge the difficulty of teaching a second language and culture without the institutional support of schools, teachers, and textbooks. My late mother, who had no pedagogical training, had to juggle teaching Vietnamese classes with her full-time job and household chores. I have vivid memories of her pausing her lectures on Vietnamese poetry to check the stove or stir the soup pot. I also struggled to learn the language due to the dearth of age-appropriate reading materials and the absence of a sizeable Vietnamese-speaking peer group. Nevertheless, our community must shoulder the task of maintaining Vietnamese as a vibrant, living language in the United States because too few universities offer Vietnamese instruction. Beyond our community, we can also support the field by donating to universities and research institutes that promote Vietnam studies.

More broadly, if Vietnamese-Americans want to influence the collective historical memory, then we must value the humanities, the social sciences, and the arts. These are the fields that shape how a society remembers the past. Our community needs historians to interpret our experience, anthropologists to analyze our rich culture, literary critics to keep our long tradition of oral and written literature alive, and filmmakers to tell our stories on the silver screen. The problem is that Vietnamese-American elders often dissuade young people from pursuing those fields in favor of conventional careers in medicine and engineering. My own relatives frowned upon my decision to become a historian when I was in college, and even Vietnamese-American peers puzzled over my choice to major in history, though I was lucky to have my parents' full support. Some of my Vietnamese-American colleagues recount that their decision to pursue graduate studies in the humanities provoked a family crisis, and their parents responded with lectures, entreaties, and orchestrated interventions. It is understandable that refugees who have weathered profound dislocation would nudge their children into lucrative, high-status occupations. Doctors and engineers certainly do laudable work. But if our community blocks its young people from alternative careers, we are actively contributing to the erasure of our experiences from the historical memory. After all, would Ham Tran have made *Journey from the Fall* if he had decided to become a pharmacist?

Lastly, we as a community must support intellectual freedom because it is vital to historical memory. Virtually every government in modern Vietnamese history has to some degree suppressed dissent, enforced censorship, and tried to shore up its power by manipulating history. We must recognize that the serious examination of the past will render multiple interpretations. Moreover, the Vietnamese-American community is increasingly diverse, and members harbor varied perspectives on the war and on the RVN.[11] We should choose polite debate rather than trying to silence those with whom we disagree. My elders understood how it felt to be ignored by the dominant discourse and insisted that their perspective deserved to be acknowledged. As we attempt to incorporate our stories into the collective memory, we must also make room for the histories of others. Their viewpoints, like ours, will enrich the understanding of the past.

Notes

1 Oliver Stone's *Heaven and Earth* (1993) was the only mainstream American feature film produced in the late 1980s and 1990s that focused on the Vietnamese experience of the Vietnam War.

2 Michael Renov, "Imaging the Other: Representations of Vietnam in Sixties Political Documentary," in *From Hanoi to Hollywood*, ed. Linda Dittmar and Gene Michaud (New Brunswick: Rutgers University Press, 1990), 255–68; Doug Williams, "Concealment and Disclosure: From 'Birth of a Nation' to the Vietnam War Film," *International Political Science Review* 12, no. 2 (1991): 37–38; David Dresser, "'Charlie Don't Surf': Race and Culture in the Vietnam War Film," in *Inventing Vietnam: The War in Film and Television*, ed. Michael Anderegg (Philadelphia: Temple University Press, 1991), 86–97; Andrew Martin, *Receptions of War* (Norman: University of Oklahoma Press, 1993), 99–100.

3 Gabriel Kolko, *Anatomy of a War: Vietnam, the United States, and the Modern Historical Experience* (New York: Pantheon Books, 1985); James Carter, *Inventing Vietnam: The United States and State Building, 1954–1968* (Cambridge: Cambridge University Press, 2008); Seth Jacobs, *America's Miracle Man in Vietnam: Ngo Dinh Diem, Religion, Race, and the US Intervention in Southeast Asia, 1950–1957* (Durham, NC: Duke University Press, 2005). See also George Herring, "Our Offspring: Nation Building in South Vietnam, 1954–1961," chap. 2 in *America's Longest War: The United States and Vietnam, 1950–1975* (New York: Wiley, 1979); Marilyn B. Young, *The Vietnam Wars, 1945–1990* (New York: Harper Perennial, 1991); George Kahin, *Intervention: How America Became Involved in Vietnam* (New York City: Anchor Books, 1987).

4 For a concise overview of this period in Vietnam studies, see Tuong Vu, "Vietnamese Political Studies and Debates on Vietnamese Nationalism," *Journal of Vietnamese Studies* 2, no. 2 (Summer 2007): 187–203.

5 David G. Marr, *Vietnamese Anticolonialism, 1885–1925* (Berkeley: University of California Press, 1971); David G. Marr, *Vietnamese Tradition on Trial, 1920–1945* (Berkeley: University of California Press, 1980); William J. Duiker, *The Communist Road to Power in Vietnam*, 1st ed. (Boulder, CO: Westview, 1981); Huỳnh Kim Khánh, *Vietnamese Communism, 1925–1945*

(Ithaca: Cornell University Press, 1982); Carlyle Thayer, *War by Other Means: National Liberation and Revolution in Viet-Nam, 1954–60* (Boston: Allen and Unwin, 1989).

6 Philip Catton, *Diem's Final Failure: Prelude to America's War in Vietnam* (Lawrence: University Press of Kansas, 2002); Edward Miller, *Misalliance: Ngo Dinh Diem, the United States, and the Fate of South Vietnam* (Cambridge, MA: Harvard University Press, 2013).

7 Jessica Chapman, *Cauldron of Resistance: Ngo Dinh Diem, the United States, and 1950s Southern Vietnam* (Ithaca: Cornell University Press, 2013).

8 Geoffrey Stewart, *Vietnam's Lost Revolution: Ngô Đình Diệm's Failure to Build an Independent Nation, 1955–1963* (Cambridge: Cambridge University Press, 2017).

9 For a sample of research by this cohort, see Van Nguyen-Marshall, "The Associational Life of the Vietnamese Middle Class in Saigon (1950s–1970s)," in *The Reinvention of Distinction: Modernity and the Middle Class in Urban Vietnam*, ed. Van Nguyen-Marshall, Lisa Drummond, and Daniele Belanger (Singapore: Asian Research Institute, National University of Singapore, in cooperation with Springer Publishing, 2012), 59–75; Jason Picard, "Renegades: The Story of South Vietnam's First National Opposition Newspaper," *Journal of Vietnamese Studies* 10, no. 4 (Fall 2015): 1–29; Phi Vân Nguyen, "Fighting the First Indochina War Again? Catholic Refugees in the Republic of Vietnam, 1954–59," *Sojourn* 31, no. 1 (March 2016): 207–46; Nu-Anh Tran, "South Vietnamese Identity, American Intervention and the Newspaper *Chính Luận* [Political Discussion], 1965–1969," *Journal of Vietnamese Studies* 1, nos. 1–2 (February/August 2006): 169–209.

10 Notable memoirs by diasporic Vietnamese men relating to the RVN include but are not limited to Nhị Lang, *Phong trào kháng chiến Trình Minh Thế* [The resistance movement under Trinh Minh The] (Boulder, CO: Lion Press, 1985); Bùi Diễm with David Chanoff, *In the Jaws of History* (Boston: Houghton Mifflin, 1987); Đỗ Mậu, *Việt Nam máu lửa quê hương tôi* [Vietnam, my warring country: political memoirs] (Mission Hills, CA: privately published, 1986); Huỳnh Văn Lang, *Nhân chứng một chế Độ* [Witness to a regime], vols. 1–2 (Westminster, CA: Văn Nghệ, [2000?]); Hà Thúc Ký, *Sống còn với dân tộc* [Live and die with the nation] (n.p.: Phương Nghi, 2009); Nguyễn Công Luận, *Nationalist in the Vietnam Wars* (Bloomington: Indiana University Press, 2012). The most prominent memoirs by diasporic Vietnamese women that discuss the RVN are Duong Van Mai Elliott, *The Sacred Willow* (New York: Oxford University Press, 1989); Le Ly Hayslip, *When Heaven and Earth Changed Places* (New York City: Plume, 2003).

11 For an overview of recent changes in the composition of Vietnamese-Americans, see An Tuan Nguyen, "More Than Just Refugees: A Historical Overview of Vietnamese Migration to the United States," *Journal of Vietnamese Studies* 10, no. 3 (Summer 2015): 87–125.

Chapter Sixteen

Political, Military, and Cultural Memoirs in Vietnamese

Tuan Hoang

Tuan Hoang is assistant professor at Pepperdine University and teaches in the History and Great Books Programs. His research has focused on noncommunist and anticommunist Vietnamese in South Vietnam and the postwar diaspora. Among his publications are "The Early South Vietnamese Critique of Communism," in Dynamics of the Cold War in Asia: Ideology, Identity, and Culture, *ed. Tuong Vu and Wasana Wongsurawat (Palgrave Macmillan, 2009); "From Reeducation Camps to Little Saigons: Historicizing Vietnamese Diasporic Anticommunism,"* Journal of Vietnamese Studies *(2016); and "Ultramontanism, Nationalism, and the Fall of Saigon: Historicizing the Vietnamese American Catholic Experience,"* American Catholic Studies *(2019). He has also edited the following volumes for the Association of Core Texts and Courses:* Tradition and Renewal: Continuity and Change in Core and Liberal Arts Programs *(forthcoming); and (with Daniel Nuckols)* Bridging Divides, Crossing Borders, Community Building: The Human Voice in Core Texts and the Liberal Arts *(forthcoming).*

Since the end of the Vietnam War, many former government officials, military officers, and prominent cultural figures from the Republic of Vietnam (RVN) have published memoirs. Researchers have exploited some of these memoirs, especially those in English such as *In the Jaws of History* by Bùi Diễm, the former ambassador to Washington. In the diaspora, and to a lesser extent, there have been many more Vietnamese-language memoirs targeted at Vietnamese readers. An example comes from a contributor to this collection: the two-volume memoir by Vũ Quốc Thúc. For linguistic and other reasons, however, only a small number of scholars and researchers have used these memoirs.

There are several problems among these memoirs, especially those written by political and military figures. They include the strong intention of the authors, stated or otherwise, to justify their action in the past. Rather common among people on the losing side after a long and complex armed conflict, the memoirists tend to absolve themselves from contributing to major problems during the war and the eventual demise of South Vietnam. They instead place the blame for those problems on the communists, the Americans, and other noncommunist South Vietnamese, including the RVN leadership at the top. Having Vietnamese readers in mind, the memoirists also tend to affirm and assert their personal virtues such as righteousness and patriotism as another way to dislodge criticism of their actions and decisions in the past. Then there is the issue of selectivity, as the memoirists sometimes focus on certain periods and neglect others. This issue is related to the problem of reliability, particularly the trickiness of memory and the revision of one's original understanding or interpretation of events. There is also neglect of certain subjects. With rare exceptions, for example, the memoirists write little about their experiences of the peasantry and the conditions of rural South Vietnam. It might be the result of selective memory as much as a lack of depth and understanding about the countryside, whose fate was affected by communist control and U.S. bombing and search-and-destroy missions. Consequently, researchers should be very cautious when using these memoirs. At the least, they should compare the memoirs to information found in official records and other sources.

These limits notwithstanding, Vietnamese-language memoirs serve at least two purposes that are potentially helpful to researchers. First, they provide many details about personalities and events that may not show up in official records and other primary sources. Equally if not more significantly, they help to illustrate broader themes and patterns about the background, politics, and culture of South Vietnam. Below are several discernible themes that come from the list of selected Vietnamese-language memoirs at the end of this chapter. The first section focuses on memoirs by RVN officials and high-ranking officers of the Republic of Vietnam Armed Forces (ARVN), and the second section on memoirs from writers, artists, and other prominent figures in the realm of culture.

The first theme is the violence ascribed to the August Revolution. Only some of the memoirs discuss the period before 1954. Among those that do, they typically consider the revolution to be a period of enormous losses among nationalist groups at the hands of the Việt Minh. The encounters might have varied in kind and degree, depending on the age, political status, and area of residence of the memoirists. Nonetheless, sections on personal experiences and recollections of the revolution include many of the most graphic descriptions of violence, if not the most graphic, of the respective memoirs. One example comes from the memoir of Đỗ Mậu, who became a solid supporter of Ngô Đình Diệm when they first met in 1942. Mậu was captured by the Việt Minh in central Vietnam not long after he was out of French imprisonment. Although he was let go a few months later, many other noncommunist revolutionaries during this period were not so fortunate. In central Vietnam, Mậu's brother-in-law had helped to organize a local noncommunist group that enlisted officials, functionaries, officers, and soldiers from the colonial regime. They attempted to make contacts with nationalist groups in northern Vietnam, but the Việt Minh found out and executed or imprisoned some in the leadership. Many of those prisoners, including one of Mậu's brothers and another of his brothers-in-law, were executed during the early phase of the First Indochina War, as the Việt Minh ran away from the French advances and did not want to take along their prisoners.

Another supporter of Diệm, Nguyễn Trân, later the RVN's chief in two provinces, was arrested and nearly killed during the "white terror" in Quảng Ngãi. According to Trân, some eight thousand people were killed during this period of forty days before and after the August Revolution. A different example is Nguyễn Bá Cẩn, later a chairman of the lower house under the Second Republic. Although only a schoolboy at the time of the August Revolution, Cẩn witnessed in and around his native city of Cần Thơ public executions of Hòa Hảo officials, Vietnamese associates to the colonial regime, and other rivals of the communists. On one of the rivers, he also saw three bloated and floating corpses tied together by barbed wire, clearly meant as warning to the local people not to support French collaborators or anticommunist groups.

Taken as a whole, recollections and reflections about this period suggest a relationship between revolutionary violence on the one hand and, on the other hand, the creation of and trajectory for the First Republic. It would be too far to say that the repression committed by Việt Minh forces under Võ Nguyên Giáp, Nguyễn Bình, and other leaders led to the ideologically anticommunist foundation of the State of Vietnam and the RVN. However, the ruthlessness experienced by Ngô Đình Diệm and other nationalists during 1945–46 might offer a partial explanation for his own government's ruthless if ultimately counterproductive Denounce Communists Campaign. Diệm's weaknesses and the well-known factionalism among the nationalists were among the major reasons for the difficulties of fighting communism in South Vietnam. Nonetheless, the memories found in these books confirm the genealogy of revolutionary violence described in many official histories of communist organizations published since the end of the Vietnam War. It is not to deny the complexity of this situation, for some of the anticommunist nationalists proactively engaged in violence and at times succeeded in attacking, kidnapping, and killing the communists. But the intra-Vietnamese violence during 1945–46 tipped the scale to the Việt Minh. It contributed to the organization's political successes in rallying more Vietnamese to its anticolonial cause, but also hardened the anticommunist position when Diệm began the task of nation building after the Geneva Conference.

Nation building is indeed related to the second theme, which is the continual polarization of opinions among Vietnamese regarding Diệm's government. In spite of hindsight, or possibly because of it, the memoirists remain divided over their assessment of Diệm and the demise of his regime. Not surprisingly, the most negative opinions come from former ARVN officers instrumental in the planning and execution of the coups in 1960 and 1963: Nguyễn Chánh Thi, Phạm Văn Liễu, Vương Văn Đông, and Trần Văn Đôn. (An exception is the memoir of Tôn Thất Đính, a generally pro-Diệm general who participated in the latter coup only after a skillful if deceptive effort by the coup leaders to get him to their side.) In addition to the usual charges of dictatorial rule and oppression against non–Cần Lao nationalists, they accused Diệm and the Ngô family of corruption, failure in the fight against the insurgents, and even negotiation with the National Liberation Front. This opinion is shared by some longtime supporters of Diệm, who thought that he and his brother Ngô Đình Nhu were corrupt and unacceptable for the cause of nationalism. This point is underscored in Đỗ Mậu's memoir, possibly the most controversial memoirist in the diaspora. Displaying an anti-Catholic line of argument, Mậu alleges an incompatibility between nationalism and Catholicism in Vietnamese history and contends that Diệm ultimately placed church over nation and favored Catholics over non-Catholics.

But Diệm still has his share of defenders, some of whom place some or most of the blame on Nhu for the failure of the First Republic. Among the latter is Huỳnh Văn Lang, a high-ranking member of the Cần Lao Party assigned by Nhu to be its chief fundraiser. Lang was eventually sidelined by Nhu, however, and even became a coconspirator in an unrealized coup before the successful coup in November 1963. Yet Lang's memoirs maintain his belief in the vision of the Ngô brothers. He praises Nhu for his philosophical vision, and even dedicates one of the volumes to both brothers. (Lang holds lower opinions about Archbishop Ngô Đình Thục and especially Madame Nhu.) Another defender, General Huỳnh Văn Cao, not only remained loyal to Diệm during the coup in 1963 but also professes this loyalty in both of his memoirs that were published twenty-three years apart. In recent years, Diệm's standing in history has improved thanks to archival research led by Western-trained historians as well as a gradually shifting position of the official line in Vietnam. Nonetheless, these memoirs are a reminder of the contentious long-standing debates about his status among the Vietnamese.

In comparison to opinions on the First Republic, Vietnamese-language memoirs are more uniform in holding a mostly positive view about the politics under the Second Republic, which is the third discernible theme: that this period showed democratic progress and held out promise for a desirable political culture among the anticommunist Vietnamese. It is true that the sections in the political and military memoirs on the post-1965 period are usually shorter and less insightful than the sections about the period before 1965. It is true, too, that the memoirists are divided when evaluating Nguyễn Văn Thiệu, though to a lesser extent than they are about Diệm. Most criticism of Thiệu centers generally on his authoritarianism and particularly on his manipulation of two presidential elections. Nonetheless, the fact that many of the memoirists, including several former military officers, were serving in the legislature of the Second Republic led to a more positive appraisal of political life during 1967–75. Even the anti-Thiệu memoir by the opposition politician Lý Quí Chung portrays, perhaps inadvertently, a climate of genuine if sometimes chaotic debates among legislators about the present and future of the country. Because of the fall of Saigon, it is impossible to know whether this political climate would eventually translate into a full-fledged democracy as some other noncommunist countries in Asia. Yet scholars should at least consider that this period saw the largest democratic exercise in modern Vietnamese history up to today.

Related to democratic exercise was the relative freedom in the realm of arts and letters, especially under the Second Republic but also during 1954–67. This theme is prominent in memoirs written by noncommunist writers, artists, musicians, and other noncommunist participants in the public culture of the RVN. It is not to say that the memoirists were uncritical of the Saigon government. The popular fiction writer Madame Tùng Long thought Diệm to be under the control of other members of his family. She was especially displeased by the pressure from Madame Nhu to have various women's groups join the largest government-led organization for women. Another prolific writer, Nguyễn Hiến Lê, notes in his memoir "heavy censorship" during the Second Republic on the highly respected semimonthly *Bách Khoa* (Encyclopedic). Nguyễn Thụy Long, a younger novelist and military officer, could not help but mention corruption, including his own, in one of his memoirs. Such complaints, however, are small and few. The majority of recollections tend to emphasize individual achievements and describe the cultural environment conducive to intellectual, literary, and artistic pursuits among the authors.

The qualified freedom of this environment is most palpable on the pages written by noncommunist figures that had participated in the Việt Minh–led anticolonial war. Phạm Duy, who would become the most productive musician in South Vietnam, eagerly joined this movement as a cultural cadre that wrote and performed many nationalist songs. By 1951, however, he and his wife and her siblings, who formed a beloved vocal group, left the war zone due to rapidly restrictive policies regarding what they could or could not produce. So did Tạ Ty, a rising painter during the early 1950s who became one of the most important artists in the RVN. Unlike the communist revolutionaries, these memoirists believed that bourgeois values were compatible with, even necessary for, Vietnamese nationalism and Vietnamese modernity. Having found the Việt Minh milieu antithetical to those values, they planned their escape from the communist zones and found their way to Saigon even before the signing of the Geneva Peace Accords.

There was a lot more besides ideology and belief. Collectively, the memoirs reveal, among other things, an active engagement of ideas, institutions, and travels between South Vietnam and other noncommunist parts of the world. Some of this engagement was possible due to funds and scholarships that brought young Vietnamese to Europe and the United States for studies: a point made in the contribution of Nguyễn Đức Cường, among others, in this book. But it was merely one among many examples of this global engagement, including the flow of books and magazines from western Europe, North America, and east Asia to Saigon, Huế, Cần Thơ, and other towns and cities. Many memoirists eagerly consumed those publications, then translated them into Vietnamese or made them the basis for their own books and magazine articles. Another means of this global exchange were Paris-based correspondence courses, at least for Nguyễn Hiến Lê in the 1940s and 1950s. (During the 1930s, Madame Tùng Long took a correspondence course that contributed directly to her writing career, albeit one run by Vietnamese in Indochina.) Like other urbanites, the memoirists watched movies from Hollywood and Bollywood, from Hong Kong and France and Britain and other countries. They listened to records of Western and Asian popular music played in cafés and private residences, and they created a vibrant if somewhat eclectic popular musical culture of their own. Studies and travels abroad provided another venue toward their making of Vietnamese modernity. The poet Nguyên Sa came back to Vietnam at the start of national division and became an advocate for a postcolonial form of French existentialism. Around the same time, Phạm Duy saved enough money from his work in Saigon so he could go to Paris for a year and learn musicology to further his song-writing skills. During the 1960s, the ethnic Chinese museum director Vương Hồng Sển visited Taiwan, France, and other countries to collect antiques and meet with foreigners who shared the same interests. These and other examples from the memoirs illustrate the eager activities among the noncommunist elite in South Vietnam, who engaged the larger bourgeois and capitalist modernity in the wider noncommunist world to create their postcolonial and nationalist culture.

The growth of this culture was organic for the most part. The educational system provides an example. As shown in the memoir of the "youth music" (nhạc trẻ) organizer Trường Kỳ, many proponents of this music were students within the informal network of private schools started during colonialism and run by Catholic religious orders (but welcoming Catholic and non-Catholic students alike). Certainly, the educational system in the RVN saw many adaptations and changes reflecting a nationalist, republican, and postcolonial ideology. It did not mean, however, an uprooting of curriculum or even administration as was the case in the Democratic Republic of Vietnam. Similarly, the proliferation of journalism, where Nguyễn Thụy Long and many other fiction writers first made their names, grew out of the largely noncommunist press during colonialism. The contents of numerous dailies, weeklies, semimonthlies, and monthlies reflected new or evolving political, intellectual, and artistic sensibilities. But the structure, organization, and entrepreneurialism of this press were not dissimilar to those from late colonialism.

In recent years, the rise of social media has contributed to a strong nostalgia about the RVN in general and republican Saigon in particular among Vietnamese in the country and the diaspora. Much of this nostalgia derives from visual and audio forms—photographs, video clips, original recordings of popular music—but some also from diasporic representations of South Vietnam. Historians and scholars must guard themselves against the temptations of nostalgia due to the possibility of exaggeration and even falsification of the historical records about South Vietnam. At the same time, the historical records should be examined or reexamined in the context of both dominant *and* alternative perspectives. For the reasons described above, Vietnamese-language memoirs by prominent figures in the RVN offer alternative perspectives to the dominant and orthodox interpretations in both Vietnam and the United States. They will help researchers to grasp better the complexity of the Vietnam Conflict, if not also to help explain some of the reasons behind the nostalgia for the republic lost to the communists in 1975.

Selected Memoirs

Đỗ Mậu, *Việt Nam Máu Lửa Quê Hương Tôi: Hồi Ký Chính Trị* [Vietnam, my warring country: political memoirs] (Mission Hills, CA: Hương Quê, 1986; Westminster, CA: Văn Nghệ, 1993). This is one of the first and longest memoirs to be published by a former general in the ARVN. It provides many details about his support for Diệm prior to 1954, his work in the Diệm government and the military, and his involvement in the 1963 coup. It is critical of the Catholic Church in general and the Ngô family in particular, and it interprets Diệm to have held a pro-Catholic position at the expense of non-Catholic nationalists. Although the book remains controversial among Vietnamese in the diaspora, it also offers an insider's look into Diệm's activities in building support for his movement during the 1940s.

Huỳnh Văn Cao, *Lòng Ái Quốc* [Patriotism] (Saigon: Fatima, 1970); and *Một Kiếp Người* [A lifetime] (Chantilly, VA: self-published, 1993). Out of about twenty generals during the rule of Ngô Đình Diệm, Cao was one of three Catholics. He remained loyal to Diệm during the 1963 coup, and these memoirs give his reasons for this loyalty. The first memoir was published in Republican Saigon, around the time that he was running for reelection in the upper house of the legislature. The second memoir recounts the same events and adds those that occurred after 1970.

Huỳnh Văn Lang, *Nhân Chứng Một Chế Độ* [Witness to a regime], 3 vols. (Westminster, CA: Văn Nghệ, 2000); and *Ký Ức Huỳnh Văn Lang* [The memoir of Huynh Van Lang], 2 vols. (Westminster, CA: self-published, 2011–12). The Southern-born Catholic Lang was still in his twenties when he was invited by Diệm to run the Office of Foreign Exchange. He became a member of the Cần Lao Party and led its successful fundraising. The three-volume memoir focuses on 1954–63; and the two-volume memoir covers his childhood, youth, student years, and the entire period of the Republic of Vietnam (RVN). (Of the latter memoir, a planned third volume on his exile after 1975 has yet to appear.) Given the secrecy surrounding the Cần Lao, these memoirs are especially valuable for the information on Ngô Đình Nhu's activities during the 1940s, including Nhu's initial development of personalism as a guiding philosophy.

Lý Quí Chung, *Hồi Ký Không Tên* [Memoir without a name] (Ho Chi Minh City: Trẻ, 2004). This memoir is the only political or military memoir on this list that was published in postwar Vietnam. The author began his adult life as a journalist. He was elected to the lower house in the Second Republic and became one of the opposition politicians to President Thiệu in the legislature. Due to self-censorship as well as official censorship, the book is much more circumspect than most memoirs on this list when it comes to criticism of the postwar government. Most valuable to researchers are probably the sections on his activities against the Thiệu government during the 1970s.

Nguyên Sa, *Hồi Ký* [Memoir] (Irvine, CA: Đời, 1998). The author of possibly the most famous poem published in South Vietnam, Nguyên Sa studied in France during the First Indochina War and returned to Vietnam to teach philosophy and literature at a prominent high school in Saigon. This memoir is unconventional in that it is not chronological but jumpily topical. Nonetheless, it includes some interesting recollections on two prominent periodicals in the RVN, plus a long section on Trần Kim Tuyến, a central figure in the Personalist Party run by Ngô Đình Nhu. More indirectly, the memoir is a good example of Francophile influence on intellectual life in South Vietnam.

Nguyễn Bá Cẩn, *Đất Nước Tôi: Hồi Ký Chánh Trị* [My country: political memoirs] (Derwood, MD: Hoa Hao Press, 2003). Before becoming penultimate prime minister of the RVN in 1975, Cẩn was an official at the provincial level, then in the national legislature. He rose to be the chairman of the lower house, and this memoir is most detailed about this period of his life. It also describes the collaboration between the Confederation of Vietnamese Labor and smaller political groups toward the formation of a new political party.

Nguyễn Chánh Thi, *Việt Nam: Một Trời Tâm Sự* [Vietnam, a sky full of confidences] (Los Alamitos, CA: Xuân Thu, 1987). Thi was not yet a general at the time of the 1960 failed coup against Diệm, but his role was important and became a subject of intense debate for many years. This memoir is his attempt to present his side of the story. For this reason, it covers the years 1955–66 but is most detailed on the coup and its aftermath. The book also gives his strong criticism against other military officers, especially Lieutenant Colonel Vương Văn Đông, one of the instigators of the failed coup, and General Nguyễn Cao Kỳ for his action during the Buddhist Struggle protests in central Vietnam. The second event made Thi a hero among the Buddhists but also led to his exile in the United States in 1966.

Nguyễn Hiến Lê, *Hồi Kí* [Memoir], 3 vols. (Westminster, CA, 1988–89). Lê was the most prolific author in South Vietnam, and his hundredth book was published five days before the fall of Saigon. A self-taught intellectual well respected by communist and anticommunist authorities alike, he is cool-headed and factual in describing his experience in teaching, writing, publishing, and private life. The first volume concerns his upbringing, education, and early career under colonialism and decolonization. The second is on his work and life in the RVN, and the third is about his experience in and observations of postwar Vietnam. The second volume is most direct and detailed about the RVN, and the last volume further shows his perspective on the differences between the Northern and Southern intellectual and publishing cultures during 1954–75.

Nguyễn Thụy Long, *Thuở Mơ Làm Văn Sĩ* [Dreams of becoming a fiction writer] (Irvine, CA: Tuổi Xanh, 2000). The author grew up in Hanoi and moved to Saigon in 1952, when he was still a teenager. The book recounts his life as a student in the North in 1950 to his employment at one of the best-known Saigon weeklies during the mid-1960s. In between are recollections of his enrollment in a military school, his inadvertent involvement in the 1960 coup against Diệm that landed him in jail, and his relationships with budding and established writers alike.

Nguyễn Trân, *Công và Tội: Những Sự Thật Lịch Sử, Hồi Ký Lịch Sử Chính Trị Miền Nam 1945–1975* [Merits and guilt: truths about history, political memoirs about South Vietnam, 1945–1975] (Los Alamitos, CA: Xuân Thu, 1992). One of the more effectual provincial chiefs during the First Republic, Trân was known for holding public debates with communist prisoners. This long book recalls those episodes and offers information not commonly found in other memoirs, probably because Trân's early roles were neither in the military nor the cabinet but at the provincial level. There is more about rural conditions than perhaps any other title on this list. Trân was also different from most other memoirists for being pro-Diệm and anti-Thiệu, having run unsuccessfully against the latter in the 1971 election. He was a leading organizer behind the anticorruption movement in 1974, and the book includes a long section about his activities in this movement.

Phạm Duy, *Hồi Ký* [Memoir], 3 vols. (Midway City, CA: PDC Musical Productions, 1989–91). The most important Vietnamese musician from the twentieth century also published one of the most informative memoirs about the urban culture of South Vietnam. These volumes cover his life from childhood in colonial Hanoi in the 1920s to the fall of Saigon. The third volume begins with his departure from the Việt Minh zone in the early 1950s and ends with his departure to the United States during the fall of Saigon. In between were his prolific production of song-writing, recording, performances, and travels, including trips to France and the United States. Along with the memoir by Trường Kỳ, this memoir is indispensable for understanding the growth of popular music in South Vietnam.

Phạm Văn Liễu, *Trả Ta Sông Núi: Hồi Ký* [Give back my country: memoir], 3 vols. (Houston: Văn Hóa, 2002–4). Colonel Liễu is best remembered for his involvement in two controversies: the failed coup of 1960 and the post-1975 diasporic anticommunist organization National United Front for the Liberation of Vietnam. Not surprisingly, the memoir is most detailed on these two subjects. The first two volumes cover his life until 1975 and the third volume thereafter. A member of the largest Đại Việt political party, Liễu also sprinkles this memoir with information and observations about its members as well as the evolution of the party in South Vietnam.

Tạ Ty, *Những Khuôn Mặt Văn Nghệ Đã Đi Qua Đời Tôi: Hồi Ký* [Past figures in arts and letters in my life: memoir] (San Jose, CA: Thằng Mõ, 1990). Similar to Phạm Duy, this painter and military officer participated in the anticolonial struggle led by the Việt Minh but left it in the middle of the First Indochina War. Like the musician, he had very large circles of friends in arts and letters in Hanoi during the war and in South Vietnam afterward. This memoir is about them as much as it is about himself. Surprisingly, there is little on painting in South Vietnam during the 1960s and 1970s. On the other hand, there are some recollections about the art scene in Hanoi before 1954, plus the transition of the noncommunist press from Hanoi to Saigon after the Geneva Conference.

Thế Phong, *Hồi Ký Ngoài Văn Chương* [Memoir beyond literature] (Westminster, CA: Văn Nghệ, 1996). Because of warfare, a number of writers and artists enlisted or were drafted into the ARVN. Thế Phong was one, and his memoir traverses between the realms of military and arts and letters, illustrating some of the close relationships between them in South Vietnam. While it focuses on his life from the mid-1960s to the early 1970s, it also includes many citations and notes about publications and literary figures in South Vietnam.

Tôn Thất Đính, *20 Năm Binh Nghiệp* [Twenty years in the military] (San Jose: Chánh Đạo, 1998). General Đính is forever linked to the 1963 coup, and the book describes and discusses his role in the coup at length. Moreover, he is notable among the military memoirists for giving the least self-justifying and most self-critical reassessment of the past. Đính considers Diệm and Nhu capable if flawed, and he stresses their effort to keep South Vietnam from becoming an American colony. Stopping the memoir at the end of the coup, he voices criticism of ARVN's performance during the early 1960s and also the growing U.S. military influence in South Vietnam.

Trần Văn Đôn, *Việt Nam Nhân Chứng: Hồi Ký Chính Trị* [Vietnamese witness: political memoir] (Los Alamitos, CA: Xuân Thu, 1989). Đôn was among the principal plotters of the coup in 1963. Having published a memoir in English in 1978, he wrote this one to give a longer and more elaborate explanation of his background, relationship with Diệm, involvement in the successful coup, and the aftermath. There are shorter sections about his time in the upper and lower houses during the Second Republic, the fall of Saigon, and a visit of Bảo Đại to the United States after the war was over. Similar to many military memoirists, there is surprisingly little about his experience with the U.S. military.

Trường Kỳ, *Một Thời Nhạc Trẻ: Bút Ký* [An era of youth music: recollections] (Montréal: self-published, 2002). This highly informative memoir comes from the most successful promoter of "youth music" in South Vietnam. The author knew virtually all figures of this movement in Saigon, and he provides many details about the background, origin, and developments of this music. The book illustrates the closeness of this movement to the broader noncommunist youth and student culture in urban South Vietnam. It also highlights the tension between its advocates and older and more traditional Vietnamese, and the impact that the Americanization of the war had on the movement. There is also a rich collection of photographs of "youth music" bands and people.

Tùng Long, *Hồi Ký Bà Tùng Long: Viết Là Niềm Vui Muôn Thuở của Tôi* [The memoir of Madame Tùng Long: writing is my lasting happiness] (Ho Chi Minh City: Trẻ, 2003). Tùng Long published about seventy novels and novellas of popular fiction, many of which were initially serialized, plus an influential newspaper advice column where readers sent her questions about work, romance, and family life. The memoir is unique for having come from a woman, and also for describing the upbringing, education, marriage, and work of someone from the central province Quảng Ngãi rather than Saigon or Huế. The memoir glosses over her life after 1963. It is most informative on her rise to fame during the 1940s and 1950s, showing a bustling market for readers as well as writers of popular fiction.

Võ Long Triều, *Hồi Ký* [Memoirs], 2 vols. (Fresno, CA: Người Việt, 2009–11). Triều had a diverse career in teaching, journalism, and politics. He served in Nguyễn Cao Kỳ's cabinet as head of the Department of Youths, then published a major newspaper and ran successfully for a seat in the lower house. This memoir was serialized in the largest diasporic Vietnamese newspaper over several years, and it is somewhat messy in organization and jumpy in chronology. Covering his life from childhood to postwar imprisonment and release, it is perhaps most useful to researchers on the fluidity between political life and civilian life under the Second Republic.

Vũ Quốc Thúc, *Thời Đại Của Tôi* [My era], 2 vols. (Westminster, CA: Người Việt, 2010). In his capacity as the RVN's director of postwar planning, Thúc was best-known to Americans as coauthor of the David Lilienthal-Vũ Quốc Thúc Report (1970) on postwar prospects for economic reconstruction. He also worked as director of the Vietnam National Bank and taught at the School of Law in Saigon. Of this two-volume work, the first volume presents Thúc's perspective on Vietnamese history, and only the second volume is a memoir of his life from childhood to exile in France after 1978. Many pieces of information presented in Thúc's contribution to this book come from this memoir, which is especially long and detailed about his family background and his education under the colonial system.

Vương Hồng Sển, *Hồi Ký 50 Năm Mê Hát* [Memoir of fifty years following musical theater] (Saigon: Phạm Quang Giai, 1968); and *Hơn Nửa Đời Hư* [More than half of a wasted life] (Ho Chi Minh City: Nhà Xuất Bản Thành Phố Hồ Chí Minh, 1992). Most cultural memoirists on this list came from Northern Vietnam. The author of these two memoirs, however, was an ethnic Chinese born and raised in the South. A well-known antique collector, he was director of the national museum in Saigon for over fifteen years. The first memoir was published four years after his retirement from the museum. It is a valuable source on the history of the genres of reformed musical theater (*cải lương*) and classical Vietnamese opera (*hát bội*) during colonialism, and also illustrates a more open cultural climate in Southern Vietnam that saw continuity in the RVN. The second memoir is longer, more comprehensive, and more informative about South Vietnam during the First Republic. It includes recollections of Sển's education and initial interest in antiques, his work at the national museum, his travels in Asia and Europe, and his meetings with Ngô Đình Diệm and other members of the Ngô family about collecting antiques.

Vương Văn Đông, *Binh Biến 11-11-1960: Khởi Điểm Một Hành Trình* [Coup attempt of November 11, 1960: starting point of a journey] (Westminster, CA: Văn Nghệ, 2000). The author was one of the primary planners and instigators of the failed coup against Ngô Đình Diệm. This memoir consists of two parts. Written in 1970 when he was living in France, the first part is about the background of the coup and the events of the coup itself. The second part was written thirty years later to tell about his life following the coup, which included exile in Cambodia. The memoirist argues forcefully that the 1960 coup was a completely Vietnamese affair and there was no American involvement or support.

About the Editors

Tuong Vu is director of Asian studies and professor of political science at the University of Oregon and has held visiting fellowships at Princeton University and the National University of Singapore. His books include *Vietnam's Communist Revolution: The Power and Limits of Ideology* (2017) and *Paths to Development in Asia: South Korea, Vietnam, China, and Indonesia* (2010), both published by Cambridge University Press. The latter book received an Honorable Mention in the competition for the 2011 Asia Society Bernard Schwartz Award. Vu is also a coeditor of *Dynamics of the Cold War in Asia: Ideology, Identity, and Culture* (Palgrave, 2009) and *Southeast Asia in Political Science: Theory, Region, and Qualitative Analysis* (Stanford University Press, 2008). His articles have appeared in many scholarly journals, including *World Politics, Journal of Southeast Asian Studies, Journal of Vietnamese Studies, Studies in Comparative International Development, Communist and Post-Communist Studies, South East Asia Research,* and *Theory and Society.*

Sean Fear is a lecturer in international history at the University of Leeds. He was awarded a PhD in history from Cornell University in 2016 and has held postdoctoral positions at Dartmouth College and McGill University. Fear's work has been published in *Diplomatic History* and the *Journal of Vietnamese Studies*. He is currently working on a book manuscript, under contract with Harvard University Press, exploring South Vietnam's domestic politics and foreign relations between 1967 and 1975.

INDEX

Abrams, Creighton, 75, 89
Accelerated Miracle Rice Production Program (AMRPP), 51–53
Adams, Eddie, 78–79
Agency for the Development of the Da Nang Area, 44
agricultural development
   expansion of rural credit, 53–54
   Green Revolution, 51–55
   in Thúc-Lilienthal Postwar Development Report, 22
   See also land reform; rice
Agricultural Development Bank of Vietnam (ADBV), 53–54
Alpha Film Studio, 169–70
American media, 132–34
   bias of, 131, 134–36, 173–74
   spies' influence over, 132
Á Nam Trần Tuấn Khải, 157
Antiriot Police, 72, 73, 74–75
antiwar bias of foreign press, 130–31, 134–36, 173–74
Armed Forces of the Republic of Vietnam (ARVN)
   before and after Allied intervention, 91–92
   and American military performance and command, 88–91
   Bùi Quyền's reflections and analysis of, 84–88
   courage of, 129–30
   development of, 82–83
   expansion of, 37–38
   reorganization of, 81
   during Second Republic, 83–84
   size of, 1
   training of, 84
Armed Forces Vietnam Network (AFVN), 170
arts. See cinema; culture and arts
Asia Film, 167
Asian Film Festival, 171
Association of Journalists, 149
Association of Newspaper Publishers, 148
August Revolution, 180–81
austerity program, 19, 36–37
Âu Trường Thanh, 18–19

banking, and economic development between 1955–1965, 15. See also central banking
Banknote Exchange Scandal, 32–33
Bank of Indochina, 29–30
bank runs, preventing, 21
Banque Française d'Asie, 30
Bảo Đại, 3, 4, 28
Bến Cũ (The old station), 168
Berg, Dennis, 116n7
Berger, Samuel, 39
Berman, Larry, 132
Bích Hợp, 161
Binh Biến 11–11–1960 (Vương Văn Đông), 188
Bình Xuyên, 81–82
black market, 18–19, 39–40
book burning, 161–62
Boon, Ronald, 134
Borchgrave, Arnaud de, 64
Boulevard of Horror, 130
Bowden, Tim, 132, 134
Brezhnev, Leonid, 63
Bùi Diễm, 6, 168–69, 179
Bunker, Ellsworth, 17, 41, 48, 50, 63, 65–66
Bush, George W., 136

Cách Mạng Quốc Gia (National revolution) newspaper, 118
Cai Lậy elementary school bombing, 135
California State University in Fullerton (CSUF), 115
Calley, William, 134
Cần Lao Party, 181
Cánh Đồng Ma (The haunted field), 167
Cao Văn Thân, 2
Cao Văn Viên, 61
Caravelle Group, 119
Catholic Church, influence of, 120
Catton, Philip, 175
censorship, 1–2, 121, 131–32, 140, 161–62, 177
central banking
   and Banknote Exchange Scandal, 32–33
   and Four-Party Conference, 25–28
   and National Bank of Vietnam, 28–30
   United States' involvement in, 30–32
Central Commissariat for Intelligence, 72
Champeaux, Louis de, 30, 31, 32
Chân Trời Tím (The purple horizon), 171
Chapman, Jessica, 175
Châu Kim Nhân, 69
cheap money, 40
Chế Linh, 161–62
Chennault, Anna, 60

children, teaching Vietnamese language and culture to, 176
Chính Luận, 145, 148
Chợ Lách District, 113–14
Chờ Sáng (Waiting for daybreak), 169
Chu Mạnh Trinh, 161
Chu Tử, 141, 142, 143, 160
cinema, 165–66
    depiction of Vietnam war in American, 173–74
    growth of Vietnamese industry, 170–72
    from 1954 to First Republic, 168–70
    significant milestones in history of, 166–68
    underdevelopment of Vietnamese industry, 166
cinematographe, 166, 167
Civil Operations and Rural Development Support (CORDS) program, 75–76
Clifford, Clark, 60
colonialism, 3, 84–85, 93, 106
Commercial Import Program (CIP), 30–31, 32
Committee for Freedom of Press and Publishing, 146, 151
Committee on Examination Reform, 100
community colleges, 97–98, 112–13, 114–15
comprehensive high schools, 95–96
Công và Tội: Những Sự Thật Lịch Sử, Hồi Ký Lịch Sử Chính Trị Miền Nam 1945–1975 (Nguyễn Trân), 186
Cooper, Charles, 41–42, 43
corruption
    and death of Hà Thúc Nhơn, 141
    of journalists, 136
    reporting on, 125
"counterinsurgency war" model, 88–89
courage
    of ARVN, 129–30
    of war correspondents, 127–28
Credit Commercial Bank of Vietnam (Việt Nam Thương Tín), 15, 31–32
Cronkite, Walter, 134
culture and arts
    and collective historical memory regarding war, 176–77
    following war, 161–62
    in Vietnamese-language memoirs, 182–83
    before war, 155–58
    during war, 158–61
    See also cinema
currency
    Banknote Exchange Scandal, 32–33
    cheap money, 40
    common, for Indochina, 27
    devaluation of, 15–16, 18–19, 39–40
    tearing, 81
    transfer from Indochina currency to Đồng, 29

Đại Dân Tộc, 148
Đà Lạt University, 112
Đặng Thị Tám, 151
Đào Hữu Ngạn, 113
Đất Khổ, 160–61
Đất Nước Tôi: Hồi Ký Chánh Trị (Nguyễn Bá Cẩn), 185
"decent interval" concept, 62–63, 69
Democratic Republic of Vietnam (DRV), 3–4
    economy of, 17
    logistical support for, 85
    strategy of, 84–86
    transition to communist administration in, 17
    violates peace accords, 67
    See also Paris Peace Accords (1973)
Điện Tín (Telegraph), 122, 123, 148
Directorate General of Exchange, 27
Directorate General of Planning (DGP), 16
Directorate of Elementary Education (DEE), 101
Đoàn Kế Tường, 143
Đỗ Bá Khê, 97, 112
Đỗ Cao Trí, 129–30
Đời Mới, 157
Đỗ Mậu, 180, 181, 184
Đồng
    Banknote Exchange Scandal, 32–33
    devaluation of, 15–16, 18–19
    introduction of, 29
Đông Hồ, 157
Đỗ Tiến Đức, 172
Dương Tấn Tài, 27
Dương Thu Hương, 161
Dương Văn Minh, 120, 121, 122
Duyên Hải Community College, 97–98, 112–13

Easter Offensive (1972), 62, 143
economic development, 13–15
    challenges to, 23
    between 1955–1965, 15–17
    between 1965–1975, 17–22
    price liberalization and market stabilization, 55
    See also agricultural development; land reform; Vietnamization
Edison, Thomas, 166
education, 105–6
    background of Vietnamese, 93
    community colleges, 97–98, 112–13, 114–15
    comprehensive high schools, 95–96
    and economic development between 1955–1965, 16
    elementary schools, 97
    Faculty of Education, 107–9
    growth of public and private universities, 112–13
    national examinations, 99–101
    National Wards Schools (QGNT), 109–10, 115

between 1954–1975, 102
after 1975, 114–15
philosophies of, 94–95
polytechnic universities, 98–99
reorganization of Ministry of Education, 113–14
teacher training, 101–2
Thánh Mẫu Gia Định Catholic School, 110–12
in Vietnamese-language memoirs, 183
Vietnamization of, 106–7
Education Administrative Offices, 114
elementary school bombing, 135
Elementary School Office, 114
elementary schools, 97
examinations, national, 99–101
"Exhibition Hall of Mỹ Ngụy Crimes," 161

Faculty of Education, 107–9
Faculty of Letters, 159
Fallaci, Oriana, 127
Fiery Summer, 62
First Indochina War, 156
First Republic
ARVN during, 88
education under, 107, 109–10, 113
end of, 58–59
journalism under, 117–20
Strategic Hamlet program under, 86
in Vietnamese-language memoirs, 181–82
See also Republic of Vietnam (RVN)
floating exchange rate, 40
foreign exchange rate, 18–20, 39–40
Formosa Hà Tĩnh Steel Corporation, 125
Four-Party Conference (1954), 15, 25–28
France
and cinema, 166–67
colonial regime of, 84–85
and Four-Party Conference, 26–27
public security under, 72
transfer of authority to RVN from, 14, 15
and Vietnamese education, 93, 98, 102, 106, 108–9
war between DVR and, 3–4

General Directorate of Security and Police, 72
Geneva Accords, 26
Giao Chỉ Studio, 171
global engagement, 183
Greene, Graham, 168
Green Revolution, 51–55
Gromyko, Andrei, 63

Hà Huy Hà, 160–61
Haig, Alexander, 66
Harlan, Robert, 38, 39, 41
Harriman, William, 60
Hà Thế Ruyệt, 146–47
Hà Thúc Cần, 163n3
Hà Thúc Nhơn, 141

Hiếu Chân Nguyễn Hoạt, 118, 162
high schools, comprehensive, 95–96
Hoà Bình (Peace), 144–45
Hòa Hảo University, 112
Hoàng Đức Nhã, 132, 145, 146–47
Hoàng Quỳnh, 120
Hoàng Vĩnh Lộc, 168
Hồ Biểu Chánh, 157
Hồ Chí Minh, 3–4, 85, 133
Hồ Hữu Tường, 161–62
20 Năm Binh Nghiệp (Tôn Thất Đính), 187
Hồi Chuông Thiên Mụ (The bell of Thiên Mụ pagoda), 168–69
Hồi Kí (Nguyễn Hiến Lê), 185
Hồi Ký (Nguyên Sa), 185
Hồi Ký (Phạm Duy), 186
Hồi Ký (Võ Long Triều), 188
Hồi Ký 50 Năm Mê Hát (Vương Hồng Sển), 188
Hồi Ký Bà Tùng Long: Viết Là Niềm Vui Muôn Thuở của Tôi (Tùng Long), 187
Hồi Ký Không Tên (Lý Quí Chung), 184–85
Hồi Ký Ngoài Văn Chương (Thế Phong), 187
homelands, mass exoduses from, 130
Hồ Văn Đồng, 160
Hubler, Clark, 109, 110
humanism, 94–95
Hùng Cường, 171
Huỳnh Trung, 142
Huỳnh Huy Dương, 145
Huỳnh Văn Cao, 181–82, 184
Huỳnh Văn Lang, 2, 28–29, 181, 184

import license applications, 18
Indictment No. 1, 122, 149, 150
Indochina Film Studio, 167
insecure areas, 86
interest rates, increased, 39–40
International Rice Research Institute (IRRI), 52

Jefferson, Thomas, 152
Jet Fighter Squadron, 83
Johnson, Hiram, 136
Johnson, Lyndon, 22, 59, 89
Joint Development Group, 22
journalism
American media's understanding of war, 132–36
and austerity tax, 37
battlefield observations, 129–31
birth of Sóng Thần, 141–43
under First Republic, 117–20
freedom of press under RVN versus modern-day Vietnam, 123–25
Martial Law 005/72, 143
Press Law 007/72, 123, 139, 143–45, 147
Press Law 019/69, 121–23, 140–41, 147
Press Law 103/2016/QH13, 124–25
purpose of, 136–37

journalism *(continued)*
   Reporters Go Begging Day, 123, 149–50
   under Second Republic, 120–21, 140
   of South Vietnamese media during war, 131–32
   spies' influence over American media, 132
   training and education in, 128
   in Vietnamese-language memoirs, 183
   war correspondents, 127–29
   wartime changes in, 158–59
   See also *Sóng Thần* (Tsunami)
Journey from the Fall, 166, 174, 177

Kennedy, John F., 5
Khái Hưng, 156
Khánh Ly, 159, 160, 161–62
Kiếp Hoa (The fate of flowers), 168
Kim Vân Kiều, 167
Kissinger, Henry, 61–62, 63–64, 65–66
Komer, Robert, 75

Lâm Lễ Trinh, 2
land reform
   and economic development between 1955–1965, 16–17, 21
   and economic development between 1965–1975, 22
   Land to the Tiller program, 17, 21, 47–51
   See also agricultural development
Land to the Tiller program, 17, 21, 47–51
Lansdale, Edward, 168
League for Great Unity, 120
Lê Công Chất, 148
Lê Đức Thọ, 61, 63
Legion of Activist Lawyers, 149, 150, 151
Lê Hoàng Hoa, 171
Lê Hữu Bôi, 159
Lê Hữu Từ, 120
Lê Kim Hiền, 142
Lenin, Vladimir, 48–49
Lê Quang Mỹ, 82
Lê Quang Uyển, 21
Lê Thương, 160–61
Lê Trọng Nguyễn, 160–61
Lê Văn Đệ, 156
licensing control, 18
Liên Ảnh Company, 171
limited warfare concept, 89
literature. *See* culture and arts
Lòng Ái Quốc (Huỳnh Văn Cao), 184
Lý Đại Nguyên, 148
Lý Quí Chung, 150, 182, 184–85

Mặc Thu, 118
Malaysia, counterinsurgency methods employed in, 86
Manila Summit (1966), 22
Mao Zedong, 84, 89
Maritime Boat Force, 83
Martial Law 005/72, 143

McCain, John, 152
McNamara, Robert, 89
memoirs
   list of selected, 184–88
   problems among, 179–80
   purposes of, 180
   themes in, 180–84
Mendès France, Pierre, 26
military. *See* Armed Forces of the Republic of Vietnam (ARVN)
Miller, Edward, 175
Minh Đức University, 112
Ministry of Culture, Education, and Youth (MCEY), 114
Ministry of Economy, 13–14, 18
Ministry of Education (MOE), 96, 98, 100–101, 105, 107
Ministry of Education and Training (MOET), 113, 115
Ministry of Information, 68
Ministry of Mass Mobilization and Open Arms, 68
Ministry of Open Arms, 68
miracle rice, 51–53, 54
Movie Producers Association, 171
Mưa Rừng (Forest rain), 169–70
Mỹ Vân Studio, 172

Nhất Linh Nguyễn Tường Tam, 157
nạp bản, 140, 144
National Agricultural Center, 112
National Bank of Vietnam, 15, 21, 27, 31–32
National Council on Monetary Policy and Credit, 32
national examinations, 99–101
National Film Center, 169, 170
National Food Administration, 55
National Institute of Administration, 112
National Institute of Technology, 112
nationalism, 94–95
National Liberation Front, 119–20
National Police
   and Civil Operations and Rural Development Support (CORDS) program, 75
   history of, 71–74
   and Phoenix program, 75–76
   and Tết Offensive, 77–79
   training of, 74–75
   See also public security
National Police Academy, 74
National School of Administration, 112
National Wards Schools (QGNT), 109–10, 115
nation building
   defined, 2–3
   postcolonial context of, 3
   preceding Paris Peace Accords, 60–61
   in Republic of Vietnam, 1–7
   as theme in memoirs, 181
new Vietnam War scholarship, 175–76
Nghiêm Xuân Thiện, 119

Ngô Đình Diệm, 4–5
    attempted assassination of, 120
    and Banknote Exchange Scandal, 33
    and Bình Xuyên rebellion, 81–82
    and birth of central banking, 25, 26, 28
    and founding of Republic of Vietnam, 3
    opposition to, 5, 119–20
    overthrow of, 5, 120
    press control under, 118
    reorganizes armed forces, 81
    and replacement of Bank of Indochina employees, 29–30
    scholarship on, 175–76
    in Vietnamese-language memoirs, 181–82
Ngô Đình Nhu, 118, 119, 181
Ngô Đình Vận, 145
Ngô Trọng Hiếu, 29
Ngô Vương Toại, 160
Người Tình Không Chân Dung (The faceless lover), 171
Nguyễn Bá Cẩn, 180–81, 185
Nguyễn Bá Trác, 155
Nguyễn Bích Huệ, 36
Nguyễn Cao Kỳ, 22
Nguyễn Chánh Thi, 119, 185
Nguyễn Đăng Hải, 53
Nguyễn Đức Cường, 38–39, 69
Nguyễn Duy Xuân, 109
Nguyễn Gia Hiền, 120
Nguyễn Gia Trí, 156
Nguyễn Hải Chí, 160
Nguyễn Hiến Lê, 182, 185
Nguyễn Hoạt, 118, 162
Nguyễn Hữu Hanh, 15, 32, 36
Nguyễn Khánh, 121
Nguyễn Kinh Châu, 143
Nguyễn Lan Hương, 167
Nguyễn Liệu, 147–48
Nguyễn Mạnh Côn, 161–62
Nguyễn-Marshall, Vân, 141–42
Nguyễn Ngọc Loan, 78–79, 134
Nguyễn Phúc Bửu Lộc, 26
Nguyễn Phú Đức, 61, 64–65
Nguyễn Quang Lãm, 120
Nguyễn Quốc Cường, 145
Nguyên Sa, 183, 185
Nguyễn Tân Dân, 151
Nguyễn Thanh Liêm, 2, 113, 114
Nguyễn Thụy Long, 182, 185–86
Nguyễn Trân, 180, 186
Nguyễn Trung, 160
Nguyễn Văn Bình, 149
Nguyễn Văn Cử, 120
Nguyễn Văn Lực, 120
Nguyễn Văn Thiệu
    brain trust of, 58
    and economic development during Vietnamization, 35–36
    and events preceding Paris Peace Accords, 58–59

and Green Revolution, 51, 52
Indictment No. 1 directed at, 122
and Land to the Tiller program, 47–48, 49
and 1971 presidential election, 6
and oppression of Vietnamese press, 149, 151
and Paris Peace Accords, 60, 61, 63–65
and Press Law 007/72, 123, 143
and Press Law 019/69, 121, 140
and psychological warfare, 67–68
and Rural Development program, 86
in Vietnamese-language memoirs, 182
Nguyễn Viết Thanh, 129
Nguyễn Xuân Hoàng, 159–60
Ngy Thanh, 143
Nhân Chứng Một Chế Độ (Huỳnh Văn Lang), 184
Nhân Văn-Giai Phẩm Affair, 156
Nhất Linh Nguyễn Tường Tam, 125n2
Nha Trang Air Force Training Center, 82
Những Khuôn Mặt Văn Nghệ Đã Đi Qua Đời Tôi: Hồi Ký (Tạ Ty), 186
Nhượng Tống, 156
Như Phong, 118
Nixon, Richard, 6, 61, 62, 63, 67
Nông Lâm Súc, 16
normal colleges, 101
North Vietnam. *See* Democratic Republic of Vietnam (DRV)

Office of Exchange, 28
Ohio University, 95
oil reserves, 21–22
Open Arms program, 75
open mind for changes, 94–95

Palmer, Bruce Jr., 85
Paris Peace Accords (1973)
    aftermath of, 68–69
    beginning of negotiations, 59–60
    and "decent interval" concept, 62–63, 69
    disagreements in negotiations, 61–62, 66–67
    discussions in Saigon, 63–66
    events preceding, 58–59
    nation building preceding, 60–61
    North Vietnam's approach to, 62
    North Vietnam violates, 67
    and psychological warfare, 67–68
    terms of, 6
Passage to Freedom, 168
Pathé Studio, 167
PEN Vietnam, 144, 145–46, 158
People's Front against Corruption, for National Salvation and for Building Peace, 146
People's Warfare strategic concept, 84, 89
petroleum crisis, 21
Phạm Đăng Lâm, 64–65
Phạm Duy, 157, 160, 182, 183, 186
Phạm Kim Ngọc, 15, 19, 22, 32
Phạm Ngọc Chi, 120
Phạm Quỳnh, 155

Phạm Tăng, 118
Phạm Tấn Nằm, Louis, 110
Phạm Văn Đồng, 64
Phạm Văn Liễu, 186
Phạm Xuân Ẩn, 132
Phan Huy Quát, 121
Phan Khôi, 156
Phan Trọng Chinh, 90
Phan Văn Hùm, 156
Philippines, 53
Phoenix program, 75–76
Phùng Sanh, Anthony, 110
Phú Thọ Polytechnic University, 112
police. *See* National Police; public security
polytechnic universities, 98–99
Popular Forces (PF), 82, 83, 86–87
port congestion, 17–18
Presidential Decree no. 503, 97
press. *See* journalism
Press Law 007/72, 123, 139, 143–45, 147
Press Law 019/69, 121–23, 140–41, 147
Press Law 103/2016/QH13, 124–25
price crisis, between 1965–1975, 20
private schools, 110–12, 113
Program Law (1970), 19–20, 39
psychological warfare, 67–68, 75, 84, 85
public security
　general situation from 1965 to 1975, 76–77
　1966 upheaval in central Vietnam, 77
　See also National Police

Quiet American, The (film), 168
Quiet American, The (Greene), 168

refugees, 16, 21, 44, 168, 173
Regional Forces (RF), 82, 83, 86–87
Reporters Go Begging Day, 123, 149–50
Republic of Vietnam (RVN)
　founding of, 3–4, 32
　loses war, 79
　nation building in, 1–7
　neglect of, in American historical memory, 173–77
　nostalgia regarding, 183–84
　transfer of authority from France to, 14, 15
　See also First Republic; memoirs; Second Republic
revolutionary violence, as theme in memoirs, 180–81
rice
　Accelerated Miracle Rice Production Program (AMRPP), 51–53
　crises between 1965–1975, 20
　discovery of high-yield varieties, 52
　and Land to the Tiller program, 21
　price liberalization and market stabilization, 55
Riverine Assault Force, 83
Rogers, William, 61

rural credit, expansion of, 53–54
Rural Development program, 86–87

Safer, Morley, 163n3
Saigon, congestion at port of, 17–18
Second Republic
　ARVN during, 83–84, 86, 88
　birth of, 19, 107
　economic development under, 19–22
　education under, 107, 110
　journalism under, 120–21, 140
　policy making under, 32
　rural revolution under, 55
　in Vietnamese-language memoirs, 182
　See also Republic of Vietnam (RVN)
social media, 183–84
Society of Young Fine-Arts Painters, 159
Sóng Thần (Tsunami), 139–40
　birth of, 141–43
　and Press Law 007/72, 144
　trial and revocation of license of, 146–52
Sơn Nam, 160–61
South Vietnam. *See* Republic of Vietnam (RVN)
Soviet Union, 133
spies, 132
Stalin, Joseph, 133
Stewart, Geoffrey, 175–76
Strategic Hamlet program, 86
Sully, Francois, 130
Summit on Vietnam War, 130–31

Tạ Ty, 182, 186
tax, austerity, 36–37
tax collection and revenues, 20, 40–43
teacher training, 101–2
television, 170, 173–77
Testing and Guidance Center, 100
Tết Offensive (1968), 6, 35, 77–79, 85, 159
Thái Lân, 145
Thái Thanh, 157
Thái Thúc Nha, 168, 170
Thanh, Father, 122, 148, 150, 151, 153n11
Thanh Lãng, 144
Thánh Mẫu Gia Định Catholic School, 110–12, 115
Thế Phong, 187
Thích Tâm Châu, 120
Thích Thiện Hoa, 120
Thích Thiện Minh, 120
Thích Trí Quang, 77, 120
Third Film Festival, 171
Thời Đại Của Tôi (Vũ Quốc Thúc), 188
Thời Luận, 118–19
Thời Nhạc Trẻ: Bút Ký (Trường Kỳ), 187
Thúc-Lilienthal Postwar Development Report, 22
Thủ Đức Demonstration High School, 95–96, 100–101
Thủ Đức Polytechnic University, 99, 112

Thuở Mơ Làm Văn Sĩ (Nguyễn Thụy Long), 185–86
Tiền Giang Community College, 97, 98
"Tình Ca" (Love song), 157
Tin Sáng (Morning news), 122
Tố Hữu, 133
Tôn Thất Đính, 145, 187
Tôn Thất Trình, 69
Tran, Ham, 174
Trần Cự Uông, 36, 38
Trần Dạ Từ, 158, 159, 162
Trần Du, 120, 144
Trần Hữu Phương, 33
Trần Hữu Thanh, 146
Trần Kim Phượng, 61, 64–65
Trần Kim Tuyến, 118
Trần Quang Minh, 55
Trần Quốc Bửu, 149
Trần Tấn Quốc, 144
Trần Thiện Khiêm, 19, 61, 69
Trần Văn Đỗ, 26
Trần Văn Đôn, 187
Trần Văn Hương, 61, 121, 146
Trần Văn Khởi, 22
Trần Văn Lắm, 61, 65
Trần Văn Tấn, 108, 109
Trần Văn Tuyên, 118–19
Trả Ta Sông Núi: Hồi Ký (Phạm Văn Liễu), 186
Treaty of Pau (1950), 26
Triều Giang, 151
Trịnh Công Sơn, 158, 159, 160
Trinquier, Roger, 48
Trọn với Tình, 167
Trump, Donald, 152
Trung Tâm Văn Bút Việt Nam (PEN Vietnam), 144, 145–46, 158
Trương Công Cừu, 108
Trương Khuê Quan, 110
Trường Kỳ, 183, 187
Từ Chung, 142, 160
Tự Do (Freedom) daily newspaper, 118
Tùng Long, 182, 183, 187
Tự ý đục bỏ, 122, 140, 143, 144, 145, 146, 147

Union of Southern Journalists, 149
United States
  advantages of military forces, 89
  and birth of central banking, 30–32
  Bùi Quyền's reflections on military performance and command, 88–91
  disadvantages of military forces, 90–91
  and economic development during Vietnamization, 37–39
  and escalation in war, 5, 35
  and events preceding Paris Peace Accords, 59–60
  impact on economic development, 14–15, 22
  and Land to the Tiller program, 49–50
  neglect of RVN in American historical memory, 173–77
  and Paris Peace Accords, 61–68
  and port congestion, 17–18
  reduced presence in RVN, 6
  and tax collection under Vietnamization, 41
universities
  growth of private and public, 112–13
  polytechnic, 98–99
U.S. Agency for International Development (USAID), 18, 37, 43, 44, 49, 95, 102
U.S. Mission Operations (USOM), 94
Ut, Nick, 130
Uyên Thao, 141

value-added tax (VAT), 20, 42–43
Văn Cao, 156
Vạn Hạnh Buddhist University, 112
Vann, John Paul, 90–91
Việt Minh, violence against nationalists, 180–81
Vietnam Children's Funds (VCF), 166
Vietnam Cinema Association, 171
Vietnam Cinema Day, 171, 172
Vietnamese Communist Party, 124
Vietnamese language, 176
Vietnamese People Watch Vietnamese Films Movement, 172
Vietnamese Union of Reporters, 149
Vietnam Film, 167
Vietnamization, 35–36, 44–45
  austerity program during, 36–37
  of education, 106–7
  employment of refugees under, 45
  floating exchange and interest rates during, 39–40
  impact of, 43–44
  launched by Nixon, 62
  tax collection during, 40–43
  U.S. involvement in, 37–39
Việt Nam Máu Lửa Quê Hương Tôi: Hồi Ký Chính Trị (Đỗ Mậu), 184
Việt Nam: Một Trời Tâm Sự (Nguyễn Chánh Thi), 185
Việt Nam Nhân Chứng: Hồi Ký Chính Trị (Trần Văn Đôn), 187
Việt Nam Thương Tín (Credit Commercial Bank of Vietnam), 15, 31–32
Vietnam War
  American approach to, 88–89
  Americanization of, 5, 14–15, 35
  American media bias, 132–36, 173–74
  antiwar bias of foreign press, 130–31
  and "decent interval" concept, 62–63, 69
  global nature of, 133
  journalists' battlefield observations, 129–31
  journalists covering, 127–29
  new Vietnam War scholarship, 175–76

Vietnam War (continued)
   outcome of, 79
   public opinion turns against, 6
   scholarship on, 1, 2, 9–10, 174–77
   South Vietnamese reporting on, 131–32
   televising of, 133
   See also memoirs; Paris Peace Accords (1973); Vietnamization
Vĩnh Linh, 142
Voice of Freedom (VOF), 131
Võ Long Triều, 2, 188
Vũ Đình Đa, 33
Vũ Hoàng Chương, 161–62

Vũ Ngọc Trản, 39
Vương Hồng Sển, 183, 188
Vương Văn Đông, 119, 188
Vũ Quốc Thúc, 2, 14, 15, 188
Vũ Thành An, 160–61

Westmoreland, William C., 88–89

Xuân Thủy, 61

youth music, 183

Zhou Enlai, 63